Transforming the Teaching of Shakespeare with the Royal Shakespeare Company

RELATED TITLES

Creative Shakespeare: The Globe Education Guide to Practical Shakespeare: Fiona Banks

Shakespeare for Young People: Productions, Versions and Adaptations: Abigail Rokison

Teaching Shakespeare and Marlowe: Learning versus the System: Liam Semler

Transforming the Teaching of Shakespeare with the Royal Shakespeare Company

Joe Winston

Bloomsbury Arden Shakespeare
An Imprint of Bloomsbury Publishing Plc

BLOOMSBURY

LONDON · NEW DELHI · NEW YORK · SYDNEY

Bloomsbury Arden Shakespeare

An imprint of Bloomsbury Publishing Plc

Imprint previously known as Arden Shakespeare

50 Bedford Square	1385 Broadway
London	New York
WC1B 3DP	NY 10018
UK	USA

www.bloomsbury.com

BLOOMSBURY, THE ARDEN SHAKESPEARE and the Diana logo are trademarks of Bloomsbury Publishing Plc

First published in 2015

© 2015 Joe Winston

Joe Winston has asserted his right under Copyright, Designs and Patents Act, 1988, to be identified as author of this work.

British Library Cataloguing-in-Publication Data
A catalogue record for this book is available from the British Library.

ISBN: HB: 978-1-4081-8335-9
PB: 978-1-4081-8397-7
ePDF: 978-1-4081-8587-2
ePub: 978-1-4081-8466-0

Library of Congress Cataloging-in-Publication Data
A catalog record for this book is available from the Library of Congress

Typeset by RefineCatch Ltd, Bungay, Suffolk
Printed and bound in India

*To my granddaughter, Meri, born while this book was
being written.
May her life be lightened by the stories and poetry of
Shakespeare and enlivened by a love of theatre.*

CONTENTS

TABLES AND FIGURES

Tables

Figures

ACKNOWLEDGEMENTS

There are a number of very busy people I need to thank for their time and help in the completion of this book. Jonathan Bate, Cicely Berry, Michael Boyd, Tim Crouch, Jackie Devine, Maria Evans, Rachel Gartside, Tracy Irish, Mary Johnson, Catherine Mallyon, Jonothan Neelands, Jacqui O'Hanlon and Michelle Thresher were all generous with their time in allowing me to interview them. Their considerable and varied professional achievements are referenced in the book; here I simply offer them my gratitude.

A few of the above were also kind enough to read and comment upon draft chapters; my thanks to Maria, Tracy, Mary and Jacqui for this and also to Andy Kempe and Miles Tandy, who similarly offered me their honest opinions and critical comments.

I am particularly grateful to the British Academy for their financial support and to Hannah Grainger-Clemson, Caroline Parker and Matthew Winston for their assistance with various technical, clerical and analytical tasks. My thanks also to the University of Warwick for granting me study leave in order to research and complete the book.

A special thanks, too, to the educational team at the Royal Shakespeare Company. In addition to Jacqui O'Hanlon, the Director of Education, and Miles Tandy, the Head of Professional Development, I would like to acknowledge Fiona Clayton, Sarah-Katy Davies, Rob Elkington, Natasha Goodge, Sophie Hobson, Fiona Ingram, Sarah Keevill, Jamie Luck, Holly Parker, Lizzie Rawlinson, Rae Seymour and Hannah Uttley.

Sections of Chapters 5 and 8 were previously published in 2013, in the summer issue of *The Journal of Aesthetic Education*, vol. 47, no. 2, in the article ' "Play is the thing!": Shakespeare, Language Play and Drama Pedagogy in the Early Years'. They are reproduced here with the permission of the University of Illinois Press.

Introduction

The Royal Shakespeare Company is one of the best known theatre companies in the world, with a history of theatre-making in Stratford-upon-Avon that has been well documented by critics and academics alike. Less well known is the history of its educational work. This certainly dates back as far as 1948 and its first summer school for teachers, a highly successful partnership with the Shakespeare Institute that continues to this day. It is, however, the Company's recent, innovative educational work that forms the subject of this book, work that has involved long-term partnerships with clusters of schools and regional theatres at a national level; the provision of sustained professional development, accredited by a high-ranking UK university; the touring into schools of edited versions of Shakespeare's plays, specifically targeted at young audiences and directed by internationally acclaimed theatre practitioners; and, in particular, the development and articulation of a particular form of pedagogy, anchored within a conceptualization of the rehearsal room as a communal space for creative learning. Other major theatres, such as the Globe in London, have developed their own specific approaches to the teaching of Shakespeare and have provided excellent and informative publications that detail their work for teachers.[1] This book is different inasmuch as it attends to structural and policy issues as well as describing, theorizing and investigating the particular form of rehearsal room pedagogy that the RSC promotes. Crucially, the Company has encouraged and commissioned research to gauge the impact of its long-term work with schools. Much of this is available on its website and has informed a number of academic publications. I will be drawing upon this published material as the book progresses, with the aim of providing a comprehensive and comprehensible narrative to describe and explain the nature of the Company's work with teachers and students and its considerable achievements.

Chapter 1 contextualizes the educational work of the RSC within its own history, paying particular attention to the vision of Michael Boyd, who was artistic director of the Company between 2002 and 2012. It was during this period that the education department expanded, was drawn into the heart of the Company's policy-making and was given the freedom to develop ambitious projects of long duration. This eventually resulted in the creation of the Learning and Performance Network in 2006, a unique partnership between a major cultural organization and schools at a national level. The chapter presents an overview of these and other key developments in this period, in particular the *Stand up for Shakespeare* manifesto of 2008. It also looks at the thinking behind initiatives intended to bring actors from the Company's ensemble into closer collaboration with its educational role. The *Young People's Shakespeare* productions that began in 2009 were a key part of this, as was the accredited training of actors to work with young people which ran alongside the accredited programme for teachers. Much of this chapter is historical and descriptive and is aimed at readers interested in issues of vision, policy and Company strategy.

To present a book about the teaching of Shakespeare without reflecting on its importance would be to write within an intellectual vacuum, so Chapter 2 begins with an overview of historical perspectives that address this question before presenting a rationale for Shakespeare's continuing centrality to contemporary cultural life and hence to young people's education. In doing this I draw upon the arguments of two celebrated figures, both of whom were with the RSC during a crucial ten-year period. One is Michael Boyd himself, as noted above, and the other the academic and author of several works on Shakespeare, Professor Jonathan Bate, who was on the RSC's governing body at the time of these developments.

These theoretical arguments, I suggest, are complemented in practice by the rehearsal room pedagogy that the RSC actually articulates and promotes. Chapter 3 investigates the origins and development of this pedagogy, attending to active drama approaches developed outside of the RSC but principally to the work of the legendary voice coach, Cicely Berry, which provides it with its distinctive quality, and to the work of Mary Johnson, the RSC practitioner most influential in developing Berry's work in ways that could connect with classroom practice.

Chapter 4 then presents a detailed look at this pedagogy by tracking the narrative of a weekend workshop – led by Miles Tandy, currently the Company's Head of Professional Development – for teachers and actors from the Learning and Performance Network in 2013. I then present my own theoretical rationale for this work in Chapter 5, in which I draw upon a range of educational theorists to explain the appeal and effectiveness of these approaches, anchored as they are within the language play, physicality and communal creative processes of successful rehearsal room practices.

In Chapter 6 I turn briefly away from pedagogy to examine the *Young People's Shakespeare* productions, or *First Encounter*, as the Company now calls these edited versions of the plays that tour schools and regional theatres before performing for a week at the Swan Theatre in Stratford. In particular, I take an in-depth look at *The Taming of the Shrew* and *King Lear*, both directed by Tim Crouch, and consider their artistic achievements and the responses of young people to them.

In the following two chapters I look specifically at what research tells us about the impact of the Learning and Performance Network (LPN) in transforming learning and teaching in the schools that collaborated in this partnership. Chapter 7 concentrates on teachers and draws upon two research reports specially commissioned by the RSC to gauge this impact. It also draws from research projects conducted by teachers themselves as part of their accreditation process and from the detailed oral accounts of two teachers involved in the LPN, one newly qualified and one a head of department. Chapter 8 focuses more directly on the impact on students. It begins by looking at evidence drawn from a series of large scale quantitative surveys commissioned by the RSC that indicate that core involvement in the LPN resulted in significant improvements not only in children's attitudes to Shakespeare but also in their overall attitudes to school. I then look at two contrasting case studies, both based in primary schools, in order to investigate and theorize how and why this might be the case, concentrating in particular on the effect of this work on children's language development. My own conclusions from this chapter speculate on the specific benefits that would appear to accumulate from a playful engagement with Shakespeare's language and stories, and the cultural nourishment this can afford young people.

In the final chapter I look at current and planned developments in the Company's education strategy since the arrival of Gregory Doran as artistic director in September 2012. In particular I consider the plans to develop and expand the Learning and Performance Network as the RSC tries to ensure a sustainable future.

1

Education at the Royal Shakespeare Company

Introduction

When Michael Boyd completed his tenure as artistic director of the RSC in 2012, the consensus within the Company and among audiences and cultural commentators alike was that it had been a particularly vibrant and successful period. Finances were in a much healthier state than they had been when he had taken up the position ten years earlier; he had successfully overseen the rebuilding of the Royal Shakespeare Theatre in Stratford-upon-Avon; morale within the Company was high; and artistically there had been many celebrated productions, his own cycle of the History Plays receiving particular praise. These successes were achieved within a vision that reaffirmed the RSC's core values, expressed at its foundation in 1961,[1] in particular the twin ideas that Shakespeare's plays could be re-interpreted and staged in ways that allowed their themes to resonate directly with contemporary concerns; and that this was best achieved by actors who could work, rehearse and learn together over a period long enough to establish communal understandings and a shared work ethos through the spirit of the 'ensemble'. There was general agreement that Boyd had demonstrated the continuing relevance of Shakespeare, and of the RSC itself, to the nation's contemporary cultural and political life. What was remarkable, though little commented upon, was the extent to which education had been integral to Boyd's aspiration that the Company should reach out to all parts of the country, to all classes, ages and cultures.[2] Throughout his time as artistic director, he defined the RSC as a learning institution, with the rehearsal room at the heart of this learning process, as a place where educational and artistic values should coincide. The transformations he oversaw in the Company's education department managed to connect this particular vision with practice in classrooms at a national level.

Education had long been seen as part of the RSC's remit, of course; but, as with many theatre companies and cultural organizations, it had hitherto struggled to find a valued position and to be regarded as integral to the Company's overall strategy. A brief and selective look at this history will not only contextualize Boyd's period of tenure but also serve as a thematic prelude to it, showing how a number of tensions and challenges, as well as key qualities and aspirations, had been pervasive over time but never fully addressed.

Education at the RSC 1961–2003: a very brief history

Before and after the Second World War, the Shakespeare Memorial Theatre (later to become the Royal Shakespeare Theatre) had ventured into educational programmes without in any way regarding them as central to its mission. School parties attended matinee productions and leading academics were invited to give public lectures but the introduction of regular summer schools for teachers, begun in 1948 and continuing to this day, established two important precedents that remain core principles within the Company: first, that its work with teachers was key to its educational strategy; and second, that this work should relate closely to its own artistic processes. This was expressed as early as 1949 in an internal report, in which it was stated that the Company 'should seek to make Stratford a recognized centre of study in which the principal item of the curriculum would always be the study of the plays in the Theatre itself'.[3]

A second key precedent, that of bringing the RSC's actors into its educational work, was established in 1965 with the introduction of *Theatregoround*. This was, in effect, a small touring company of twelve actors with an accompanying show bus, whose aim was to bring live theatre to audiences otherwise unlikely to access it. Their venues included schools, libraries, recreation centres and community halls and among the young actors who toured in their first season were some who went on to become household names, notably Ian Richardson and Michelle and Roy Dotrice. After the performances, the actors would engage in straightforward, post-performance Question and Answer sessions, a form of pedagogy that was hardly original and not always successful, as actors were not trained to handle the challenging behaviour of some children in the audiences.[4] *Theatregoround* closed for financial reasons in 1971 but was recalled by Boyd as embodying the 'founding virtue' of education at the RSC; that of being 'rooted in theatre practice'.[5] Nevertheless, the recognition that actors did not necessarily have the skills to lead workshops with young people was one that the Company was to address directly when it re-introduced the practice of touring productions around schools during Boyd's tenure.

Between 1975 and 1982, the Company's education work was co-ordinated by Maurice Daniels, a very popular outgoing and enthusiastic figure who had been working at the Stratford theatre since the 1950s. It was during this period that the RSC began its Newcastle residency as a cost-effective way of taking its work further afield from its usual bases in Stratford and London. Daniels proved to be highly successful at persuading actors involved in this residency to give of their time and contribute to workshops, where they would discuss the plays and their performances with teachers, A-level students and undergraduates. This was not a contractual obligation and actors were not paid extra for doing the work, but Daniels was both persuasive and respected as an established part of the Company and as a man of the theatre. One of his most significant long-term achievements was to persuade the Company's voice coach, Cicely Berry, to begin working with school children. The pedagogies she went on to develop whilst working with sixth formers in London and in local Stratford schools were highly innovative and would prove to be foundational to the approaches later used by the RSC, both in the rehearsal room and in their educational work. It is to her seminal work, as much as to anything else, that Boyd was referring when commenting on how the Company's education work at its best was rooted in its own traditions of theatre practice.

It was not until Daniels retired that the Company actually set up an education department and appointed an administrator to run it. This was in part following the lead of the National Theatre and also responding to the climate of increasing accountability that all subsidized cultural organizations had to face in the early years of Margaret Thatcher's Conservative government. In 1983, in fact, the Arts Council published a paper stipulating that education should be part of the role and function of any arts organization in receipt of a government subsidy. The new post focused explicitly on work with schools and Local Education Authorities but for much of the 1980s and 1990s, the establishment of a specific department paradoxically led to education work becoming less integrated within the Company as a whole as actors lost the kind of contact they had had through the person of Maurice Daniels. Nevertheless there were some highly innovative and creative projects during this period. In 1992, for example, six young people's theatre groups from around the UK worked regionally on Sophocles' play *Antigone*, collaborating with professional playwrights and directors to produce their own modern versions, which they then performed regionally and over a weekend residency in Stratford. Despite the success of the project, which had young people collaborating with the likes of Mike Shepherd, director of *Kneehigh*, and playwrights of the calibre of Nick Darke in Cornwall and Noel Greig in the North West, it was not repeated, even though sponsorship would likely have been available. Ironically, it was the National Theatre that later took up the idea to develop a similar programme that continues today in the form of *National Theatre Connections*.[6]

In 1997 the department re-organized and this resulted in new appointments that would turn out to be highly significant for future developments. In particular, Mary Johnson was given responsibility for developing programmes for teachers. Like Maurice Daniels before her, she worked hard at drawing actors into educational programmes for teachers, but her key influence on the future direction of the Company's educational work lay in the approaches she developed connecting the work of Cicely Berry with the needs of teachers, specifically around the issue of interpretive choices. Both teachers and students can have difficulties with the idea that there are no simple right or wrong ways to make sense of – or interpret – a scene from a Shakespeare play, yet this is seen as a foundational value in the RSC rehearsal room. The strategies Mary developed to help teachers manage this were to become core activities in the RSC's later work, which was committed to bringing the values of the rehearsal room directly into the classroom.

Mary Johnson was joined at the time of her appointment by Maria Evans, who would later be the Company's director of education between 2004 and 2007. Maria found her early years at the RSC frustrating as she felt that education was positioned to the side, rather than at the heart, of the Company. In fact she found Michael Boyd, who had only recently arrived as associate director, to be one of the few people on the artistic side willing to co-operate with her. 'Nobody at the time was able to champion education or be heard at a senior enough level,' she recalls. 'Michael was one of the few even to allow people from the education department to go into rehearsals.'[7] Nevertheless, in 1999, the then artistic director, Adrian Noble, did make a very high status appointment intended to signal the importance of education to the Company. Clare Venables, who had formerly been artistic director of Theatre Royal Stratford East and was founding director of the Brit School, was appointed as director of learning. For the rest of the education team, however, the appointment proved to be a difficult one. Michael Boyd explained how her revolutionary ideas had a number of unintended negative consequences, 'completely giving up on any remit to improve the quality of teaching in the classroom', something he saw as 'an intolerable loss'. Although each would return with major roles in the department, both Maria Evans and Mary Johnson resigned in the wake of this appointment.

Such was the situation that Boyd inherited when he became artistic director: an education department suffering from a confused strategy, low morale and a loss of touch with core values. The history related briefly here, however, is one of significant virtues as well as persistent challenges. From the outset and from the early days of *Theatregoround*, education at the RSC had been rooted firmly in theatre practice. There had long been a tradition of working with teachers as well as with young people but much of this work, however creative and inspirational, had been in the form of short-term, one-off projects with no long term capacity. The Newcastle residency had shown that the RSC could, over a long period of time, target specific areas away from its traditional hubs in order better to fulfil its national remit but other parts of the country, including far-flung rural areas and urban pockets of social deprivation, remained largely beyond the Company's educational reach and there had never been a coherent strategy to engage proactively with them. The Company had demonstrated, as with the *Antigone* Project, that it could work with young directors and playwrights from outside in ways that fused education with the kind of artistic experimentation that could fuel its own creative impulses; but the overall dichotomy between the artistic and the educational remained deeply ingrained in the institution and strategically unaddressed. In other words, education had not been structurally integrated into the mainstream so that its work, successful or otherwise, failed to inform how the Company evaluated its national impact. All of this was about to change.

Establishing a long-term strategy: the learning and performance network

'The structural, managerial approach to changing the RSC and to making the Learning and Performance Network were compatible, in harmony, conceived together.'

MICHAEL BOYD

Although Michael Boyd's vision for education within the RSC was very different from that of Clare Venables, any serious conflict was avoided when, soon after he became artistic director, Claire became seriously ill with breast cancer and tragically died twelve months later. Maria Evans was appointed in 2004 to the vacant post. Boyd was also instrumental in bringing Vikki Heyward from the Royal Court Theatre to the RSC as its new executive director. She too believed that education had a place at the centre of cultural organizations and Maria identifies her as 'absolutely pivotal' at management level in transforming the Company from one that, in 2003, had no coherent strategy for working with schools, no real national presence and little influence on how Shakespeare was being taught.

At this time, the study of Shakespeare was not only compulsory in all state secondary schools but was also examined as one of the Standard Assessment Tests (SATS) for English taken by all students at the end of Year 9. These had been introduced in 1991 and critics from both cultural and educational quarters were increasingly concerned that, far from gaining a cultural entitlement to Shakespeare through this study, large numbers of young people were being alienated by the way they were being taught, finding him difficult, irrelevant and boring. Shakespeare was being examined through students' reading comprehension and writing skills and many teachers, it was claimed, were teaching almost exclusively to the test, ignoring the set plays as a whole, concentrating on the stipulated scenes and spending long periods of time desk-bound, analysing them line by line.[8] Students rarely engaged in performing scenes from the plays themselves and seldom saw them performed other than in electronic versions such as Leon Garfield's *Animated Tales* and Baz Luhrmann's *Romeo + Juliet*.[9] In this climate, Maria proposed that the Company prioritize its work with teachers, particularly those in more socially deprived areas, and promote theatrical forms of pedagogy as the best means of not only making the study of Shakespeare more enjoyable for students but also as being potentially more effective in terms of test results. These aims in themselves were discussed with Boyd and had his backing and would eventually form the foundation for the Learning and Performance Network.

The idea behind a national learning network had first been mooted in the 1990s by Wendy Greenhill, then head of education, and had developed informally over time in conversations between a number of education officers, notably Mary Johnson, Maria Evans and the newly appointed Jacqui O'Hanlon, who arrived at the Company from the National Theatre in 2003 and who, by 2005, was given the leading role in creating what was then being called the Learning Network. The idea was to build up long-term relationships with schools throughout the country, particularly schools in disadvantaged areas or in areas with poor access to arts organizations, in order to achieve a transformation in teachers' appreciation of Shakespeare and in their confidence and ability to teach him well. Such aspirations chimed with Boyd's policy of creating an ensemble of actors on a three-year contract; three years were needed, in Boyd's mind, for the RSC to become an effective catalyst for learning, for it 'to earn its mythical, special place in the firmament as a career changing place for actors'. As three years was the optimum period for actors, the same was probably true for schools. He agreed with Jacqui that any school joining such a partnership with the RSC would need to be willing to embark on a rigorous learning journey, which would involve residencies at Stratford, school-based support from RSC practitioners and young people performing Shakespeare both regionally and – very importantly to Boyd's mind – on the stage at Stratford itself, so that they could learn to feel at ease inside what might otherwise seem a remote, middle-class institution. In every sense this would mark a bold break from the one-day in-service programmes and one-off projects that had previously characterized the Company's education initiatives. It would need to draw the organization's artistic resources and personnel into the programme and be rooted in pedagogical practices in harmony with the RSC's own approaches to learning and discovery in the rehearsal room. Such an ambitious initiative would need to be funded, however, at a time when the RSC was already in debt.

The first, partial source of funding for the Learning Network came obliquely, via a grant awarded to Warwick University in 2005. The well-known academic and Shakespeare scholar, Jonathan Bate, had joined the board of the RSC in 2002 and was shortly afterwards offered a Chair at Warwick on the understanding that he would help forge a closer connection between the university and the Company. In 2004 this took the form of a project, funded by the Higher Education Funding Council for England (HEFCE), which had emerged from conversations between Boyd and himself about the rehearsal room experience.

> Our idea was that the effective classroom bears analogy to the effective rehearsal room; that a rehearsal room is a learning experience; that in some senses the director is like a teacher but he or she is a teacher who brings on a class, the acting company, through collaborative work, through asking questions, playing games, through trust, through exploring ideas together and respecting different opinions.[10]

The acronym for this project was CAPITAL – Creativity and Performance in Teaching and Learning. Funding was generous and led, among other things, to £20,000 a year for five years being set aside to assist with the development of the Learning Network. The RSC wanted to use this allocation to develop a professional learning programme for teachers and Jacqui began by discussing the possibilities for an accredited programme with Jonothan Neelands, Professor of Drama and Theatre Education at Warwick's Institute of Education. He had previously worked with other theatre companies to develop similar programmes for teachers, so a model for accreditation was readily adapted into a Postgraduate Certificate in the Teaching of Shakespeare. This would be assessed by academic staff at the university but taught chiefly by practitioners from the RSC, drawn from both its educational and artistic teams. The funding was sufficient for a first cohort of twenty teachers to be accredited and this was recruited for the academic year 2006– 07. Large grants were later secured by the RSC, namely £300,000 from Creative Partnerships and £280,000 from the Paul Hamlyn Foundation. These not only guaranteed the future of the Learning and Performance Network (LPN) for a full ten years but also provided funds for the Company to research and evaluate the impact it was having.

The stated aims of the LPN were to develop a pedagogy for the teaching of Shakespeare clearly rooted in theatre-based approaches and the spirit of the ensemble; to develop, through dialogue with RSC artists, teachers' understanding of the interpretive choices that actors and directors make in order to access and own Shakespeare's text; and to develop confidence in and enjoyment of the learning and performance of Shakespeare for young people and their teachers.[11] In order to ensure sustainability, a small number of hub schools would be selected from different regions to send two lead teachers to follow the Postgraduate Certificate. These teachers would be required to take a lead not only in their own schools but also with an identified cluster of schools with which they would organize regional Shakespeare projects. The length of the partnership would ensure that the hub schools received the kind of planned, structured and regular support necessary to help them become increasingly autonomous and able to offer regional leadership beyond the initial three years.

The choice of the hub schools would be key to the success of the LPN. The selection criteria were: the quality of the vision expressed by individual schools for working with the RSC; their social and economic circumstances; the need to ensure a high level of cultural diversity across the network as a whole; and the need to ensure a broad geographical spread across the country to represent the national remit of the RSC.

The first year of the programme would consist of a series of intensive residential courses in Stratford, immersing teachers in rehearsal room pedagogy and preparing them to complete an accredited research project in their own schools. In addition, RSC practitioners would provide three days of bespoke in-service training in the hub and cluster schools. The second year would concentrate on Shakespeare in performance, with local performance projects organized by hub schools being supported by RSC practitioners. The work would culminate in a Schools Festival in Stratford involving one school from each of the clusters. The final year of the partnership involved schools in a collaborative project with the Company specifically intended to prepare them for a more autonomous role in their region.

The appeal of the network is borne out by numbers. In 2009, for example, sixty-four schools made inquiries, of which forty-two applied to join, a process that involved considerable preparatory work for the applicants. Twenty-one schools were shortlisted for interview from which eleven were selected. By 2010 eighty-one teachers had obtained the postgraduate qualification. By 2013, 423 schools were part of the network, of which sixty-one had acted as hub schools. A total of 124 teachers had by this time followed the PG Certificate programme with a further 988 involved with the LPN on a non-accredited basis. Sixty-three schools had performed as part of the regional schools celebrations and over 400,000 young people had participated in LPN activities.

Through the LPN, the RSC could see itself beginning to meet a number of its policy aspirations for education. It was taking on a national role, engaging proactively with schools who might otherwise find access to Shakespeare difficult; it was involving actors and directors in the work as well as educational practitioners, thus bringing education closer to the Company's artistic heart. The three-year involvement for schools, while striving for developmental coherence in itself, also reflected the way the Company conceived of learning for its actors, a 'community of practice' that mirrored the principles of the ensemble and for the same reasons – to demonstrate commitment and provide individual schools and teachers with time to develop and grow in partnership with the Company, not only helping them work towards performances but also providing them with a specific pedagogy. The desire to spread this pedagogy and transform children's experiences of Shakespeare on a broader, national stage was to inform the education department's next major initiative.

Standing up for Shakespeare

Following extensive consultations with the Qualifications and Curriculum Authority (QCA), the Department for Children, Schools and Families (DCSF), subject associations and theatre companies, the RSC launched its *Stand up for Shakespeare* manifesto in March 2008. This sought to gain wide national coverage for what was now thought to be a coherent educational strategy to which the entire company could subscribe. The key driver of the manifesto was once again Jacqui O'Hanlon, who had by now picked up the baton as director of education when Maria Evans left the position in 2007. In a short, colourful document, readily available online and widely publicized, the manifesto spelt out in the unashamed language of advocacy what RSC education stood for and why, summed up in three, pithy sound bites: 'Do it on your feet; See it Live; Start it Earlier.' The opening words of Boyd's introduction to the manifesto were equally catchy. 'Shakespeare wrote plays and young children are geniuses at playing',[12] at once emphasizing the connection between theatre, playfulness and enjoyment and a belief that, given the right approaches, even very young children can connect with Shakespeare's theatricality. But if Boyd was unashamedly Romantic in his tone, the manifesto itself was careful to argue its case in the educational language of problem-solving and learning styles whilst emphasizing the RSC's particular remit as a theatre-making organization to inform and connect with these approaches.

> The best classroom experience we can offer is one which allows young people to approach a Shakespeare play as actors do – as an ensemble, using active, exploratory, problem-solving methods to develop a greater understanding and enjoyment of the plays. . . . These active, theatre-based approaches acknowledge the importance of kinaesthetic learning – learning through doing and feeling.[13]

The manifesto is confident and sure of what RSC education stands for. If somewhat evangelical in its tone, as a political document it succeeded not only in gaining national attention but in convincing the entire organization of the RSC that this was a message they could understand and support. 'The world needs enthusiasm and vividness,' Boyd told me, 'and this was a moment when the whole organization understood the significance of what the education department was doing'.

The aspiration to start Shakespeare early – no later than the age of eleven, the manifesto stipulates – was once again highly pragmatic, recognizing the statutory nature of his study in the early years of secondary school.

The later Shakespeare is introduced the harder it can seem. Perhaps the most challenging time for first contact is early teenage years, when self-consciousness can inhibit the active ways of working most likely to foster a positive initial understanding. Teenagers with no earlier experience of Shakespeare are at greater risk of forming negative opinions.[14]

In contrast to this, the ease with which primary-school-aged children are willing to engage in playful, drama-based approaches to learning is emphasized and, as with any marketing campaign, the document is peppered with enthusiastic comments, including those from young children, but also from renowned actors such as Judi Dench, Tamsin Greig and Ian McKellen. 'A seven-year-old told me', comments McKellen, 'having seen the RSC's latest *Lear*, it was "the best play he had ever seen" in his entire life. I'm glad that the RSC is encouraging other youngsters to share his enthusiasm.'[15] The winning charm of such comments was intended to convince the Company as much as the nation that what this manifesto was advocating carried due cultural weight and was thus something they could readily support.

McKellen's comment leads us to the third strand of the campaign: that young people should see Shakespeare live. The manifesto emphasizes that: 'the sensory act of hearing, seeing and feeling the sounds, rhythms and words aids comprehension in a way that reading the play cannot . . . There is no substitute for the shared experience of seeing Shakespeare live.'[16] Not many seven-year-olds will, of course, be privileged enough to be taken to see a theatre production. For this reason the Company was set to begin another major initiative, the *Young People's Shakespeare* (YPS) in which young directors from outside the RSC would be invited to work with actors drawn from the ensemble on shortened versions of the plays. These would tour and play in school halls and culminate with a week of performances in the Swan Theatre in Stratford.

The young people's Shakespeare

The immediate antecedents to the YPS were two productions for young people mounted in the early years of Boyd's tenure: a shortened version of Dominic Cook's *Macbeth*, which toured schools in 2004; and a *Twelfth Night* in 2007–08. Reminiscent as these were of *Theatregoround*, the YPS was always more artistically ambitious and served to mark out the education department as part of the RSC's creative, experimental wing. Jacqui O'Hanlon recalls it being initially driven by the Company's desire to work with theatre-makers 'whom actors would be excited to work for and who were themselves interested in the challenge that a young audience presents'.[17] Boyd was in no doubt of its strategic significance as a way of getting education 'into the bloodstream of the organization' and saw it as fundamental to the national remit and the cultural health of the RSC.

The YPS gave us access to the nation as a whole. Theatre is viewed as having very high social status, as being quite a middle-class preoccupation, still very white for instance, and one of the most wonderful things about our education work is that, suddenly, your audience is a real audience. You can feel the pulse of the actual culture beating when you are working there.

The first YPS production – *The Comedy of Errors* in 2009 – was directed by Paul Hunter and Hayley Carmichael and was a co-production with *Told by an Idiot*. For the press performance, a number of established reviewers were transported to a primary school in Walsall. The *Daily Telegraph*, for one, gave the production a very positive review and Lyn Gardner of the *Guardian* was also impressed. 'It does the job with such zest', she wrote, 'that I doubt you could see it without feeling Shakespeare is your contemporary, whether you are nine or 99.'[18]

Given the success of *Errors*, the Company followed up very quickly in 2010 with a YPS production of *Hamlet*. Tarell Alvin McCraney was at the time the Warwick/RSC's International Playwright in Residence. Born in 1980, McCraney had grown up in very disadvantaged circumstances in one of Miami's poorest housing projects and has spoken candidly of how a theatre company coming into his school completely transformed his life by giving him a life in art.[19] His *Brother/Sister* trilogy of plays has won awards in the US, where he has been hailed by the *New York Times* as the best playwright since Eugene O'Neill, but he was previously inexperienced as a director. 'Tarell didn't need to work with young people,' Michael Boyd told me, 'he wanted to, for biographical and socio-political reasons.' He added: 'Should you have to make a choice between working with young people, with communities, and making good art? I don't think so.' *Hamlet* is not, of course, the first play that might spring to mind as suitable for primary or secondary school students, but McCraney's edited version was extremely well received by young people and critics alike.[20] Jonathan Bate was particularly impressed by it, and for artistic reasons. 'There is an aspiration for pace, for brevity that is often not realized in productions of Shakespeare,' he told me, 'but the *Young People's Shakespeare* did realize it. I thought *Hamlet* was terrific.' It also provided the RSC with its first British Asian Hamlet in the person of Dharmesh Patel, a casting decision that McCraney, an African American, had insisted upon.

It was hugely important for me to cast a Hamlet of colour. We're in London, for God's sake, where around 40% of people are non-white. Something happens when your first theatre experience is at a young age. But if you're from a minority and, in the first show you see, everyone is white, followed by another that's the same and so on, you think: 'Oh, this is for them.' A pattern builds. And it's difficult to overcome.

'In short', commented Nosheen Iqbal in the *Guardian*, 'McCraney embodies the purpose of the RSC's *Stand up for Shakespeare* manifesto – to encourage as many young people as possible to develop a lasting connection with theatre, especially if they don't come from a background where doing so can be taken for granted.' As a result of their success, both YPS productions were taken to New York later in 2010, where they played as part of the Company's Park Avenue Armoury season, a tradition that has continued since.

The next two YPS productions – *The Taming of the Shrew* and *King Lear* – were directed by the avant-garde playwright, Tim Crouch. These will be looked at in depth in Chapter 6 as case studies, examining specifically the ways in which serious artistic and educational thinking were integral to the production process and how young people responded to this. After *Shrew*, a key strategic decision was taken to link the YPS more closely to the work of the Learning and Performance Network by touring *Lear* to all partner theatres and hub schools in the 2012 cohort. This did signal a break from the practice of casting actors currently in main house productions, something that had hitherto limited the touring to schools local to the Stratford area. The added partnership possibilities were seen to outweigh this loss, however, and these were developed still further in the next production, in which the YPS was renamed *First Encounter*, reflecting a refocusing of the vision behind it: as the plays were touring to theatres as well as schools, the emphasis was now not simply on introducing young people to Shakespeare but also anyone in these communities who might never have seen one of his plays before. Michael Fentiman, an associate director at the RSC who had recently directed *Titus Andronicus* in the main theatre, directed another version of *Shrew* as the first of these productions, which also introduced further innovations. The play toured as a two-hour experience, with a pre-performance induction into its story and a post-performance talk with the company. Teachers in the LPN were also included in the pre-production research, Mike Fentiman joining them during their September residential programme to discuss any concerns they had about the play and the issues they thought it might raise for their students. Even the audition process was integrated into the LPN, with actors being invited to join in student workshops at one of the schools before deciding whether they wished to join the production or not. Other future developments envisaged as part of the continuing development of the LPN will be discussed further in the final chapter.

Actors working with young people

Through the *Young People's Shakespeare*, actors in the Company had been brought into contact with young people (and vice versa) and Boyd was very keen on taking this contact further. In a further collaboration with Warwick University, a postgraduate award (PGA) for actors was introduced in 2007, specifically for those who were part of the Company and interested in leading Shakespeare workshops with young people.

In 2009, a special centrefold included in the programme for the then current production of *A Winter's Tale* was public testimony to this development's significance for the Company. The piece, written by Jonothan Neelands, explained the rationale behind the award and pointed to the fact that a quarter of the cast in this particular production had already taken it. Neelands was careful to make it clear that this was no superficial training module formulated simply to pass on a series of workshop skills. Actors were not intended to switch roles and become teachers; rather were they being encouraged to share the social and artistic values of the ensemble rehearsal room in their engagements with young people. He articulated a set of ideas very close to Michael Boyd's: that working with young people can provide theatre-makers with the kind of direct energy often found to be much fainter in 'normal' theatre audiences; that the rehearsal room is essentially a space of learning; that playfulness is a key both to learning about and also to making theatre; and that there is a constant need to re-interpret and make Shakespeare fresh again if we are to continue to find him relevant.[21]

Of course such visionary language proves its worth only if it has practical, tangible results. Jacqui O'Hanlon is in no doubt of the significance of this programme in terms of how the organization as a whole began to appreciate the work of the education department. She comments:

> One of the most memorable incidents for me was being in the green room during one particular show and overhearing one of our PGA actors talking to another actor about *Bloom's Taxonomy*! When the final, long ensemble of actors finished their contracts with the RSC in 2011, 30% of the company had acquired a post graduate award in the teaching of Shakespeare. That is a statistic we are all immensely proud of and actors from the Company tell me today that the post graduate award training was one of the most significant achievements of their time at the RSC.[22]

The importance of research

Since the 1980s cultural organizations have been increasingly under pressure to provide evidence of public value to justify public subsidy. The best measures by which they can do this have provoked continuing debate among economists, cultural theorists, think tanks and policy-makers and the argument tends inevitably to revolve around the contested nature of cultural value itself.[23] Should such value be seen as intrinsic – something worthwhile in itself, related to the personal and subjective responses people offer to describe how, for example, a specific production of *Hamlet* has affected them? Should it be more instrumental, relating to objective measures of economic well-being or public good, expressed through statistics and in the language of impact and outcomes? Furthermore, there is the concept of

FIGURE 1.1 *Dharmesh Patel as Hamlet, Simone Saunders as a female Horatio, with Gruffudd Glyn and Dyfan Dwyfir as Barnardo and Francisco, in the 2010 YPS production of* Hamlet.

institutional value, rooted in an organization's own ethos of public service. In this sense, the question might be: how far does the RSC succeed in operating as an active agent, as a creator in its own right of what the public values?[24] In all three senses – the intrinsic, the instrumental and the institutional – questions of cultural value can be seen significantly to overlap with those of educational value.

From the outset the RSC decided that an initiative as innovative, ambitious and costly as the LPN would need to be properly and objectively researched in order accurately to assess its value. In addition to the subjective reports and quotes from teachers, young people and company actors that could illustrate the intrinsic value that involvement with the LPN had had for them, there was a need for data to provide harder, more statistical evidence of its instrumental impact. If positive, this would in turn bolster the RSC's own institutional value, both in its own eyes and in the eyes of a broader public. *Stand up for Shakespeare* had made very public the organization's vision of its educational remit; researching the LPN would provide evidence of how this had impacted on teachers as professionals, schools as institutions and young people as learners.

In response to feedback from teachers and as a result of observations made by its own practitioners, the Company began by focusing on student attitudes to Shakespeare and whether these changed for the better when teachers began to use RSC approaches in the classroom. The University of Warwick's Centre for Educational Development and Research (CEDAR) was commissioned to conduct this research and Professor Steve Strand (who later moved to the University of Oxford) designed a questionnaire to test not only students' attitudes to Shakespeare pre- and post-school involvement in the LPN, but also their more general attitudes to school and to learning. As the results were so interesting, this was actually commissioned twice between 2007 and 2011. The Teacher Development Agency (TDA) then commissioned CEDAR specifically to explore the impact of the accredited training on teachers. This report, published in 2009, so engaged Paul Collard of the UK-based charity Creativity, Culture and Education (CCE) that he commissioned further research from a different group of academics to evaluate comparatively the impact of the LPN on teachers in hub schools and those in cluster schools, and results were received in 2010. The mixture of qualitative and quantitative data that these reports present has provided the Company with an unusual and unique evidence base about the impact of their work and much of Chapters 7 and 8 is devoted to examining their findings and what they imply.[25]

Michael Boyd was in no doubt of the importance of this research in finally convincing the whole of the RSC, including the likes of its then Chair, Sir Christopher Bland, to value the education department and see its activity as core to the institution. He recalled in particular the results of a survey conducted as part of the second CEDAR report being presented to the board and the fact that the completion rate for teachers taking the PG Certificate was 97 per cent as compared to a national average of 47 per cent in similar postgraduate courses for teachers; 43 per cent had gained promotion during or immediately after their involvement in the LPN. 'You couldn't argue with that!' he commented.

You can, of course, argue with statistics and people often do. This 97 per cent, for example, amounted to 26 teachers, which might in itself be seen as a small sample, and the twelve or thirteen members who achieved promotion could have done so for a variety of reasons, perhaps because they displayed the kind of energies and desire for professional improvement that would have marked them out for promotion anyway.[26] It is hard to believe that the likes of Christopher Bland – wryly described by Michael Boyd as a 'tough old bird' – were unaware of this, yet they nonetheless found the results impressive in ways that, if presented as bald statistics, they might not have. The reason, of course, as Boyd made clear to me, is that the overall impact of the education work on the Company had been gradual and cumulative and the amount of evidence gathered through research was, in the end, substantial. Both qualitative and quantitative in nature, it provided rich accounts as well as statistical headlines that helped confirm at the highest level the Company's belief that the impact of its educational projects were indeed significant and thus worth celebrating.

Conclusion

This chapter has attempted to show how the policies that drove the RSC during a period of creative and critical success cannot be separated from those that shaped its educational endeavours in a similarly transformative way. The challenges facing Boyd when he took up his post were considerable and were neatly summed up at the time by Colin Chambers, who was then completing a history of the Company. Chambers pointed to how the organization needed to rediscover its core values within the framework of a coherent vision and seek greater coherence in its activities; how it needed to forge a new relationship with its audience, treating them less as consumers and more as partners, while seeking to extend the social and cultural mix of this audience in order to fulfil its remit as a national company; and how it needed to rebuild its internal culture, showing greater care for actors by re-establishing the primacy of the rehearsal room as a site for learning and discovery.[27] The work of the education department was not only reflective of this process but also integral to making it happen – in Boyd's words, the artistic and educational changes were 'compatible, in harmony, conceived together'. Bringing the education department into the centre of the Company worked against fragmentation in a structural sense, drawing theatre artists and educators together in a variety of ways. The structure of the Learning and Performance Network ensured that teachers and young people of mixed ethnicity and from schools in socially deprived areas became involved in a new form of partnership with the Company, with theatre artists and education practitioners working in the schools and young people being offered the opportunity of performing in one of the Stratford theatres. The principles of the ensemble rehearsal room which re-invigorated the Company's culture of care were not only central to the actors' learning experiences but also made available to teachers and young people through a strongly articulated pedagogy.

Of course, the RSC has not been the only UK theatre company in recent years to position education more centrally in its priorities and Helen Nicholson has written about these growing 'cultures of participation', commenting that: 'in the most forward-thinking theatres in the twenty-first century, theatre managers are placing education and learning central to the ethos of the entire cultural organization'.[28] She notes that some see this as a cynical move; after all, school parties can at least provide a sizeable captive audience. However, she herself refutes such cynicism and hails it as a political inheritance from the 1960s, when such radical initiatives as the Coventry Belgrade Theatre spawned the Theatre in Education movement. She sees the current commitment to education as inherited from this political spirit, a 'genuine commitment to find inventive ways to invite people from all sectors of society into their performing spaces'.[29] Her insightful comments are particularly apt with regard to the RSC, for Boyd himself makes this very connection when talking of how he first became interested in education as part of the remit of a theatre company.

As a trainee director, my first job in Britain was in the Coventry Belgrade in 1979, when their Theatre in Education company had such vigour and reputation. So it was very natural for me to see a healthy connection between learning, memorability and good art, and experiment and good art, and community and good art – all of which, at one time or another, the Belgrade TiE team exemplified.

And, although it may not have been unique in its enhanced focus on education, the RSC has gone further than most cultural organizations in establishing a structure to consolidate long-term relations with schools and in commissioning a programme of research to evaluate its impact and inform future policy.

2

Why Teach Shakespeare?

Historical perspectives

The manifesto *Stand up for Shakespeare* was able to express its aims with such confidence and energy in part because of an existing political consensus in the UK: as the only compulsory author in the National Curriculum for English, Shakespeare is an educational entitlement for all young people, so finding ways to help them enjoy and succeed in the study of his plays is surely justification in itself. There is, however, 100 years of history behind the mask of this apparent consensus, very well summarized in two brief studies, one by Martin Blocksidge and the other written specifically for the RSC by Tracy Irish.[1] Both reveal the ideological controversies and pedagogical struggles that have characterized arguments among and between university academics, educationalists and politicians as to why and how Shakespeare should be taught, and these are arguments that still resonate today. This book is specifically concerned with pedagogy – the *how* of this equation – but to separate completely the *how* from the *why* would be to reduce teaching to a technical process and teachers to technicians concerned merely with servicing young people to a value agenda with which they need not concern themselves. So, although it is not necessary here to revisit in detail the history of Shakespeare in education, some key historical pointers will nonetheless provide a necessary context before we consider the values that underpin the RSC's vision about why Shakespeare matters. We will proceed to look for these values in the words not only of Michael Boyd but also of Jonathan Bate, whose tenure as a governor of the RSC coincided almost exactly with Michael Boyd's as artistic director. Their expressions of *why* will, I believe, illuminate and rationalize what we will later read about the *how*.

Why teach Shakespeare? To many, the answer may seem obvious: because he is the greatest poet and playwright in English (if not world) literature. But where does this greatness lie exactly and is he primarily a poet – and therefore to be studied as literature – or a playwright – and therefore best taught within a drama curriculum? Historically, Shakespeare has always been firmly entrenched in the curriculum for English. It is only in recent years, since the 1970s, that Drama and Theatre Studies have successfully decoupled themselves from English departments within the academy and Drama still remains outside of the National Curriculum in the UK, often as a marginal subject in state schools. So when we seek out the history of Shakespeare in schools, we must primarily look within the English curriculum; and to understand how he has traditionally been valued we need to consider philosophical ideas that have underpinned the teaching of English literature.

In the early days of mass education, Matthew Arnold argued that a society could be united by the enlightened study of culture in ways that religion no longer had the power to; and, that Shakespeare, as England's foremost national poet, should be central to this educational endeavour to provide the nation with a unified sense of moral purpose.[2] Shakespearean scholars in the early twentieth century, such as A.C. Bradley and Walter Raleigh, helped entrench this idea of Shakespeare as a national cultural icon, celebrating what they saw as the profound moral wisdom and universal truths at the heart of his work – in Bradley's case, as character studies of the main protagonists – and offering their analyses of his plays as interpretations of where this wisdom lay.[3] With the establishment of the English Association in 1906 in order to promote the teaching of English as a rival to classics in schools, this understanding of Shakespeare's greatness began to permeate from universities into the classroom.[4] The general belief was that the works were receptacles of universal moral truths, and to gain access to them was in itself a source of cultural and moral uplift for the future citizens of Britain. Later influential literary critics such as T.S. Eliot and F.R. Leavis, both of whom used moral terms to theorize the value of great literature, added further weight to the idea that Shakespeare mattered because to study him would provide a moral education as well as an aesthetic one. Given these articles of faith, Shakespeare remained unchallenged in educational policy as the supreme example of the civilizing power of literature until the later part of the twentieth century.

In practice, for the vast majority of young people in schools, whether such a belief in the moral imperative of studying Shakespeare was well founded or not was irrelevant. The fact remained, as both Blocksidge and Irish point out, that very few schoolchildren were being given any kind of effective education in his plays, with the result that by the mid-1960s the idea of Shakespeare's centrality in English education began to be challenged. Influential books by J.W. Patrick Creber and Frank Whitehead both embraced the child-centred educational philosophies dominant during this period, seeing young people's own interests and values as of paramount importance and suggesting that teachers should prioritize texts with which their students could most readily engage.[5] In other words, they questioned the relevance of Shakespeare for all and it is important to note that, despite his cultural dominance, Shakespeare's plays were never in fact a compulsory part of the UK examination system for sixteen-year-olds until the 1990s.

We can now look back on the period of the 1960s as one of major social and cultural upheaval, when many established values were being challenged and the distinction between higher and lower forms of culture began to be questioned. The general spirit of iconoclasm was also apparent in the theatre with the emergence of new playwrights, such as Edward Bond and Harold Pinter, who deliberately set out to shock the cultural establishment with works such as *Saved* and *The Homecoming*, the latter premiering at the RSC in 1965.[6] It was, however, also evident in the RSC's productions of Shakespeare by directors such as John Barton and Peter Brook, who were consciously seeking striking new ways to make Shakespeare relevant to contemporary audiences. Later productions by Charles Marowitz in the early 1970s continued this radical agenda, with iconic works such as *Hamlet* and *Macbeth* being cut and collaged in an attempt to make their essential energies more tangible. Jan Kott's book *Shakespeare Our Contemporary*, published in 1965, perfectly captured this new vision, one that prioritized relevance over reverence. The fact that the teaching of Shakespeare was not necessarily determined by an overly prescriptive examination system did allow adventurous teachers to experiment and draw upon these radical artistic ideas as inspiration for their own teaching approaches. One student to benefit from this was the young Jonathan Bate, whose drama teacher introduced him to Marowitz's adaptation of *Macbeth* at the age of fifteen. As if to refute the purists who saw in these versions a mutilation of the great master and a cheapening of his timeless poetry, Bate recalls performing in this version of *Macbeth* as the single most significant educational experience to stimulate his interest in Shakespeare. 'The language just got under my skin,' he told me, and he still regards *Macbeth* as the Shakespeare play he knows best to this day.[7] This kind of exciting intervention, potentially life-shaping, was unfortunately not available for most young people at the time.

The intentions of Whitehead and Patrick Creber were pragmatic rather than political. Neither was challenging the iconic status of Shakespeare but they doubted his suitability, interest and relevance for most secondary-school students. In the 1980s, however, a number of university academics did set out overtly to challenge Shakespeare's supremacy within English studies, together with the critical approaches of Bradley, Raleigh, Eliot, Leavis and others, who had for so long influenced how teachers understood and appreciated this supremacy. Described as the 'New Iconoclasts' by Jonathan Bate,[8] these academics, who included Alan Sinfield and Jonathan Dollimore in the UK and Stephen Greenblatt in the US, were heavily influenced by critical theory. They read Shakespeare through the theoretical lenses of cultural materialism or new historicism and were intent on exposing the hidden ideologies that underpinned the long-established cult of 'bardolatry', which they saw as politically partial, overtly nationalistic, inherently right wing and evidently servile to a conservative establishment.[9]

Their arguments gained vigour, energy and a good deal of venom through their oppositional stance to a Conservative government on the verge of establishing a National Curriculum which was to set out by law what young people would be taught in each subject area, with Shakespeare becoming the only author whose study was to be compulsory. That Conservative ministers such as Kenneth Baker and Michael Portillo began to promote Shakespeare as the upholder of values they defined as British, but that were self-evidently Tory, deepened the political rift between the literary academy and politicians, an increasingly bitter spat referred to as 'The Battle of the Bard' by sections of the British press.[10] In policy terms it was the government that won, of course, as Shakespeare was not only instated as a compulsory part of English but also, by 1991, as an integral part of the new Standard Assessment Tests (SATS) to be taken by all students at the end of Year 9, their third year in secondary school.

With the landslide return of a Labour government in 1997 there was a new cultural expansiveness that was less stridently nationalistic but Shakespeare remained central to both the curriculum and the examination system. The new iconoclasts had, however, disturbed entrenched views about the established canon of great literature, shaking to the core ideas of authorial genius, universal truths and the fixed nature of textual meaning, and arguing for the primacy of historical and social interpretations over individual aesthetic response. Above all they had foregrounded the political in Shakespeare, critiquing the plays and arguments in favour of their genius through the various perspectives afforded by critical theory. The RSC had always prided itself artistically in revising and reviewing Shakespeare in order to find contemporary relevance in his work, but its educational vision, too, needs to be seen as responsive to changes in how Shakespeare is culturally and intellectually valued. If Shakespeare was not simply another author whose pre-eminence had been largely constructed and perpetuated for political purposes, then what was the intellectual justification for his continuing centrality to English culture and education, upon which the RSC's very existence was founded?

Jonathan Bate and *The Genius of Shakespeare*

However arguments about a national curriculum might ebb and flow in the years to come, Shakespeare's pre-eminence is secure. Yet in order to earn it, he needs to be re-made over and over again, just as he re-made his characters . . . Bate's book does just that.[11]

Jonathan Bate's book *The Genius of Shakespeare* was published in 1997 to great acclaim. The praise cited above by the then poet laureate, Andrew Motion, was echoed by figures as diverse as the eminent Shakespearean scholar and member of the Board of the RSC, Stanley Wells, the left-wing academic and iconoclast, Terry Eagleton, the biographer and novelist, Peter Ackroyd, and the first artistic director of the RSC, Peter Hall. The latter's comment, describing the work as 'an extraordinary monument to common sense in a sea of nonsense' is telling inasmuch as it is indicative of the hostility and exasperation felt by many theatre practitioners for the more extreme arguments of cultural materialists such as Alan Sinfield, who had singled out the RSC for particular attack. Such criticisms were felt to demonstrate little understanding of theatre as an art form and echo the rift between academia and RSC practitioners in the past, made famous by the scathing comments of Peter Brook in his seminal work *The Empty Space*, in which he attacked the type of scholar who emerges from a production of Shakespeare 'smiling because nothing has distracted him from trying over and confirming his pet theories to himself'. Such an academic, he suggests, 'lends the weight of his authority to dullness'.[12]

Bate's book is important for a number of reasons. At the time he was King Alfred Professor of English Literature at the University of Liverpool, a post formerly held by both A.C. Bradley and Walter Raleigh and thus symbolically associated with visionary and influential studies of Shakespeare. In the tradition of his post, Bate sets about re-inventing the case for Shakespeare as *the* giant of world literature. What Peter Hall describes as his 'common sense' lies in the clarity of his language and the way his arguments are based on historical and literary scholarship rather than fashionable ideological theory. Importantly for the RSC and for other theatre practitioners, it also demonstrates an understanding of theatre performance and an appreciation of how Shakespeare's literary genius is actually centred in his theatricality. Bate provides telling evidence from history that, far from regarding him as the property and servant of right-wing elitism or cultural imperialism, we should see in Shakespeare's work opportunities for the disadvantaged and oppressed to find a voice; and, whilst never denying that Shakespeare's plays are constantly political, he reclaims their ethical authority by redefining them as an education in humanity rather than in traditional morality.

Bate demonstrates that there is a radical tradition of what he calls 'Popular Shakespeare' that originated in the eighteenth century and with the early nineteenth century essayist, William Hazlitt, as its greatest champion. This, he argues, has always offered an explicit challenge to 'Establishment Shakespeare' by appropriating his language for its own purposes. 'Classical quotations are among the most polished badges of the elite', he writes; 'most obviously they bespeak an expensive education. Hazlitt makes Shakespeare his classic as a way of fostering a counter tradition.'[13] This counter-tradition was nurtured in dissenting academies established in the eighteenth century when religious non-conformists – those who did not belong to the established Church of England – were forbidden access to the elite universities of Oxford and Cambridge. In these academies, which preceded the educational writings of Matthew Arnold by some decades, we find the early foundations of a liberal education, with English literature in general, and Shakespeare in particular, at its centre as a radical force for democratization and an engine of social mobility. He re-enforces this argument in a later work, *English Literature: A Very Short Introduction.*

> Its beneficiaries were not the ruling classes, who continued to be schooled in the Greek and Roman classics until well into the twentieth century, but middle-class non-conformists, women and soon the working classes . . . and colonial subjects.[14]

The key textbook in these academies was *The Speaker*, written by one William Enfield. Published in 1774, it consisted largely of extracts from Shakespeare and was intended, in Bate's words: 'to make people articulate, adept with language; to use Shakespeare's amazing linguistic facility, fertility, to give language as a form of power to the poor, the dispossessed, the lower classes.' Bate is evidently angry at the idea that Shakespeare should be seen essentially as part of an elitist culture, seeing him instead as a force for empowerment. 'To give people from disadvantaged backgrounds language,' he told me in interview, 'to give them Shakespeare as a tool to think with, to speak with, is an enormously powerful thing.'[15]

This capacity within Shakespeare to present a language for radical thought extends to dissenting voices beyond the shores of the UK and even beyond its own former colonies. Bate uses *The Tempest* as an example of how Shakespeare continues globally to be a positive force in cultural renewal despite the attacks mounted by postcolonial criticism on the Eurocentric tradition. In his own reading of the play, Caliban is not only a rebel but a poet, the character who has the most beautiful lines and the one able to hear the music of the island, the '*Sounds and sweet airs that give delight and hurt not*'. This, he suggests, opened the space for the voices of rebellious Caribbean poets to engage with the play, in particular Aimé Césaire, the inventor of the term 'negritude' and the teacher of the radical writer Frantz Fanon, whose own book *Black Skin, White Masks* became a foundational text for black consciousness. Bate sees Césaire's rewriting of the play, *Une Tempête*, first performed in 1969, as one of the great creative revisions of our time, 'smuggling into the European tradition the voice of Caliban' and using Shakespeare's plot and characters to consider the question of how to break the white man's totalitarian grip on power. In this sense Shakespeare, far from being an instrument of what Pierre Bourdieu would call 'symbolic violence', was re-interpreted through Césaire to become the voice of a recovered black identity.[16]

Just why Shakespeare is able to speak so powerfully to the imaginations of different people in different eras and with different political aspirations is approached in the final chapter entitled *The Laws of the Shakespearean Universe*. 'Shakespeare', he writes 'has proved himself peculiarly adaptable to a world of ambiguity, uncertainty and relativity.'[17] (Such a world, of course, is the one we find ourselves living in today). History rather than ideology shows us that no one, fixed meaning can be imposed on a Shakespeare play; after all, he has been core curriculum in communist Bulgaria as well as the icon of conservative England. In order to understand the value of Shakespeare, then, we need to see the power, intensity and very variety of the 'Shakespeare effect' as inherent to the plays themselves, as part of their very purpose. Taking his lead from Wittgenstein and J.L. Austin, Bate describes the plays as games whose purpose is the performance itself and not any specific conclusions they are logically designed to elaborate. And just as games are guided by rules that are beyond the invention of the players, the world of Shakespeare's plays has rules or laws beyond the invention of the reader, player or audience; so meanings cannot be imposed or drawn out of them that are not already embedded within them. 'Shakespeare can be thought of as a vast collection of games', Bate suggests, 'in which the oldest and most enduring stories . . . are made new.' But there are, he suggests, two laws that all the plays obey and which account for their lasting appeal and for Shakespeare's enduring genius.[18]

The first of these laws is the 'aspectuality of truth', an idea for which he is again indebted to Wittgenstein. This means that oppositional truths can exist at one and the same time but that they cannot both be *seen* at one and the same time. In his grammar school education, Bate argues, Shakespeare learned rhetoric, the art of presenting different, contrasting arguments as persuasively as possible. Rhetoric is essentially a performance, designed to work on an audience and persuade them of the truth of the voice they are hearing. Shakespeare subsequently took the art of rhetoric to new heights in the theatre. Like no other artist before or since, he was able to bring into existence and animate oppositional voices through the vividness and range of his characters and through the inventive power of his language. So in *The Tempest*, for example, there is a Prospero aspect and a Caliban aspect, both of which are truths that co-exist but that cannot be apprehended simultaneously. Keats recognized this creative gift, one that 'took as much delight in conceiving an Iago as an Imogen' and called it 'negative capability' – the capacity to hold contradictory ideas in the mind at the same time, essentially to remain in uncertainty and doubt and to make this the very centre of one's art.[19]

Keats saw this quality as a characteristic of all great art. As a concept, it works directly against any idea that an understanding of Shakespeare or any other great artist can be reduced to their peddling of pre-conceived moral or political ideas. It is also, Bate points out, why Shakespeare has been adopted by so many different political causes since his death. But on its own it does not account for Shakespeare's genius. This is dependent upon the way that the first law of his universe, the aspectuality of truth, is inextricably interwoven with the second law, that of performativity. 'The performative truth of human being', writes Bate, 'is that being and acting are indivisible.'[20] One of the fundamental features of drama as opposed to literature is that the authorial voice is dispersed, so that no one character can ever be singled out as the embodiment of what the author considers to be true. Shakespeare's richness of characterization and extraordinary powers of language added a range and depth to this process with the result that he animated more characters more vividly than any other dramatist before or since; as Hazlitt put it: 'his genius shone equally on the evil and the good, on the wise and the foolish, the monarch and the beggar'.[21] More than this, many of his most memorable characters are acutely conscious of themselves as performers; in the lies they tell, the disguises they wear, the deceits they mount, the games of wit they play, in the rituals they stage, in the way they constantly imagine themselves as actors. The idea of the world itself being a stage permeates his theatre to such an extent that game-playing, performing, acting and being all fuse into one and blur the barriers between reality, performance and dream. As such, I would add, his world is a particularly playful one and a particularly fascinating one to play with. It is through this active playfulness that we tap into the twin energies of its aspectuality and performativity and can come to see its value; or rather, to quote Gloucester from *King Lear*, we come to 'see it feelingly', for it is the kind of value we need to feel emotionally if we are to understand it intellectually. Bate writes:

> The meaning of a performance is to be found in the process of performance, which requires both writer and reader, actor and spectator. The genius of Shakespeare . . . is certainly not the wisdom that can be extracted from Shakespeare. It is the process of Shakespeare, that which is performed by the performance . . . The working through does not *lead to a conclusion*, it *performs the point*.[22]

Bate is clear, then, that we should not be searching for moralistic conclusions or universal truths in the plays but for something to be found in the process of performance itself and this, he told me in interview, is 'not morality but humanity'. He elaborated on this with reference to *King Lear*.

> The point about *Lear* is that the people who try to moralise and draw lessons about good and evil, about appropriate behaviour, about how we ought to run a state, run a family, whatever, they are constantly proved wrong and all the attempts to organize experience in a sort of moralizing way are subverted and in the end you are just left with this raw sense that all that matters is to try to be human.[23]

Shakespeare can draw us into a world in which, for a short period, we inhabit a range of other people, in different times and places, with different problems and urgencies, yet whose humanity in all its guises – from Iago to Imogen, Beatrice to Isabella, Leontes to Macbeth – shines through the intensity of their language, the complexity of their feelings, the obstinacy of their struggles and the immediacy of their actions. A good education in Shakespeare is a good education in what it means to be human and that, above all, is its point.

Michael Boyd on why Shakespeare matters

Early in my interview with Michael Boyd, he recalled a moment from his career as a young assistant director at the Belgrade Theatre in Coventry, when he was participating in a Theatre in Education programme about the Irish Potato Famine of the 1840s.

> I remember sitting in a year four-ish primary school classroom, being teamed up with quite a serious-faced young kid and the pair of us being given a dilemma. We had a potato, it was a seed potato, and the dilemma was to eat it now and solve our hunger, because we were on the edge, or keep it and thereby hope to have a crop next year. I was all for eating it, so that I could stay alive in the hope that something might come up, but the kid was saying: 'we can't do that, we'll starve next year'. That sort of blistering, impossible, irresolvable dilemma is the very stuff of great drama, and very Shakespearean, actually.[24]

As a theatre artist rather than an academic, Boyd's thoughts about the value of Shakespeare are traceable principally through the spoken rather than the written word. He did, however, write a brief foreword to the RSC's edition of the Complete Works, published in 2007, in which he offers what he calls 'a few recommendations on how to read this book' from which we can glean much about where and how he thinks we find value in Shakespeare. First and foremost, as we might expect, he urges the reader to regard the plays not as literature but primarily as 'blueprints for performance to a live audience and parts for actors to learn and embody'. He continues: 'There's an extent to which you shouldn't "read" this book at all, but rather speak the parts out loud.' Secondly he suggests that any difficulty in the language is far less to do with the difference between modern and Elizabethan English and more to do with the 'linguistic compression of passionate thought, be it erotic love or political rage'. A character might be being deliberately misleading or obscure, but the clues are always there in the language itself; and if you trust the author, Boyd advises, he will 'take you to places you had previously not imagined or understood'. Finally he counsels us to avoid trying to seek out any 'essential' authorial voice.

> One of the most essential secrets of Shakespeare's survival and brilliance as an artist is his utterly successful sublimation of himself into the constantly conflicting voices of his characters. Thus he avoided . . . stifling his living dramas with the authorial voice of an essayist. Don't try to

decide what the plays are about. Let them be rowdy, lyrical, dirty and inconsistent in your head ... and enjoy the ride on Shakespeare's dangerous contradictions.[25]

It is chiefly in this area of 'dangerous contradictions' that Boyd has pointed to the continuing cultural relevance of Shakespeare in our own time. When interviewed by Charlie Rose in New York,[26] he referred back to John Barton's emphasis on Shakespearean 'antithesis' as the great gift that Shakespeare has bequeathed us: his refusal to judge or tell an audience what to think, or to 'tie these great dilemmas up in a bow'. Instead, he lures us to that place where we are empowered to give such dilemmas serious thought and are demanded to do so. Boyd sees Shakespeare as embodying a divided worldview both as a human being and as an artist: Catholic and Protestant; town and country; privileged and unprivileged; heterosexual and homosexual. His sensitivity to such divisions – religious, social, sexual – makes him 'appallingly contemporary'. He describes this graphically as 'a bag of rats: you open it and they are still wriggling today'. It is in this refusal to be a polemicist or a teacher that we find Shakespeare's humanity as he tries to populate the land in between the great divisions as well as represent those faultlines both fully and truthfully. Shakespeare is always concerned, he suggests, with how we should best behave without ever suggesting that he knows the answer. In *Macbeth* he takes us to the darkest places, 'not to wallow in evil but trying to be fully human'. In Iago and Edmund we are presented with two people who have learned the wrong things from their pain; they have both felt it deeply but their reactions are disastrous as they seek to deny it, control it and manipulate those around them. Shakespeare's moral universe is messy and that is what makes him true to life.

The 'blistering, impossible, irresolvable' dilemmas are populated by characters big enough and memorable enough to embody them, who speak in words that are equally memorable, for both actors and audiences. Simon Schama has commented on how Shakespeare is 'the greatest language enhancer of all time', joining words together, making new words and Boyd agrees. But his poetry, he insists, is never decorative but comes out of a need: it has 'grit and mud' in it, and endures because it is not sentimental. This is because he was never elitist and Boyd reminds us how his fellow playwright, Robert Greene, educated at Cambridge, referred to him as an 'upstart crow'.

Finally, of course, Boyd takes us back to the fact that Shakespeare wrote for the theatre and that theatre has its own, key gift in being an intensely emotional, communal experience. To have the same group of people sit together and breathe the same air, share the same great emotions, the same great ideas, this can never be captured by watching a DVD, he suggests, the experience of which is 'hollow and empty without the conspiracy of the audience' that one finds in live theatre.

When I interviewed Boyd, he spoke at length about what he considered to be Shakespeare's abiding importance for young people both nationally and globally. He commented on the aptness of introducing his work to primary school children, for whom playing with new and rhythmic vocabulary is 'meat and drink'. He spoke, too, of how at all levels of education, the very strangeness of his language can act potentially as a great leveller, as all children will be challenged by it, be they first or additional language users. The fact that Shakespeare is culturally of high status and is known to be, can, he believes, have a very powerful impact on those young people who are inspired to connect with his language and stories. 'That stuff is revolutionary,' he said:

> That moment when you move from being excluded and stupid to included and noticed in an academically positive sense. It's like a slow and controlled explosion that has ripples throughout all your work at school, and also your relationships and well-being.

And, given the fact that 'English has become the Latin or Greek of our time', he believes that Shakespeare provides a space where we can discourse across languages and cultures, in ways that can unify rather than divide us.

> Ultimately he's a poet of a time of great division, whose dramatic language could acknowledge and digest the conflict and the grief of that, while keeping the candle lit for harmony and resolution, which in itself makes him valuable. And while he digests that conflict and grief, and while he keeps the candle alight for resolution, he doesn't resolve anything within the work, which is why it is still alive and incandescent now.[27]

A shared vision of Shakespeare's value

Although Michael Boyd's terminology and examples are different from Jonathan Bate's, I think they share many understandings as to the continuing value of Shakespeare. Both see the plays as embodying contrary perspectives on deeply rooted social, moral and political questions that continue to resonate today, questions that Shakespeare vividly animates yet never attempts to resolve in any didactic manner. In this sense, as Bate explained to me, they both share 'that sense that a Shakespeare play is a debate; is a posing of questions'. He went on:

> The archetypal Shakespeare encounter is where you've got two people putting different points of view, whether it's a pair of bickering lovers or a political debate or whatever, and that sense that everybody has their truth and truth overall has many aspects to it. You see things one way, you see it another, and in the end knowledge comes not through articulating a proposition or a position but working through an argument,

performing experience. I think those two things – aspectuality and performativity – are for me, as I said in *The Genius of Shakespeare*, the message of Shakespeare. I think those are things that Michael also believes and that they've shaped a lot of his work.[28]

Both see the cultural effect of Shakespeare in political terms, viewing him as a playwright of direct and immediate relevance as much to the disadvantaged and dispossessed as to the establishment and neither sees any place for elitism in an education in Shakespeare. In different ways they describe him as offering a voice to those whose first language may not be English. Both point to the language of Shakespeare as being central to his appeal and view the challenge it affords young people in positive terms, as something from which they can derive great feelings of achievement.[29] Both stress that, when considering the big questions, Shakespeare takes us into dark places not to moralize but to offer us a broad education in humanity. Boyd stresses the importance of play and playfulness when approaching a Shakespeare script, and play is inherent to the concept of performativity that Bate sees as key to the message of Shakespeare and the various games that his stories play out for us. Closely related to this is the value of theatre itself, which both appreciate in similar terms, as the process of theatre is the process through which these games, these stories, are continually re-interpreted and renewed. Boyd, as we have seen, sees the communal experience of theatre as something uniquely special and Bate spoke of the essentially collaborative nature of theatre, specifically as it relates to Shakespeare, as an understanding he believes he shares with Boyd.

> There is something very special about theatre because it is a communal activity in which the creative work and the receptive audience share the same space and time. It's different from the cinema where you are looking at a two-dimensional representation of a piece of completed work; it's different from a novel that is consumed in the head; it's live, it's risky it's that shared space.

He views the Shakespearean theatre as 'the first place in modern times where a public comes together to witness, to hear about, to debate big questions of politics, society, justice, law, life, death, family, all the big questions'. Like Boyd, he sees the theatre as still possessing this role, as still being the only live public forum where these questions are played out in collective form – hence its political significance.[30]

Conclusion

What I have tried to demonstrate here is the considerable overlap between the ideas of Boyd, the artistic director, and Bate, a leading Shakespeare scholar, both coincidentally at the RSC at almost exactly the same time. This consistency, I will suggest, allows us to draw on both of these leading figures when considering a theoretical grounding for the pedagogy the RSC was already developing during this period. These principles can be outlined as follows:

- The pedagogy will present a Shakespeare play in a way that prioritizes intensity and variety of effect so that the language can be felt strongly and interpreted differently.
- It will encourage different interpretations and due examination of the contrasting visions and perspectives of the characters.
- It will refrain from imposing an over-arching didactic or moralistic vision on the plays and will not shy away from the big questions they are asking.
- It will approach the plays performatively, that is to say, actively and playfully, seeing the experience of this process as key to the learning.
- It will be collaborative and communal in its approach, making space for performance and reception as well as reflection.
- It will seek out ways to make the language part of this performative process so that finding one's voice in the lines of Shakespeare is enjoyable and rewarding as well as challenging.
- It will seek to be inclusive and have no truck with elitism.

I am offering these principles as explanatory rather than foundational; in other words, I am not suggesting that the pedagogy was devised during some managerial brain-storming session or that it derives from some concocted corporate statement – of course not. There were precursors within the RSC who shaped the Company's pedagogic approaches, as did outside influences, and we will examine these in the next chapter. There is, too, a body of theory from outside of the world of Shakespeare, from education in general and from drama education in particular, that will further our theoretical understanding of its processes once we have explored its practice. What I am suggesting is that during the Michael Boyd years there was an organic coming together of educational and artistic policies, theoretical understandings and practical approaches, of academic, educational and theatrical expertise, brought about through an opening up of the Company's internal structures and the presence of some inspirational figures. We have seen in the last chapter how Boyd went about structurally integrating the education department into the artistic culture of the Company and how Jonathan Bate promoted the RSC's rehearsal room approaches for teaching purposes as a central idea of the CAPITAL project.[31] Mary Johnson recalls leading workshops at Warwick University during the early days of CAPITAL, which Bate attended, and spoke warmly to me of the support and understanding he showed for her work. When I asked Bate whether he thought that the *Stand up for Shakespeare* pedagogy was appropriate to his own theories of why Shakespeare matters he was in no doubt: 'Yes, I absolutely think it is,' he replied.[32] We now need to turn directly to this pedagogy, the genesis and nature of which will be examined in the next two chapters.

3

Developing a Rehearsal Room Pedagogy at the RSC: Key Influences

Introduction

While signalling the importance of Michael Boyd and Jonathan Bate to a theory of Shakespeare's value that can underpin the pedagogy of *Stand up for Shakespeare*, I have been at pains to emphasize this relationship between theory and practice as explanatory rather than foundational. The pedagogy itself emerged organically and fluidly, through practice and over time. Although it now offers a sure set of principles and tried-and-tested strategies it should still be regarded as developmental and not as fixed, and certainly not as any kind of orthodoxy. In considering its genesis we need to consider the work of influential practitioners and the creative approaches generated from their passions, insights and experience. We begin within the RSC itself by looking at the rehearsal room approaches of Cicely Berry before turning away from the Company to examine the groundbreaking work of Rex Gibson. Next we will consider the work of RSC practitioner Mary Johnson; of pivotal importance, she has brought specific theatrical understandings to her extensive work with teachers and found ways of adapting Berry's approaches to suit classroom practice. Finally we will consider the pedagogical practices of the wider drama education community by attending to the work of Jonothan Neelands and its contribution to – and differences from – the RSC's own approaches.

Cicely Berry

When considering internal influences on the RSC's pedagogy, there is really only one place to begin and that is with the legendary work of their long-standing voice coach, Cicely Berry. Eighty-seven years of age at the time of writing, she has been with the Company for over forty years, joining it in 1970. Her work has been recognized through the award of numerous honours, including two honorary doctorates, an OBE and a CBE, and noted as inspirational by directors and actors as celebrated as Peter Brook, Emma Watson and Sam West, all of whom testify to her ability to help actors connect personally with the language of Shakespeare, and to discover their own interpretations of his text rather than have them dictated from outside. In Sam West's words: 'She gives the power and freedom back to the actor without any sense of being imposed upon.'[1] She achieves this through a variety of vocal and physical approaches that are hugely playful but always shrewdly purposeful and acutely responsive to the sounds and rhythms of the text and based upon her own conviction – a conviction drawn from many years' experience – that the opposition between the intellectual and the physical that is so deeply rooted in our culture works against our ability to feel the power and the meaning of Shakespeare's plays through the language itself. As Michael Boyd sees it: 'her achievement has been to rubbish the meaningless opposition of thought and physicality, of mind and body, teaching us instead to embody thought in rigorous and responsible childlike play'.[2]

Berry believes that the era in which we live is overly literal; that the private experience of reading for meaning is prized too highly and runs counter to our ability to connect with the sounds, the rhythms, the music of Shakespeare's language at a deep level of feeling. If we are able readers, we tend to rush into sense making; we fail to *hear* the language and consequently fail to grasp how sound and meaning are subtly related.

> Reading Shakespeare simply to make sense of the language and to find the various possible meanings of words in the end emasculates the language. Of course we have to know what it means in a literal way and explore the possible variations in the text, but we must not leave it there, for then we engage only our minds and do not allow our imaginations also to be engaged, alert, and active. We talk about the images but do not let the images affect us.[3]

The way to get the images to affect us, to penetrate our imaginations, is through tapping into the sensual qualities of the language so that they work on our instincts. 'Words should disturb, delight, and provoke the hearer', she writes, 'not merely make sense.'[4] Berry is fond of citing the statistic that in Shakespeare's own time only eight per cent of the population was literate. They did not come to the theatre to appreciate the actor's interpretation of a play they had already studied or read, but to listen and be taken on an emotional journey through the story, their emotions aroused by the sounds and rhythms of the language through which it was being told. She thinks that we still share this same, primal human need; 'as people, as humans', she told me, 'we are still drawn by sound and by what sound does to us'.[5] Like

Michael Boyd, she accounts for the popularity of rap among young people in similar terms:

> I think the great thing about Shakespeare, [is] he had this sense of a beat underneath. We talk intellectually about the iambic pentameter, but it's more than that, it's something that draws us to listen, the sense of that beat, and what you can do with it. Peter Brook said that there's a million ways of saying one line, but you keep that beat underneath and it draws us. I think rap does that: it draws you and yet the variety on the top of that beat is just unlimited.[6]

Berry works principally with actors in the rehearsal room, of course, and it is with actors that she has developed most of the approaches she has written about and that are demonstrated on DVD.[7] But before we consider some examples, we should bear in mind that she has also used the same approaches when working in schools, prisons and with disadvantaged young people in the favelas of Brazil. 'I get a great kick working with young people just to get them to feel the language in their bodies,' she told me, 'and they get so surprised about how they understand it that way rather than by reading it.'[8] In fact it was while working with the RSC in schools during the 1970s that she first began to develop her particular approaches in response to problems she came across while working with groups of fifteen- to eighteen-year-olds. Some classes she found to be very able readers, others much less so. With the latter she developed communal activities to slow down the reading and give the students time to gain confidence with the language – 'to feel the excitement of passing the language on to each other', she writes, 'a collective response, so they could forget what they felt were their own inadequacies'.[9] In the process she noticed that these 'less advanced' students seemed to respond to the imagery and hence understand the meaning of the text at a deeper level than those who were more academically inclined, who read without effort but remained relatively unmoved by the text.

A breakthrough moment that she described to me – and which she has written about on more than one occasion – came during a workshop with sixteen-year-old boys who were studying Act 3 Scene 3 of *Othello*, in particular the speech in which Othello's jealousy is unleashed and, swearing revenge, he compares his feelings to the Pontic sea, '*Whose icy current and compulsive course / Ne'er feels retiring ebb*'. She explains:

> The students all knew perfectly well what it meant and understood all the allusions but they were not moved by it. In my frustration at their apparent lack of involvement in Othello's dilemma, I got them all to stand up, link arms and pull against each other as they read. That exercise got rough and desks fell over but one studious young man afterwards said to me, 'I see how he feels – he is drowning in his feelings'. That

confirmed to me the need to involve the body as well as the mind in order to elicit the layers of meaning in the text.[10]

Hitherto Berry's work had been entirely experimental and reactive to particular problems; from this point on she began to be more systematic in developing physical approaches for the rehearsal room that were specifically designed to draw actors into feeling the emotive power of the language and deliberately worked against what she felt to be overly literal approaches. The work was at once artistic, experimental and educational, an early example of how learning in the classroom can feed into the artistry of the rehearsal room and vice versa. Her various books describe examples of her work in detail and in *Working Shakespeare*, published in 2004, there is a particularly illuminating series of DVDs in which we see her leading a two-day workshop with a number of British and US actors, many of whom, such as Lindsay Duncan, Toby Stephens and Samuel L. Jackson, were already established stars of stage and screen. 'What makes this so special,' explains Jeremy Irons in a brief introduction, 'is that we see them working together and finding a collective response to Shakespeare's language. You will see them discovering layers of meaning and rhythm in the text for themselves,' he continues, 'and also – and this is important – finding the joy in the language'.[11] Playful exploration, a collective or ensemble work ethic, and an emphasis on the pleasure and enjoyment to be found in the language itself: all central tenets of *Stand up for Shakespeare* and already present here.

One of the earliest exercises she does with the group centres around the prologue to *Romeo and Juliet* – the sonnet '*Two households both alike in dignity*' – and we can use it as a simple illustration of the physical, personal and collective approaches she deploys and the creative responses these elicit from the actors she works with. She begins by asking them to move about the space muttering the text aloud and explains this is to help them become familiar with it without feeling any pressure to do it right. She then asks them to sit in a circle and read it together, beating out the iambic rhythm as they do so – 'tee-*tum*-tee-*tum*-tee-*tum*-tee-*tum*-tee-*tum*' – and to notice those places where the rhythm of the meter and the rhythm of the sense do not coincide. It is quickly evident that this happens in the very first words – '*Two households*' – where each of the syllables requires an equal stress, which makes the two words immediately stand out, signalling subliminally their absolute centrality to the coming drama. She now has the group stand up and walk through the space again, reading the text individually, this time changing direction on every punctuation mark. This, we are told, helps us realize that thought is movement and demonstrates how rapidly thought can change direction in our minds. It is a particularly good exercise when working with character, she explains. Later in the workshop, this is strikingly illustrated by the actor Paul Jesson working on Capulet's speech in Act 3 Scene 5 – '*God's bread, it makes me mad*'. Here he is remonstrating with Juliet on her refusal to marry Paris and the choppiness and volatility of the rhythm causes Jesson constantly to change direction and catch his breath, thus clearly physicalizing the emotional turmoil the character is suffering during this scene.

Back in the circle, and still working on the prologue, the actors are asked to stand close to one another and read the text again, this time jostling against one another. As well as being slightly and enjoyably anarchic, this exercise is designed 'to stop us making the voice behave in the way we think it should'. It brings out the latent violence in some of the words, words such as 'grudge', 'overthrows', 'strife', 'death-marked', as we cannot help but be playfully irritated when being jostled in this way. Then Toby Stephens volunteers to read the whole prologue from the centre of the circle while the other actors are invited, without looking at the text, to echo those words that strike them in any way. The echoes are varied and personal and one actor instigates a reflective discussion on which words appear to be ignored – the softer, more domestic and personal vocabulary as opposed to the more strident language of conflict and struggle, again an example of how within the language itself we can find the central themes of the play. At the conclusion of the work on the prologue, LaTanya Richardson confesses that, as an African American actor, she had previously found that with Shakespeare 'the words get in the way'; that she had felt they lacked the emotional, visceral immediacy that language has in her own culture. These approaches, however, had made Shakespeare's language come alive for her in a different way – a clear indication of how their playful physicality and the way they manage to displace preconceptions can help those who have felt that Shakespeare is not for them find the connection through the language, and not in spite of it.

Rex Gibson

For all of its seminal importance to *Stand up for Shakespeare*, Berry's work did not really impact on how Shakespeare was being taught in schools in the 1980s and 1990s. During this period, by far the most influential work in the UK was being carried out by Rex Gibson, director of the Shakespeare and Schools project, which began in 1986. Gibson led the project from the Cambridge Institute of Education and produced a series of newsletters, each containing articles and information intended to support the teaching of Shakespeare to all ages and abilities at secondary level. He also set up an extensive in-service programme which involved teachers returning to their classrooms and carrying out research into student responses to their teaching. This led in 1990 to a publication of papers written by a number of these teachers, *Secondary School Shakespeare: Classroom Practice*. Testimony to the positive effects of their work is provided not only by Gibson himself in the introduction but also in a quote taken from the National Curriculum English Working Group, which praised how the project had demonstrated 'that the once-traditional method where desk-bound pupils read the text has been advantageously replaced by exciting, enjoyable approaches that are social, imaginative and physical'.[12]

The project's most significant publications came in the form of school editions of the plays which began to appear in 1991, published by the Cambridge University Press. Each volume presents a full text of the play with a facing page that includes scene summaries, help with vocabulary and, most importantly, a series of suggestions for practical activities, many of which are performance-related, to help the students explore, connect with and enjoy the language, characters and plots of the plays. 'Seek to create moments of theatre', Gibson advises, 'that put some of the most powerful words of the play into the mouths of the pupils and which spur them to a range of imaginative encounters: drama, mime, painting, drawing, designing, craft work, writing, making and re-creating.'[13] By the time of Gibson's death in 2005, global sales of these editions had surpassed one million copies and the accompanying teacher's guide *Teaching Shakespeare* was established as the classic handbook for new and experienced teachers alike.[14]

Central to Gibson's pedagogy is what he calls 'active methods' and in his introduction to *Teaching Shakespeare* he clarifies what the principles behind these are. First and foremost teachers should treat the plays as plays and build what he calls 'dramatic realization' into their teaching, making room for different kinds of 'imaginative enactment'. He writes:

> The dramatic context demands classroom practices that are the antithesis of methods in which students sit passively, without intellectual or emotional engagement. Shakespeare is not a museum exhibit with a large 'Do not touch' label but a living force inviting active, imaginative recreation ... Direct experience of Shakespeare's language allows students to feel the distinctive forms and rhythms and to respond with a real sense of engagement.[15]

The book goes on to provide a set of principles for the teaching of Shakespeare, which emphasize the need for social and collective approaches to the work as well as the need to allow for choice and variety in student responses, a need which relates to the plurality of perspectives embedded in the plays themselves and the 'negative capability' of Shakespeare as an artist. Gibson is also very clear about the damaging impact on school Shakespeare from the legacy of scholarly, literary approaches that have historically dominated our understanding of how his work should be approached. As literary texts, the plays are seen as serious, difficult, authoritative, to be read passively and regarded with reverence; by contrast, if we re-cast them as play scripts then we will come to see them as texts to play with, and necessarily so, as they are incomplete without enactment. 'Scholarly editions', he writes, 'promote teaching methods that explain and analyze rather than enable students actively to inhabit the imaginative worlds that Shakespeare offers.'[16] His point here is not to condemn scholarly approaches but to argue that, however suitable they are for advanced study, they are seriously demotivating for the vast majority of school and college students. Playful approaches, by contrast, release the energies of both the students and the language.

There ensue chapters on Shakespeare's language, on his themes, characters and stories; all are written with clarity, a passion for the plays and an evident conviction that these approaches can transform the classroom experiences of children. The chapter that lists and describes the active methods themselves is particularly practical, varied and imaginative in the range of strategies it offers for individuals, pairs, groups and whole-class activities. With its emphasis on play, on social and physical activity, on treating the plays as scripts rather than literature, on engaging young people's imaginations through the language itself, Gibson's active approaches chime readily with *Stand up for Shakespeare*, so much so that the RSC has been accused of simply borrowing his clothes and adding little to them.[17] Although the Company openly acknowledges his influence, it is, however, insistent that Cicely Berry remains seminal to their pedagogy[18] and that there are major differences between Berry's and Gibson's active approaches.

Key to this is the sense that Gibson, for all his emphasis on dramatic approaches, is very much writing for a conventional classroom rather than a rehearsal room, whilst Berry is always working in a rehearsal room. With Gibson one senses the desks are still there for much of the time, particularly for many of the activities suggested on the facing pages of the playtexts published in the Cambridge School Shakespeare series. Here Gibson's scholarship and understanding of the plays and their language are impressive, accessible and hugely supportive for teachers. His suggestions for student activity are carefully intended to illuminate questions of character and motivation, language and meaning, but they are often not *that* physically active, and there is much reading aloud, talking in pairs and simple tableau work. When he suggests that students work in a group or in pairs to act out a scene, they are given precise directions but there is very much a feel of them then being expected to connect with the language and devise a performance autonomously. If such an activity were to fall flat, teachers would need to know the active methods suggested in the *Teaching Shakespeare* handbook very well if they were to choose from them to help their students re-engage with the language and the scene. There is, too, the possibility that the plays presented in this series could come to feel and be treated like textbooks rather than performance scripts; if they are worked through sequentially over a long period of time, excitement could well wane once the novelty wears off.

By contrast Berry can assume prior knowledge of the play's plot from her actors and is thus able to work on short scenes and speeches that are handed out on individual sheets of paper, very much as Shakespeare's actors would have experienced a rehearsal script themselves. Gibson is proud that the series 'does not offer a cut-down or simplified version of the play(s)'.[19] Berry, on the other hand, places a greater stress on players immersing themselves in the language of a particularly vivid scene or speech rather than on covering the ground of the play; on working in different ways experimentally with the same extract of text, to swim in the language, so to speak, to be tossed about by its rhythms and stresses and thus discover what unforeseen dramatic meanings might be brought to the surface in the process. Her physicality is often risky, perhaps too risky for some teachers, so while Gibson's restraint is highly understandable, the result is that it does lack the playful edginess and deep theatricality of Cicely Berry's work and sometimes has the feel of a rush to sense-making – something that Berry is very much against – even in those activities that appear to be adapted from her work.[20] In a section in *Teaching Shakespeare* entitled 'Acting a Scene', for example, the emphasis is on discussion and meaningful decision-making, quite contrary to the way that Berry seeks out what she calls 'displacement strategies'; in other words, physical activities that seem irrelevant to the dramatic situation yet which are chosen precisely for their potential to unleash its hidden energies.[21] Meaning is always important in her work, of course, but she searches for surprising and oblique ways to draw it out from the unconscious, whereas Gibson operates very much in the conscious, rational world of teacher planning. None of this should necessarily be read as a criticism of Gibson's work or of its remarkable achievement, but it does point to the fact that the classroom is still far removed from the rehearsal room in his pedagogy. This difference was something Mary Johnson was particularly aware of when she left teaching in schools to take up her position with the RSC and her own work was to become a key bridging point between the two learning spaces.

Mary Johnson

Mary Johnson joined the RSC in 1997 as a senior education officer with special responsibility for developing programmes of in-service work for teachers. She later became acting Head of Education for a short period and is still employed by the Company on a freelance basis to work with teachers and help with projects. She is one of the three named authors of the *RSC Shakespeare Toolkit for Teachers* and, although she herself modestly admits to being greatly influenced by those she worked with in her early days at the RSC, key practitioners in the education department today readily signal the pedagogic approaches she developed as core to their current practice.

Johnson is originally from the US and spent a number of years as an actor, actor trainer and drama teacher before joining the RSC. She quickly decided that the Company's educational work had to reflect the spirit and practices of its rehearsal rooms. She spent time in Cicely Berry's workshops, read her books and made a point of associating with actors, whom she invited to work alongside her with teachers. She became convinced that one of her core tasks was to find ways of adapting for the needs of teachers what she calls the 'physical paradigms' that Cicely Berry uses with actors to help them feel and connect with the text. She explained to me what she means by this:

> By physical paradigm I mean an activity or structure which allows the actor to discover for him or herself an important truth about the text. These exercises are physical and often reveal the non-verbal power of the text. By their nature, they help to connect thought and feeling.[22]

She exemplified this by referring to a particular workshop she was involved in, one that explored how Ophelia feels after the nunnery scene (Act 3 Scene 1) in the speech *'Oh what a noble mind is here o'erthrown'*. There was an exercise in which all of the players were asked to read the speech together, enunciating the vowels only, not the consonants, 'so you hear this is just an Irish keen, a wail – that is what Shakespeare has written'. Then, volunteering to take the part of Ophelia, Johnson was asked to read the speech as a way of putting her case to everyone else in the room; they, secretly, were told to turn and walk away from her whenever she tried to speak to them. 'I remember doing that, playing Ophelia, and I just stood there in the middle of the floor feeling absolutely desolate and it suddenly hit me how alone she was. I just felt abandoned, and of course Ophelia is abandoned.'[23] Johnson describes working in this way as 'starting from the gut instead of from the head'. She clarified how this understanding has informed her own and her colleagues' work at the RSC and essentially what makes it distinctive from Rex Gibson's active approaches.

> Rex articulated, supported, extended and made public a style of work that teachers themselves were beginning to develop and use. The RSC work is more theatre-based. It almost always needs an open space and involves much more movement than Rex's work. It promotes instinct and imagination as starting points rather than thinking and planning and offers structures which do that. It tends to follow David Kolb's experiential learning cycle – start with doing something together, so that a shared experience provides a common understanding as a foundation for discussion and debate; then reflect on and analyse that experience before applying what has been learned to the next activity. It promotes spontaneity, the affective, the unconscious, the imagination, not at the expense of the cognitive, rational and articulated, but as starting points. It tries to unite feeling and thinking, and movement is essential for the former.[24]

A *Macbeth* workshop that she originally devised in 2004 provides a range of examples that illustrate how she drew upon Berry's work and other rehearsal approaches and adapted them for teachers to make use of.[25] Many of these are now standard strategies used by the RSC's education team. First of all, it is interesting that in her notes for teachers she uses the term 'players' for those involved in the workshop – not 'teachers', not 'actors' – which recalls how actors were referred to in Shakespeare's own time whilst emphasizing the centrality of play to the rehearsal room. Like any practised drama teacher, she outlines a range of possible warm-up activities, two of which are particularly worthy of note. The first is called 'touching objects' and involves players running around the space touching five objects and calling out the names of them as they do so. The activity is immediately repeated but this time, with no prior planning, the actors have to call the objects something entirely different. Johnson told me that this is an exercise originally devised by her colleague, Sarah Downing, that helps players 'get out of their heads' and be spontaneous and inventive, reflective of that valuing of the unconscious she found so important in the work of Cicely Berry. Another warm-up exercise with a similar purpose is called 'make me a . . .'. Here players are asked to form small groups and then, without talking, make in five seconds images of a crown, a dagger, a battle scene, and a meeting of witches. Not only does this introduce players to key images from the play but it also requires them to work instinctively and makes visible from the outset what startling and vivid results can emerge from such spontaneity. To talk is to plan, she told me, and the unconscious in this context produces richer results.

The first exercises with text clearly draw from Cicely Berry's approaches. The speech is by Macbeth and is taken from Act 1 Scene 3, in which we hear his initial response to the fact that the witches' prophecies seem to be coming true. It is presented to the players in the format below.

Two truths are told
As happy prologues to the swelling Act
Of the imperial theme. – I thank you, gentlemen.
(aside) *This supernatural soliciting*
Cannot be ill, cannot be good. *If ill,*
Why hath it given me earnest of success
Commencing in a truth? I am Thane of Cawdor.
If good, why do I yield to that suggestion
Whose horrid image doth unfix my hair,
And make my seated heart knock at my ribs
Against the use of nature? *Present fears*
Are less than horrible imaginings.
My thought, whose murder yet is but fantastical,
Shakes so my single state of man
That function is smothered in surmise,
And nothing is but what is not.

The workshop leader first of all reads through the speech with the players being asked to listen with their eyes closed and to repeat any words that suggest to them that Macbeth is anxious or frightened; because their eyes are closed, the players are forced to listen and not read, and the directive focuses their attention thematically whilst still leaving space for responses to be personal and different. In order to deepen their understanding of Macbeth's internal conflict during this speech, players, working in groups of three, are then asked to do what Johnson calls the 'whispering exercise'. For this, one player sits in a chair with her eyes closed, while the other two whisper in each of her ears. One of these whispers the 'hopeful' side of Macbeth's speech (italicized in the version shown above) while the other whispers the 'fearful' side (underlined in this version). Whenever the speech is both italicized and underlined, both players are to speak at once. The leader then asks all of the players taking the role of Macbeth what it felt like for him here and what caused the feelings they describe. The exercise is essentially performative, once again placing the emphasis on hearing and feeling the language with the leader channelling the players' attention in a specific direction that prioritizes personal and group response in the process of sense-making. The players now individually read the speech as a 'punctuation shift exercise', moving through the space and changing direction on every punctuation mark. So that players can reflect upon the journey Macbeth makes from the beginning to the end of the play, this exercise is immediately repeated with a later speech, from Act 5 Scene 3 – 'Throw physic to the dogs! I'll none of it!' – and they are asked to offer single words to describe the man they have just walked.

When Johnson makes use of Berry's strategies, she adapts and extends them so that they become more structured, with the kind of precise and clearly inscribed focus that teachers need if they are to be enabled, as she puts it, to move from the head to the gut. A final example from this workshop will further illustrate how she has designed her own 'physical paradigms' to help teachers achieve this. It also serves to illustrate how she developed exercises designed to illuminate aspects of the text other than how the language works.

An exercise entitled 'bringing the news' highlights the tumultuous action of the play as Macbeth, Lady Macbeth and the witches combine to bring on the catastrophe. Macbeth or a cluster of Macbeths is chosen, or perhaps the teacher might decide to play this role. Each player is given a text scrap. Macbeth's is a short speech from Act 5 'I will not yield / to kiss the ground before young Malcolm's feet' when he realizes he has no hope. The others all have single lines, items of bad news for him that are taken from throughout the play, such as 'Most royal sir – Fleance is scaped'; 'The Queen my lord is dead'; and 'Macduff was from his mother's womb / untimely ripped'. Macbeth(s) stand in the middle of the space and the rest of the players spread out equidistant from one another and begin to walk. They maintain this equidistance as they are coached to walk faster and faster, with more energy and purpose. At a prearranged signal, the first player walks with purpose up to Macbeth and delivers his or her line of news. The other players deliver their lines in sequence in the same manner – walking up to Macbeth, giving him the news and walking away again to continue pacing through the room. Players are coached to be sensitive to the energy in the room and to increase their speed and intensity as the sequence of lines nears its climax – as the news itself becomes more urgent and life-threatening. When all the news has been delivered, Macbeth speaks his response and rushes from the space.

These and other strategies devised by Johnson have influenced the lexicon of the RSC's pedagogy. As with all teaching approaches, they need to be used carefully and in a considered fashion if they are to encourage learning and not become mere activity. Hence the order and rhythm of these activities need to be planned with aesthetic as well as learning outcomes in mind, with an understanding that the one is dependent on the other. Such an awareness of how we learn through drama was pioneered in practices outside of the RSC, in the traditions of drama and theatre in education to which we now turn.

Jonothan Neelands

Jonothan Neelands, one of the most influential international figures in the theory and practice of drama education, comes from a tradition of participatory educational drama which includes, among others, Dorothy Heathcote, Gavin Bolton and Cecily O'Neill. He is particularly well known to English and drama teachers for the range of strategies or 'conventions' he has developed to help them structure focused improvisatory drama activities into their lessons and for the inspirational workshops through which he models how these approaches can be used to great effect. His workshops, whether using playtexts, historical material, fictional stories or a mixture of all three, are principally concerned with enabling young people to work collectively in order to engage with and reflect upon questions of political and human significance. He is a passionate advocate of the importance of drama and theatre for young people as both a curriculum and a cultural entitlement and, in this sense, he views the teaching of Shakespeare as being of political significance:

> It became increasingly obvious to me that if anybody liked Shakespeare at all it was because they had been led to Shakespeare and that was likely to be through a teacher. So how you teach it makes all the difference. Bourdieu always said that works of art are only rare in the sense that the skills of being able to decode them are rare and restricted to certain groups. You can't get as much out of opera, literature, the Tate Gallery, all of those things unless someone has given you the eyes and the skills to be able to make sense of them and appreciate them and understand them.

For some that will happen at home but for most children, unless that happens in school, they will never have the choice of accessing the complex arts. And I really do think that the complex arts offer us the chance to engage in ways that reach very deeply into our sense of humanity.[26]

Given this commitment, his considerable professional experience and the fact that he is such a prominent figure in the field, it was logical for Neelands, as a professor at Warwick University, to become involved in the certificated courses for teachers and actors. His association with the RSC had begun earlier than this, however. He had previously worked over a number of years with Mary Johnson and also extensively with two other key education practitioners at the RSC, Rachel Gartside and Miles Tandy, both of whom openly acknowledge his influence on their own teaching.

There are key differences, however, between the approaches of Neelands and those that emanate from within the RSC's own artistic and educational practices. Whereas Cicely Berry begins and ends with the language of Shakespeare, Neelands approaches the plays from a different direction, more in line with his own tradition of practice and influenced by the theories of Jerome Bruner.

What excites me is 'inside out' learning in Bruner's sense; that in play we bring what we already know about the world and we adapt learning to our inner world rather than having to adapt our inner world to what's being presented to us externally. This is why I don't start with the language but come to it later. You've got to enjoy the experience and get something from it first and foremost. That for me is what is really important. My principle interest is in engaging young people in the themes and the meanings.[27]

The common bank of activities and terms in the *Shakespeare Toolkit* include a number of approaches intended to help students explore the themes and ideas of the plays without making use of their language. Some of these are long-established conventions from the tradition of drama education, such as the teacher and students working in role, perhaps as the citizens of Verona meeting to discuss what they can do to stop all the street violence. Although Neelands did not invent all of these, his work has certainly popularized them and many of the activities described here, such as 'imaging', 'sculpting', 'role on the wall', 'thought tracking' and 'voices in the head', can be traced directly back to his own publication, *Structuring Drama Work*.[28] Their significance is that, when deployed with a due sense of the aesthetic, they are themselves theatrical, making use of physicality, sound, voice and role in ways that can draw students emotionally into the world of the play and help them reflect upon it in ways other than through discussion or writing. They are intended to complement, illuminate and contextualize script work, not replace it.

A good example of the subtle ways in which Neelands uses role work can be found in a workshop he led in 2008, with an early cohort of RSC actors following the PG award and a group of female students from a secondary school in Wimbledon.[29] The award focuses principally on teaching actors how to use the deep knowledge they acquire from the rehearsal process about the text and to shape it in ways that students can access. Here, however, Neelands was modelling a way that they might use their theatrical skills in a convention commonly known as 'teacher in role'. His focus was on Ophelia and early on in the workshop participants were asked to work in pairs and create – through drawings or symbolic use of objects – a 'Circle of Love' of all of the gifts given to Ophelia by Hamlet as tokens or memories of his feelings for her. Neelands in role as Ophelia then stepped into this circle and began to improvise with the objects, letting it be known that her father had told her she must return them all to Hamlet. She is distracted and rambling, providing participants with the necessary back story of their relationship, mixing contemporary language with text scraps, including lines drawn from the songs she sings later in the play. The soliloquy sets up the parameters for her current dilemma, how she is torn between her passionate love for Hamlet and her love and duty for her father and brother; and how she no longer is sure of who loves her and why. It is careful to suggest not to tell, providing clues to be interpreted, a subtext as well as contextual information. After some discussion and reflection together on what they had just seen, participants were then divided into groups and each was given a different scenario, an 'offstage' moment to prepare for, when Ophelia was to meet either Hamlet or her father, Polonius. They were to decide what her attitude would be and what she might or might not say to each. A volunteer from each group in turn then entered the circle as Ophelia to improvise a scene with the teacher in role in what Neelands calls a 'circular drama'. In one scene Ophelia had to respond to her father as he attempted to persuade her not to see Hamlet again and to return his letters and gifts; in another she had to find ways of resisting Hamlet's entreaties and sticking to her father's demands. In each case participants were being asked to draw upon their own understandings of father / daughter and girlfriend / boyfriend relationships to make sense of the characters and their dilemmas before engaging directly in work with the text. In other words, the emphasis was on them exploring their own shared sense of humanity as a way of accessing the themes and potential meanings of the play itself.

Conclusion

A cursory glance back at the pedagogic principles proposed at the end of the last chapter will demonstrate the extent of their relevance to the work of the above practitioners as described here. It is clearly evident that all four espouse collaborative approaches, see performance, activity and playfulness as central to their practice, and welcome variety of interpretation and intensity of response, whilst guiding the parameters of such responses through the ways that they frame the activities and any subsequent reflection upon them. They see Shakespeare as a cultural entitlement for all, believing passionately that the humanity at the heart of the plays continues to be pressingly relevant today. There is a difference in how much centrality they give to the language of Shakespeare; whilst Neelands does believe engagement with the text to be essential, he tends to prioritize the issues raised by the plays rather than the language, whereas the others place the language itself at the core of a collective investigation. In doing this, both Cicely Berry and Mary Johnson see theatrical submersion in the language as the surest way for actors and young people alike to find pleasure and intensity in the work and to be provoked into engaging with the characters and their worlds. This, we shall see, has become a core principle of the RSC's pedagogy. In the next chapter we will look at how this has developed during the period of the LPN, how it has been described and presented in its educational publications, and examine a recent and detailed example of it in practice.

4

The Classroom as Rehearsal Room: An Example of Practice

The RSC Shakespeare Toolkit for Teachers

If Mary Johnson was key in beginning what could be seen as a specific pedagogy that connected classroom practices with the RSC rehearsal room, other talented practitioners have been instrumental in developing it further within the context of the Learning and Performance Network. As we have seen, Jacqui O'Hanlon, the current director of education, joined the RSC in 2003, initially as Head of Professional Development, and was instrumental in the conception and implementation of the LPN. Very early in this process she invited Rachel Gartside to work first as one of its associates and then as a leading practitioner. Rachel had trained as a drama teacher, subsequently becoming director of education at the Birmingham Rep, and brought with her a practice she describes as 'rooted in the collaborative, inquiry based, dialogic approach that characterises both a good rehearsal room and a good classroom'.[1]

The traditions of both the RSC rehearsal studio and the collaborative drama classroom are in evidence in *The RSC Shakespeare Toolkit for Teachers*, published in 2010 and written principally with secondary school English teachers in mind. The book was edited by Jacqui and co-written by Rachel, Mary Johnson and Rebecca Gould, an experienced director of young people's theatre.[2] Rachel remembers the writing of the book as a 'creative struggle' between people with different opinions drawing from their own distinctive teaching backgrounds. It consists of three lengthy chapters, each detailing a scheme of work for a different play, with a glossary of activities and common terms included at the back. The chapter on *Macbeth* is planned to illustrate how to use the approaches as a journey of discovery through an entire play; *A Midsummer Night's Dream* exemplifies a multi-sensory, multi-disciplinary approach to planning; while *Romeo and Juliet* is used explicitly to model strategies that can be transferred and applied to any of Shakespeare's plays. Each is presented in the form of detailed lesson plans, with learning objectives and suggestions for homework, and edited scenes from the plays included as photocopiable resources. The common bank of activities and terms is comprehensive and designed for teachers who will not necessarily come from a drama background. Although listed alphabetically these can roughly be divided into three types: common theatrical terms such as 'back story', 'blocking', 'staging' and 'the world of the play'; activities specifically designed by the RSC to reflect their own rehearsal room approaches, such as 'punctuation shift', 'five point chase' and 'interpolated questions'; and activities from the tradition of drama education, such as 'freeze frames', 'meeting in role' and 'voices in the head'.

In March 2013, the Secretary of State for Education, Michael Gove, gave the Company a grant to pay for a copy of the book to be distributed to every state-funded secondary school in the UK. There was some controversy about this as Gove was not a popular figure in many staff rooms. The RSC attempted to gauge the impact of the publication by emailing an online survey to every school for which it had an address on its records three months after the *Toolkits* had been delivered. Forty completed surveys were returned. Twenty-one respondents identified themselves as English teachers, the key target group, along with eleven drama teachers. Thirty-one rated the book as excellent or very good, with thirty-four stating that it had had a positive effect on their teaching and on the enthusiasm of their students. A number of warm comments were offered, with one teacher going so far as to state: 'I have to say it has been a privilege to use and at the age of 56 it has helped me rejuvenate my teaching.' As there are 3,268 secondary schools in England, however, there is no way of knowing how typical these responses are of English and drama teachers as a whole.[3]

Jacqui O'Hanlon insists that the *Toolkit* should be regarded as a transitional document, 'written at a time when we were part way through a maturation exercise, drawing as much as we could from the tradition here in the RSC but also from the broader tradition of drama in education'.[4] This maturation process reflects the Company's current aspiration that its work should concentrate chiefly on activities identifiable as practices one might find in an RSC rehearsal room. How this looks in practice is the subject of the rest of this chapter.

Rehearsal room pedagogy in action

I was able to observe and film the first of two days of the RSC working with teachers and theatre practitioners in the LPN in September 2013. Participants in the workshop included twenty-seven teachers from the current partnership, five of whom were primary teachers; and seven theatre artists from the local theatres which formed the hub around which the teachers' schools were clustered.[5] It took place in the Clore Learning Centre, situated opposite the main Royal Shakespeare Theatre, where the participants went in the evening to see the production of *Hamlet* then running, which was directed by David Farr. The workshop leader was Miles Tandy, currently the Company's Head of Professional Development. Miles has worked at the RSC since June 2011, and before that spent nineteen years as a primary adviser in Warwickshire with a particular interest in drama. He had had a long professional association with the RSC before joining them and had co-authored many books for teachers, some of which have acquired an international reputation.[6] He did, then, come to the Company with a wealth of previous teaching experience and considerable expertise, much of it in the drama education tradition. What Jacqui nonetheless admires in Miles's teaching is how he 'models and extends our capability to have an artistic narrative through our work with teachers and with students that is authentic to our rehearsal room practices'. From this point on in the chapter we will look closely at his work on *Hamlet*, which constituted the first day of the workshop. This is important because any set of lesson plans, even if as detailed as those presented in the *Toolkit*, are really no more than a loosely scripted narrative that is yet to come alive. They need to be performed for us to appreciate the pacing, subtext and patterning – indeed the *aesthetics* of the teaching and learning experience as well as its content. An examination of this will enable us to consider how the current aspirations of the RSC pedagogy take shape in practice. To this extent it is helpful that Miles was modelling practice for teachers, as throughout he provided his own commentary on the aims and intentions of particular activities.

The aims of the practical work on *Hamlet*

Miles expressed these aims as four key questions clearly focused on pedagogy, all of which evoke the co-operative nature of the work and the aspiration to make the classroom more like a rehearsal room where sharing, exploration and physical activity characterize the learning process.

1 How do we build communities in our classrooms through which we can explore Shakespeare's plays together actively? How do we develop a strong sense of 'us' rather than 'me' at the heart of this?

2 How might our classrooms become more like rehearsal rooms and what are the benefits of doing this?

3 How do we begin to share and explore Shakespeare's stories with young people?

4 How can we open up and explore Shakespeare's language through active 'on our feet' approaches?

Initial warm-up activities

The session begins with a series of games, all played in a circle and all intended to build up a sense of co-operation and togetherness – qualities we need if we are to work as a company, as Miles puts it. They also establish a relaxed atmosphere, clearly signalling that in this space we move, are playful and enjoy ourselves in our work. As he explains later, they build a sense of collective responsiveness, embedding and celebrating the co-operative spirit that makes playing games possible; and, by extension, other communal and playful activities such as theatre-making itself.

Boal handshakes

Here, the objective is to shake hands with as many people in the group and to exchange names in the process. The complication is that you do not leave go of one person's hand until you have found another. This is a loud, boisterous game that immediately introduces an element of closeness, of touch, but in a way that is comfortable since shaking hands is a social ritual that we all understand.

Name games

As a rehearsal room is a social space as well as a work space, it is important that we know and are free to use everyone's name in it. People introduce themselves and pass their names around the circle. The game is repeated twice, with each player naming themselves first as the person on their left, then as the person on their right. Again, very early on, Miles is signalling that our own identities are important but that, in a rehearsal room, we need to be prepared playfully to take on the identities of others, no matter how briefly.

Crossing the circle

In this game, one player walks across the circle, making eye contact with another player in doing so. Before the first player arrives, the second must leave their place, cross the circle, and make contact with another who then leaves their place. The pattern is continued and then another player is added, then a third. It is played again with added urgency as the players shout out the name of the person they are approaching. After the game, Miles comments on the amount of laughter it generated, not the kind of laughter that is cruel, where we laugh *at* someone, but that 'brilliant' kind of laughter where we laugh *with* one another. 'It's so much about *us*, binding us together,' he says; and of course it is important that the teacher is part of the group, included in 'us', playing the game and laughing as much as any other player.

Clapping games

A clap is passed around the circle, then is repeated at a faster pace before it is quickly followed by another, then another, so that three claps are being passed around at the same time. The game is then played once more, this time with the clap taking various rhythmic forms, thus subtly introducing the principle that rhythm, and listening and responding to it, are part of what we do in this space, a necessary endeavour when we work with Shakespeare's language.

Ensemble walking

In this activity players are asked to explore the space but to ensure that they are always spread evenly across it. Miles quickly stops the game and points out that for some young people even this is difficult: they group together; they follow one another rather than explore the space; they walk in a physically awkward, self-conscious fashion. He sees this as individuals still feeling that the work has to be about 'me' rather than 'us' and he re-emphasizes the neutrality he is looking for in the walk. He then asks that everyone become sensitive to the general pace; that they all strive to walk at the same pace and to stop and go at absolutely the same time. Can they then manage to stop and go together, without the teacher directing them? 'That was brilliant!' he exclaims, smiling at the group's efforts. Offering praise, smiling with evident enjoyment at the work, these are all an integral part of the tone of the sessions.

These introductory activities are common in drama classrooms in schools but they also reflect the authentic practices of the rehearsal room, as demonstrated in the video production diaries of *Richard II* that was in rehearsal at the RSC at that time. In the second of these, we see the director, Gregory Doran, joining in with similar games – just as Miles did – and the atmosphere is very similar: cheerful, boisterous and physically active. There is, too, no sense of hierarchy, with actors as renowned as David Tennant and Jane Lapotaire joining in freely and on equal terms with the younger members of the company. The fact that everyone sits in a circle emphasizes this. Emma Hamilton, the young actor playing the queen, reflects upon the importance of such 'welcoming games' as she describes them, emphasizing how they break the ice, bring everyone together and establish a co-operative atmosphere. 'What I want to do is to create the environment in which we can work on this play,' explains Doran and games such as these help do exactly that.[7]

Preparing for the world of the play

Go, stop, show me

Players are now asked to walk through the space and freeze in response to whatever word Miles calls out. 'Show me grief; show me madness; a king; a prince; a noble youth.' Then in twos, with no talking: 'Show me a king and a prince / brothers.' Then fours or fives: 'Show me a king and his court / a coronation / a family.' At times these images are held only briefly, with Miles making no comment; at others they are dwelt upon for a while longer. With grief, for example, Miles asks if there is ever just one way of expressing grief and points out that in the production they will see this evening, Hamlet has a very particular way of showing it.[8] He also signals that in the rehearsal room, the simple categories of right and wrong are nearly always irrelevant; instead we all have different experiences of the world and these will inform how players interpret and represent particular words or emotional states. So with 'brothers', for example, we see certain pairs displaying affection, others combativeness. 'I don't have a brother,' Miles explains, 'so I can learn from those who do have one, from what they show me here' – another example of how, even in what appears to be a simple exercise, the teacher's response can indicate that collectively we know more than we do individually. In moving effortlessly from movement in space to representation, Miles is also modelling how the warm-up activities can be used to draw the group closer to the text without yet looking at it, preparing them subtly but steadily for the world of the play itself.

Make me a . . .

Players are now asked to work in groups of five or six and to create a series of tableaux to illustrate a family. These are created successively, each time without talking, with some viewing and comment after each. The final activity requires groups to re-think and re-work their images and to show these re-workings in succession:

- a family that has just lost a father
- a family that has just lost a father and the mother has remarried
- a family that has just lost a father and the mother has remarried with her husband's brother
- a family that has just lost a father and the mother has remarried with her husband's brother and there is a grieving son
- the progression of tableaux, but this time changing the images as necessary to show that the family is a royal family

Progressively, of course, players are being introduced to the key given circumstances at the beginning of *Hamlet* but Miles also uses the images to bring out a range of general pedagogic points. With one group, for example, he points to how instinctively they have illustrated a family riven with conflict, as it is in a family context that conflicts often arise and are played out. 'They haven't had a chance to talk about anything but they have presented something we clearly understand and can read entirely through the physical spontaneity of their bodies,' he remarks, noting how they have used spatial distance to symbolize emotional distance. 'Where are these people in relationship to one another? Where do they position themselves? Where and how do they move? All of these are critical questions to consider when we are making theatre together and we are already on that road.' He also attends to the aesthetic quality of particular images, using words like 'beautiful' and 'delightful', pointing to how such simple work can nonetheless carry a strong emotional impact. We might also reflect here on how this work connects directly with Cicely Berry's idea that Shakespeare's muscular language demands more from us than cerebral engagement. It requires an intense physical involvement, which is why image-making of some kind is a key part of rehearsal room practice at the RSC.[9]

Miles has chosen to begin with families because they are a subject that every young person will know something about. 'At this point we don't know much about Hamlet,' he explains, 'but we all know about families. They are a subject about which everybody in the room will have considerable expertise. So we begin with something our students are experts in.' It is also a particular reading of the play, valid in its own right, and recalls the 1997 RSC production in which Alex Jennings played Hamlet, and that interpreted the play as a family drama and 'a personal tragedy about Hamlet, his grief and the way he coped with it'.[10] Miles now explains that in a rehearsal room the company will strive to create together a 'world of the play' that is coherent in itself but to which an audience will be able to connect by relating it to the world they know. 'This is exactly what we are doing here,' he suggests, 'helping young people connect with the world of the play by beginning from the world they know.' This knowledge includes what they will know from television news about how a royal family will behave. In the final sequence of tableaux, players instinctively change their postures and facial expressions to indicate an awareness that, as royals, their public personas will always be watched, that they will constantly be performing. As one teacher explains, 'In the first image I was sulking but as a royal I had to force a smile.' Miles nods and adds, 'Yes, you might be feeling that way but the role that life has given you requires you to behave in a different way, and we can read that, we can tell how you really feel behind that smile.' He then asks if it is still like that today. Everyone nods. 'We don't have to go too far back, do we?' he adds, recalling the death of Princess Diana, 'to remember those two young princes being expected to grieve in public as they followed their mother's coffin along the road to the abbey. Royals are expected to perform their lives.' The theme of princes grieving is, of course, a direct echo of *Hamlet* at the beginning of the play but Miles leaves the teachers to make this connection for themselves. When he does refer to the current production, he tells them to watch out for the moment when Ophelia is warned very early on in the play that Hamlet lives his life in a different world, that 'he cannot behave like the rest of us'. He then makes explicit something that this initial work has unearthed: that we are dealing with the claustrophobic intensity of an internal family conflict, a conflict that will at the same time have considerable political reverberations due to the royal status of the family in question.

Exploring the opening of the play:
Act 1 Scene 1

The group is now asked to come to the centre of the room and to sit on the floor close to one another. Four volunteers are given the roles of Barnardo, Francisco, Horatio and Marcellus, the soldiers whose lines open the play. They are asked to stand at four opposite corners, effectively forming a square around and close to the rest of the group. On being handed their scripts they are each given only their own lines and their cues, much as the actors would have in Shakespeare's own day, Miles explains. So Francisco's part, for example, is presented as follows:

> – *Who's there?*
> FRANCISCO Nay, answer me: stand and unfold yourself.
> – *the king!*
> FRANCISCO Barnardo?
> – *He.*
> FRANCISCO You come most carefully upon your hour.
> – *to bed, Francisco.*
> FRANCISCO For this relief much thanks: 'tis bitter cold, And I am sick at heart.
> – *quiet guard?*
> FRANCISCO Not a mouse stirring.
> – *good night.*
> FRANCISCO Stand, ho! Who's there?
> – *to the Dane.*
> FRANCISCO Give you goodnight.
> – *relieved you?*
> FRANCISCO Barnardo has my place.
> Give you goodnight

The four volunteers are now asked simply to read their parts aloud while the rest of the group close their eyes. 'Tell me what you heard,' says Miles, and immediately one teacher volunteers that the short, sharp lines make the soldiers sound very nervous. 'And that is without them even doing anything but read!' exclaims Miles. 'I was already tense,' volunteers one of the readers, 'waiting for my cue,' and Miles nods in agreement, underlining how this strategy makes both readers and listeners attend very carefully to the words. 'Today we go to the theatre often for spectacle,' he points out, 'but in

Shakespeare's time there was little spectacle as we know it; what mattered was the words. People went to hear as much as to see a play.' One teacher then adds that keeping her eyes closed actually sharpened her hearing. 'I am hooked into the story already,' she explains, 'just by listening to the words.'

The exercise is now repeated three times, each time with different volunteers and in a different way. First of all they are asked to whisper the lines, then to remove themselves to the far corners of the room and shout them. In the final reading, players are told that they can repeat and echo any words or phrases that stand out for them. After each reading, Miles repeats the same open-ended request, 'Tell me about that.' With the whispering, one teacher notes, there is an increase in tension, an added urgency as she had to strain her ears to listen; the shouting made the soldiers sound a lot more confident, a lot less worried, someone comments; the echoing of the words added a haunting quality to the process, says one, and another suggests that we are drawn to echo words whose sounds we like rather than those words that are of central importance to the dialogue. 'Yes, exactly,' responds Miles, 'just as young children will find a delight in the sounds of words and in what they can do with them.' What all these exercises do, he explains, is to begin a process of unlocking the power of Shakespeare's language by tuning us into it, by exciting the ear in different ways. 'Having done this work,' he tells them, 'you will hear the opening scene this evening very differently from how you would have otherwise.'[11]

Introducing the ghost: Act 1 Scene 1

Players are now asked to stand in a group together and each is given a copy of the following lines:

> **BARNARDO** Last night of all,
> When yond same star that's westward from the pole
> Had made his course to illume that part of heaven
> Where now it burns, Marcellus and myself,
> The bell then beating one, —
> *Enter Ghost*
> **MARCELLUS** Peace, break thee off; look, where it comes again.
> **BARNARDO** In the same figure like the king that's dead.

They are asked to read together through Barnardo's part as far as the entrance of the ghost and, as Barnardo is in effect telling a story, Miles suggests that they all read it again as though they were telling that story to a small child. 'Who else tells stories?' he then asks. Someone suggests a newsreader. 'Fine, let's do it as our own correspondent from Elsinore,' he responds. He then suggests that they read it as if on a TV astronomy show, pointing to a particular light in the corner of the room as they do so. Finally he asks them to read it as if it were the biggest secret in the world whereupon he unexpectedly takes on the role of Marcellus, pointing as he speaks his line to a part of the room with such conviction that a few members of the group cannot help but look in that direction. Miles then re-iterates a point made by players earlier, 'the wonderful tension' that Shakespeare has introduced simply by the way the language is used, not only here, at the moment when Marcellus interrupts, but also in all of the scene so far, where nervousness and edginess are actually written into the structure and sounds of the text.

The next exercises are offered as a different way into the play which also captures this nervousness and expectation in ways particularly suited for primary-school-aged children. First of all players are asked to get rid of their scripts and walk through the space again, then to find a pattern in their walking that involves them turning, retracing their steps and repeating this walk exactly. Miles then begins to narrate how they are to imagine themselves as guards on the castle walls at Elsinore; it is cold but they are hardened campaigners and the cold doesn't normally worry them, but tonight they sense that something isn't right and they find themselves shivering and feeling very edgy. He then narrates the appearance of a spectre dressed in armour. Seeing the apparition they stop, draw their swords and follow it in spite of their terror. They watch as the ghost turns and faces them. They notice that the visor of its helmet is raised and, to their great shock, they recognize the face of the recently dead king. Players are asked now to hold this stillness for a few seconds and are then given paper and pencil to write in no more than fifty words an entry in their soldier's diary capturing what has just happened and what he feels about it. This is done quickly and in silence and players are then asked to hold on to their writing as they gather together in a group once more. Miles now immediately takes on the role of an authority figure, evidently the captain of the guards, looking stern, snapping his fingers and gesturing for them all to gather in an orderly fashion. 'You have no shape or discipline,' he mutters, 'What is it? You are supposed to be soldiers.' Players immediately respond to this game and there is a palpable tension in the air as he takes the writing from an individual soldier, scans it and reads a selection of phrases out loud. 'I took up my sentry duty . . . I thought there was a . . .'. He sounds incredulous and stares intently into the soldier's eyes as he hands him back his paper, coldly. He repeats this exercise with three or four others before initiating a brief discussion. 'At ease. So what is it we think we have seen – a ghost that looks like the dead king? How many of you saw this?' Most raise their hands. He shakes his head 'If this really is old Hamlet, we have a decision to make. Do we tell young Hamlet or not?' After a brief exchange of opinions, he tells them all to stand down. 'You're all tired – we'll talk more about this tomorrow,' whereupon he smiles as he comes out of role, apologizing for being so horrible but asking them to note the very particular tension – highly appropriate in this case – that role play such as this can bring into the room.[12]

Miles then leads a discussion about the kind of writing we had here, pointing to two different modes of writing: that which is communicative, when we have something to say to someone else; and that which is performative, where we write in order to show that we can. Most writing in schools, of course, is performative, but here, as in many of Shakespeare's plays, writing is used to help shape the action. 'I didn't read your work and say "what a lovely sentence, I do like your use of adjectives", did I? I read it as the captain of the guards and responded with all the urgency the writing called for as an act of communication.' He points out that this exercise comes from a very particular tradition in drama education, 'which is that business of being live, in role, now, in the moment'. In terms of professional theatre practice, however, the exercise links to back story. In a rehearsal room there will be actors who have very little textual information to go on to develop a believable character who can co-create the play with as much conviction as the principal characters. In the production of *Hamlet* then running, for example, David Farr, gave each of the actors a back story for their character which they worked on through improvisation over two or three days of the rehearsal period. Miles suggests that working in this way can, when we come to engage with the text itself, 'lead us into a place where it feels as if it is here, right now, instantaneous'. The following exercise exemplifies this.

Telling Hamlet: Act 1 Scene 2

Players move in space and are asked to find a partner and greet each other as two friends from university might. This leads into an improvised dialogue between Horatio and Hamlet, with Horatio's objective being to find a way of telling his friend about the sighting of his father's ghost. At one point Miles asks the pairs to stop briefly in order to view and discuss their work in progress. He points to how some pairs have chosen the classic counselling position of indirectly facing one another, some doing this in a seated position, which he relates to an instinctive understanding of how our body language matters when we speak to someone with this kind of news. After a further two minutes the improvisations are stopped and the players who took on the role of Horatio are invited to discuss the tactics they used. One speaks of how she had reminded Hamlet of how long they had known each other, that surely he could trust his old friend, whereupon Hamlet had sensed Horatio's unease and had asked outright what the problem was. Miles points to how breaking difficult news to someone is another example of commonly shared human experiences, something young people can readily relate to, and with this established he hands out an edited version of the dialogue in Act 1 Scene 2 where Horatio greets Hamlet and tells him that he has seen the king, his father, the previous night.

HORATIO Hail to your lordship!
HAMLET Horatio – or I do forget myself.
HORATIO The same, my lord, and your poor servant ever.
HAMLET But what is your affair in Elsinore?
We'll teach you to drink deep ere you depart.
HORATIO My lord, I came to see your father's funeral.
HAMLET I pray thee do not mock me, fellow-student:
I think it was to see my mother's wedding.
HORATIO Indeed, my lord, it followed hard upon.
HAMLET Thrift, thrift, Horatio! The funeral baked meats
Did coldly furnish forth the marriage tables.
My father, methinks I see my father.
HORATIO O where, my lord?
HAMLET In my mind's eye, Horatio.
HORATIO I saw him once; he was a goodly king.
HAMLET He was a man, take him for all in all:
I shall not look upon his like again.
HORATIO My lord, I think I saw him yesternight.
HAMLET Saw who?
HORATIO My lord, the king your father.
HAMLET The king my father?
For heaven's love, let me hear.

Players are asked to not look at their scripts yet, and informed that this is something that some members of the RSC voice department often insist upon when they hand out texts for actors to work with, wishing to avoid immediate analysis and pre-conceptions in order to begin by immersing actors in the language itself. Miles says that this exercise is good for 'flattening the text out' for students, too – it prevents them from rushing to meaning, as Cicely Berry would put it; they must first of all concentrate on saying and feeling the sounds of the words. 'We can discuss the meaning of individual words later,' he explains. In order for the collective support of the whole group to provide security for those who may be less confident readers, the Horatios and Hamlets are divided into two different teams who face each other in order to read their lines. Then players group again with their partners and engage in what the RSC calls a *scene study*.

First of all partners stand back to back and read the scene out loud. 'You have to really listen when you do that,' comments one teacher afterwards, 'and you actually feel your partner's response through your body.' Miles picks up on this point, emphasizing how the voice text people at the RSC see the voice as a complex, physical instrument, an intrinsic part of our bodies. Young children often go to school, he suggests, with a highly developed if playful sense of the range and power of their own voices. But school all too often insists that they use only a small part of that voice with the result being that many become embarrassed about using the rest of it. Exercises like these, he proposes, help young people re-discover the range of their voices. The exercise is repeated, this time in a whisper, and players are asked again to comment on it. 'By limiting the range of the voice, you actually have to find more expression,' comments one teacher; another has been struck by how it seemed absolutely right for her to whisper the lines *'My lord, I think I saw him yesternight / the king, your father'*, as she felt Horatio wouldn't want anyone to overhear those words. Miles agrees and says it is a discovery she has made from actually playing within the text and wonders what discoveries might come from speaking the lines ten paces apart. After doing this, one teacher comments on how she actually found a physical release reading her part this way, as she necessarily had to use gesture, facial and vocal expression in order to communicate across the distance, and that this made everything feel more natural to her, a point which flows nicely into the final exercise.

Players are now asked to bring the text to life through movement and are explicitly invited to revisit their previous improvisations to inform the physicality and tone of the actual text. At first they are asked solely to work on the first two lines and some of the results are highly amusing. One wildly physical and laddish performance by two female teachers is contrasted with a more sombre representation. Miles says both in themselves are 'wonderful interpretations', but what the company would be searching for is whether any single interpretation is consistent with the particular kind of Hamlet being created in a particular production. 'This one would be hugely entertaining,' he exclaims, to much laughter, 'and could actually be seen to trail his later behaviour in the play, his "antic disposition".' Other examples are looked at, all very different, and Miles emphasizes once again how the distinctive interpretations reflect the fact that we will always bring what we know of the real world to our construction of a theatrical world. 'What we get is something that sits somewhere between me and what I know and Shakespeare and what he gave us over 400 years ago.' The players now return to the rest of the scene and it is clear that these reflections have had an impact on how they continue their work; the outlandishly laddish Hamlet, for example, quickly cools and becomes more serious, and there is no sense of the text being trivialized.

Before moving on to work on a new scene, Miles makes some significant reflections that explicitly relate to principles at the heart of RSC pedagogy, to the classroom as rehearsal room and to the aesthetics of theatre-making. First of all, he points out, although we have here been taking a scene forward that involves just two characters, the effort is still a collective one. In an RSC rehearsal room, he explains, the entire company might well work together on a particular scene like this and he cites the rehearsals for Gregory Doran's current production of *Richard II* as an example. 'If we can make a classroom more like a rehearsal room,' he goes on, 'different things can begin to happen in the space. We start thinking about it in a different way, specifically because these are not techniques we have invented for little people but are derived from what our actors actually do.' Jacqui O'Hanlon made the same point to me, a point which is at the very heart of the RSC's educational philosophy:

> The temperature in the room changes as soon as we say to young people that this is not work we have made up for them. This is what our actors and directors have to do to unlock the text, to free up its interpretive possibilities. And as soon as you say that, the way a student engages with it and the way a teacher engages with it changes. As soon as you put it on a professional footing, play becomes more serious.

Miles also comments on the advantages of structuring work on a play in such a way (as exemplified here) that the narrative of the lesson unfolds in parallel to the narrative of the play itself, thus provoking the same kind of curiosity and excitement that a good staging of the play might offer to young people.[13] And finally he points to the way that these exercises with the text are intent on enabling young people to 'get inside the language itself' and – echoing Jeremy Irons's comment on Cicely Berry's work – 'how to unlock its joy'.

Hamlet and the ghost: Act 1 Scene 5

The players now gather in a circle and are given the text below, an edited version of Hamlet's meeting with the ghost.

Enter GHOST and HAMLET
HAMLET Where wilt thou lead me? Speak; I'll go no further.
GHOST Mark me.
HAMLET   I will.
GHOST   My hour is almost come,
When I to sulphurous and tormenting flames
Must render up myself.
HAMLET   Alas, poor ghost!
GHOST I am thy father's spirit,
Doomed for a certain term to walk the night,
And for the day confined to fast in fires,
Till the foul crimes done in my days of nature
Are burnt and purged away. List, List, O, list!
If thou didst ever thy dear father love—
HAMLET O God!
GHOST Revenge his foul and most unnatural murder.
HAMLET Murder?
GHOST Murder most foul, as in the best it is;
But this most foul, strange and unnatural.
'Tis given out that, sleeping in my orchard,

A serpent stung me; but know, thou noble youth,
The serpent that did sting thy father's life
Now wears his crown.
HAMLET   O, my prophetic soul!
Mine uncle!

Miles introduces the next strategy as 'another way of getting the language into the air'. It is called *ensemble reading* and involves players reading around the circle from punctuation mark to punctuation mark. 'Tell me about that,' he requests when they have finished and players point to the shared responsibility for the whole passage that it encourages. 'You cannot just worry about your own line,' says one, 'as there is no way you can read ahead to find out what it will be!' 'It makes everyone listen to the whole dialogue,' comments another.

There ensues a quick activity to get players into three large groups, about ten in each. With a class of young people, Miles explains, the groups would need to be half this size, but he sees this challenge of working in a large group as suitable and a chance for the players to experience a different dynamic. The ghost's lines are shared out among the three groups and they are given the task of presenting a collective representation of the ghost which should terrify Hamlet and anyone watching. The groups then spend several minutes working intensely on this. When they are ready, Miles darkens the room and leaves through a door, explaining that when he re-enters the scene will commence, with him taking the role of Hamlet. He soon rushes back into the room, shouting his opening lines in a way that deliberately echoes Jonathan Slinger's interpretation in the then-current production, and the performance begins with great focused intensity. Two groups have chosen a similar approach – surrounding Hamlet slowly, like a snake, rushing him occasionally, shouting some phrases, whispering others, echoing one another – while the third has made an aesthetic invention based on the fact that one of its members cannot move readily as she has a broken leg. She sits on a chair with another player behind her holding her crutches and creating a diabolical, Kali-like effect in the darkness as she waves them through the air while other players snarl at Hamlet, making great play on the word 'murder' in particular, dwelling on and repeating its first syllable with a stylized vomiting motion, eventually rushing and spewing the word over Hamlet.

When the lights are turned back on there is much laughter as the tensions of performance are released. Miles congratulates the players on their work and asks for comments on what this form of collective theatre-making was like. One talks of how the task was both achievable and challenging, with the deadline providing the group with a sense of urgency that meant that ideas needed to be accepted. Miles adds that every teacher will have experienced groups of young people who have difficulties working together but emphasizes the central importance of ensuring that they *do* have

FIGURE 4.1 *Teachers improvise during the* Hamlet *workshop.*

experiences of collective theatre-making such as this that they appreciate and enjoy because they sense the success of their effect on an audience. When they have had *that* experience, they will understand that the collective effort is worthwhile. He also comments on how, because the work has been given a specific, creative focus – in this case, to make a group ghost that is frightening – the teacher can direct her feedback specifically on creative outcome rather than behaviour, both during the making process and at the end of it. So at no point does she need to say 'don't fool around' but instead can say 'You know what? If you do that, that won't scare me at all!' 'What is most important about this exercise,' he adds, 'is the relationship between the text and the creative outcome that is achieved through our joint, collective endeavour. In this very short period of time, we have actually made a performance, not just talked about or planned it.'

Creating the dumb show: Act 3 Scene 2

Having experienced a collective creation of one piece of theatre, players are now presented with the challenge of another in the form of the dumb show which Hamlet organizes to 'catch the conscience of the king'. The text, as with all the extracts the RSC uses, is taken from the version edited by Jonathan Bate and Eric Rasmussen and published by the RSC.

Enter a King and Queen very lovingly; the Queen embracing him. She kneels, and makes show of protestation unto him. He takes her up, and declines his head upon her neck: lays him down upon a bank of flowers: she, seeing him asleep, leaves him. Anon comes in a fellow, takes off his crown, kisses it, and pours poison in the King's ears, and exits. The Queen returns, finds the King dead, and makes passionate action. The Poisoner, with some two or three Mutes, comes in again, seeming to lament with her. The dead body is carried away. The Poisoner woos the Queen with gifts: she seems loath and unwilling awhile, but in the end accepts his love. Exeunt

This time in groups of six, players are asked to tackle the task seriously and to avoid parody or pantomime. In order to encourage this, Miles plays a piece of music from Bach's *Brandenburg Concertos* to set the tone while groups are preparing and it is also played when they eventually perform in an overlapping sequence. Through the use of the music, although there are many differences in each interpretation, there is an overall coherence in the final performance, which is focused and controlled, the players' movements instinctively reflecting the slow and dignified pace of the music, although never exaggeratedly so. Later one teacher comments on how Miles steering them away from pantomime made the thinking of her group become a lot more methodical. 'We started to think about what we were doing more, about the characters watching the play within the play, about how they were feeling – the effect it would have on them and upon their audience. I think it brought out a lot more empathy and understanding in our group than it would have done otherwise.'

There are many beautifully choreographed moments, I observe to myself; for example, one group copes with the challenge of removing the dead king from the stage in a deliberately non-realistic fashion, two players raising him from the ground gracefully, lifting him to his feet by holding on to a shoulder and elbow each, then walking off the stage in unison, guided by the pace and rhythm of the music. Indeed, when the performances finish (by a wonderful aesthetic coincidence, just as the music itself comes to an end) Miles is moved to talk of them in terms of their beauty, a term, he says, he is using advisedly. 'Genuinely, what you have made here, was absolutely terrific and truly beautiful. That is why I held you back from the temptation to just have a laugh with it. The notion of beauty,' he continues, 'how it has come into this room on a warm Friday afternoon, is something at the heart of what this work is all about. The aim is to help young people make something really compelling, not just in exercises like this one, but to find the beauty in the very language which Shakespeare writes for the stage, to make that language live with this kind of resonance and intensity.'

Exploring a soliloquy: *'Now might I do it . . .'*
Act 3 Scene 3

Players now engage in a series of exercises which, once again, closely reflect what actors might do in the RSC rehearsal room. Gathering in a circle, they are each handed a copy of the soliloquy from the moment in the play when Hamlet has the chance to kill Claudius whilst at prayer but chooses not to, for fear that he will go straight to heaven. Players read through the text together and are then asked to choose a word or phrase that stands out for them for any reason and to share this with the person next to them. Working in pairs, players are now asked to find a physical gesture to accompany the words and to perform them together. These are then presented in sequence around the circle. It is a light-hearted exercise and received with much laugher and enjoyment: one pair hold out an imaginary sword for the word *revenge*, then thrust their hips lewdly to represent *pleasure*; another couple choose *grossly*, indicating fatness with their arms and cheeks and *purging*, which they utter as though vomiting. What is interesting, comments Miles, is not only the variety of physical representation but in particular the variety of words chosen. Through establishing a physical connection with the words this way, through embodying them and seeing them embodied, we begin to experience the visceral power of the text rather than detach ourselves from it in the search for cerebral meaning.

Players now read the text again around the circle, passing it on at every punctuation mark and then actually physicalize this process through the 'punctuation shift' exercise, in which as individuals they take the text for a walk through the space, reading it out loud but changing direction sharply at every punctuation mark. This exercise solicits a number of immediate comments: the fact that you keep stopping conveys indecisiveness, says one teacher. Another agrees, saying its 'fidgety agitation' reflected his dilemma, whereas for another teacher it brought to her attention the rhythm between actions and consequences. 'It was like he was having a thought about an action he might do, then he was being forced in the opposite direction by considering the consequences of that action. By physically representing that, I understand it more,' she adds. Yes, suggests Miles, a clear example of how we can connect with and understand the text better as a physical rather than just a cerebral experience.

Players now examine the rhythm of the soliloquy. Miles reminds them of the iambic rhythm by tapping it (de-**dum**-de-**dum**-de-**dum**-de-**dum**-de-**dum**) and through various clapping games that help re-enforce it. But Shakespeare doesn't always keep to such a simple iambic pattern, he points out, and in pairs players are asked to go through the soliloquy and examine the rhythm carefully and consider its effect. On their return to the circle, he asks 'Were there any moments when the rhythm made you think, hey, hang on, what's that all about?' Many note the additional syllable (the feminine ending) on

FIGURE 4.2 *Teachers work on a scene study during the* Hamlet *workshop.*

lines, especially with the word 'heaven' and how every time it occurs it knocks the rhythm out, disrupting it as it does his plan for instant revenge. Others note the shorter lines as indicating pauses for thought, again a very strong example coming after the word 'heaven' and this time before the word 'O!' Miles tells them not to dismiss this short word and to listen in particular this evening for how Jonathan Slinger makes it the longest word in the speech, indicative of the intense frustration these considerations are making him feel. Throughout, Miles stresses how the sounds, rhythms and patterns of the speech can be collectively and collaboratively explored to raise questions about Hamlet's state of mind and his inability to act. As with all the work through the day, it is not about right and wrong answers; much more, it is about that constant spirit of open, collaborative enquiry into the text.

The final exercise of the day is called *interpolated questions*, in which players gather together as a group and face Miles as they read through the soliloquy once more. As they do so, Miles asks a series of questions which anticipate the sense of the following lines, which subsequently read as answers to those questions, as presented below.

Why is your sword drawn?
Now might I do it pat, now he is praying;
And then?
And now I'll do't. And so he goes to heaven,

And?
And so am I revenged. That would be scanned
Scanned how?:
A villain kills my father, and for that,
I, his sole son, do this same villain send
To heaven.
Why not do that then?
O, this is hire and salary, not revenge.
Why so?
He took my father grossly, full of bread;
With all his crimes broad blown, as flush as May,
Why does that matter?
And how his audit stands who knows save heaven?
But in our circumstance and course of thought
Why not just kill him now?
'Tis heavy with him: and am I then revenged,
To take him in the purging of his soul,
When he is fit and seasoned for his passage?
Go on . . . No!
Up, sword; and know thou a more horrid hent:
Like when?
When he is drunk asleep, or in his rage
Or?
Or in th'incestuous pleasure of his bed;
Or?
At gaming, swearing, or about some act
That has no relish of salvation in't;
Then what?
Then trip him, that his heels may kick at heaven,
And that his soul may be as damned and black
As hell, whereto it goes. *So what now?* My mother stays:
*Are you **ever** going to revenge your father's murder?*
This physic but prolongs thy sickly days

Several teachers comment on how helpful these questions are both in terms of making sense of the following lines and also in conveying the urgency of the dilemma at the heart of the soliloquy. Once again, it is aimed at making the text as alive and relevant as possible, helping players feel they are thinking these thoughts and speaking them for the very first time, right now. Miles relates this directly to the performance that the group will see in the evening, inviting them to reflect on how the work they have done throughout the day will influence and affect how they see and hear the play. Just as any good teacher might, he deliberately creates a sense of anticipation, fostering a sense that their experience of the workshop will lead to immediate, aesthetic rewards as well as be of more long-term, professional value.[14]

Conclusion

Although Miles Tandy is steeped in the tradition of drama education, his work with the RSC as typified here closely reflects its particular style of rehearsal room pedagogy. When he draws on his broader educational background, most typically in the early image-making activities, he is nonetheless reflecting the early work of the rehearsal period, using active, co-operative, dialogic activities that elide with its processes in ways designed to prepare young people to engage with the text itself. We might well expect actors to come to initial rehearsals of the play already equipped with the background knowledge that Miles explores here; we might also venture that, unlike a class of young people about to study the play, they already have a vested interest in it. The opening activities therefore are designed to fill a gap, to help young people find a connection with the play before starting to work on it like actors; and in this Miles is drawing directly from Jerome Bruner's idea of learners beginning with what they already know something about, even though they may as yet know nothing about the play.[15] He is also doing with them what any company rehearsing a Shakespeare play must do, namely make connections between the world of the play and the world we, the actors, hold in common with our audience. Players are led to consider grief and the appearance of grieving; to imagine a family with specific circumstances that mirror those at the start of *Hamlet*; and to air what they understand about royalty and how that must affect how he acts and how others will relate to him. Later, players are guided into the dialogue between Horatio and Hamlet by first of all exploring what they know about how two old friends might greet each other and the difficulties of breaking upsetting news to someone. Although some directors might make these connections through 'table work' or perhaps through discussion alone, not all will; and here active approaches are being proposed as the most suitable and engaging way for a class of young people to work them out for themselves.

The principles that guide these initial explorations remain consistent with RSC rehearsal room approaches in general: they make the body central to the meaning-making process; they stress interpretive choices, working directly from the different ideas that players offer; and they are explored in a collective fashion, founded upon the belief that we can learn about a Shakespeare play better collectively than in isolation. Underpinning them, too, is the concept of 'enabling constraints', a term much used by the American arts educator, Eric Booth, to describe the paradoxical idea that limitation can enhance freedom. 'By guiding people into a challenge that is constrained with limited choices', writes Booth, 'you can empower them to learn more, to go deeper, to find greater success'.[16] This is a form of 'scaffolding', the term used by Bruner to describe the structured interactions through which adults will lead a child towards achieving a specific goal. In the process, they will necessarily close down certain unhelpful options, reducing the degrees of freedom in order to sharpen the focus of learning.[17] This principle can be seen to permeate the entire workshop. Players are constantly given specific structures that limit their choices and focus their tasks in ways that guide them towards creative achievement. It is to further theoretical considerations of how rehearsal room pedagogy leads to learning that we now turn.

5

A Theoretical Rationale for Rehearsal Room Pedagogy

Introduction

When articulating the principles that guide their work, the RSC education team uses the language of best practice 'built on years of direct teaching and learning experiences'.[1] These, as we have seen, are designed to mirror in key ways the artistic practices of the rehearsal room: processes of playful, collaborative inquiry into the language and meaning of the text; relationships shaped by the principle of co-operative learning, whether defined in terms of an 'ensemble' or, more recently, as a 'company'; young people making personal connections with the text through considered, interpretive choices; and with active, physical involvement, making and doing, at the heart of the process, organized in such a way as to feed into reflection and understanding. This chapter takes these principles, exemplified through the practice described in the last chapter, as given and attempts to provide a brief theoretical rationale to underpin them. I begin with a look at play and playfulness, with specific reference to language play and the work of Guy Cook, before considering John Dewey's ideas that place *experience* at the centre of the learning process. This leads naturally to a consideration of the cognitive role of the aesthetic in experiential learning and also to Mark Johnson's work on the centrality of the idea of embodiment to such learning – what the RSC refer to as students' 'whole selves – bodies, hearts and minds'.[2] I then turn to the idea of collective endeavour, a concept at the heart of rehearsal room pedagogy, and consider theories of how it can foster a particular political and social vision within the classroom and enable the kind of dialogical interaction that helps young people make informed, interpretive choices. Finally I propose that we see the RSC's approaches as an example of what I have elsewhere described as a 'pedagogy of beauty', one that seeks to activate both the charms of the beautiful and the thrill of the sublime in their quest to help young people experience and appreciate the immense beauty of Shakespeare's work.

Learning through playing

'Work which remains permeated with the play attitude is art.'

JOHN DEWEY[3]

A theory of play that positions the imaginative and playful activities of young children on a continuum with the great plays of Shakespeare was, as we have seen, at the heart of Michael Boyd's particular vision as expressed at the beginning of the *Stand up for Shakespeare* manifesto. This is largely in tune with a Romantic view of childhood influenced by the writings of Rousseau, one that saw great humanizing value in children's imaginative play. This philosophy found its fullest expression in the progressive pedagogy that flourished in the 1960s, one that successive UK governments have since sought continuously and stridently to discredit and which has for a long time lost its dominance in educational practice. Although the recent vogue for creativity has gone some way towards reclaiming the value of play to creative and imaginative learning, there is still a general and pervasive scepticism about it that is easy to find in the academic field of Shakespeare studies. Kate McLuskie, former director of the Shakespeare Institute, has written dismissively about the appropriateness of playful approaches, equating them with 'dancing and not thinking'. Her particular concern is the teaching of Shakespeare in higher education but she suggests that at any level of education there is no 'easily elided continuum' between the imaginative play of young children and the work of the theatre. She sees young children's dramatic play as 'only tangentially related to drama as a script for performed theatre and different again from the plays of Shakespeare'.[4]

This attitude is not only reflective of a deep, lingering suspicion towards progressive education but also, I think, of a more general ambivalence toward the value of play that permeates our culture. Here common-sense understandings equate play with leisure time and therefore view it as the opposite of work; as pleasurable and therefore not difficult or challenging; as not serious and therefore not to be taken seriously; and as something that children do and therefore to be grown out of.[5] The writings of cultural theorists of play such as Johan Huizinga and Richard Schechner have, however, expounded a radically different perspective on play as something deeply significant to all human activity, so much so that Huizinga proposed *ludens* rather than *sapiens* – playful rather than wise – as the defining characteristic of the human species.[6] Our fascination with those who 'play' for a living, for example – musicians, actors and sports professionals – is ample evidence of the amount of value that humans globally attach to cultural forms of play, as are the huge amounts of money that the most successful players can earn for themselves.

Rather than imposing a binary opposition between the dramatic play of the child and the play of the Shakespearean actor, the RSC sees both as positioned along a continuum united by the same, basic human drive. And as playfulness is so fundamental to our human natures, it makes practical sense for them to harness for pedagogical purposes the pleasure we all generally share in playing. They strive to make use of structured forms of theatrical play in order to help young people engage with and explore the supremely sophisticated and intellectually challenging yet playful demands of a Shakespearean text. Here the analogy with the rehearsal room is highly significant for it undermines the false but pervasive dichotomy between play and work, indicating that the playing of the young people who use rehearsal room approaches is no less a serious job of work than is the playing of the actors in an RSC studio.

It is telling that those theories which promote the value of play in education tend to be concentrated on the early years. The writing of Guy Cook in the field of foreign language learning has been a notable exception. His work is particularly illuminating inasmuch as it helps us understand how Shakespeare's language, so often seen as a barrier to young people accessing his plays, can actually become a source of attraction to them.[7]

Cook argues that language play works at three interlocking levels: the formal, the semantic and the pragmatic. The formal level refers to rhythm and patterned repetition in linguistic forms, the sort of playful language common amongst children as nursery rhymes and skipping chants but one that persists throughout our lives as (for example) prayers, songs and verse. The semantic level refers to our human enjoyment of fictions and fantasies and to how we are attracted rather than repelled by novel, strange or opaque uses of language. At this level we enjoy the random, incongruous and absurd elements of language for the ways in which they free us, albeit temporarily, from conventional meaning and from the rationality that tends to govern the majority of our social interactions. The pragmatic relates to how we value and enjoy such playful uses of language for the communal ways in which they create solidarity as well as competitiveness, and build a feeling of congregation as well as intimate interaction. He uses the example of a skipping chant in a playground to exemplify how a rhythmic use of nonsense language can nonetheless suggest a boy-meets-girl scenario whilst creating a game that features both participants and on-lookers, one that provides a sense of competition as well as purposeful togetherness in which demonstrations of skill can be both admired and emulated. A religious ceremony, a song by a rap artist, the performance of a play or a televized improvization game such as *Whose Line is it Anyway?* can all be seen to demonstrate these three interlocking levels of language play at a more adult level. Cook emphasizes how this kind of language play, as opposed to the transactional processes that dominate in most classrooms, takes up most of our human energies and constitutes the greater part of our experience of language – the kind of language common in social and cultural activities, such as sharing jokes, telling stories, listening to personal fantasies, uttering prayers, singing songs and so on. He concludes that, far from being trivial and tangential, language play is central to our learning, creativity and intellectual development and should inform pedagogy accordingly.

Two key points made by Cook are that, when presented within the spirit of play, we can tolerate and indeed enjoy ambiguous or unusual language from texts that are principally driven by form rather than meaning; and that it is therefore an educational error to assume that language is learned most effectively when approached for functional rather than playful purposes. Here he draws from Wolfson's Bulge theory of social relations.[8] Wolfson proposed that in contemporary societies, the bulk of our social and linguistic interactions occur in what she calls '"the Bulge", the day-to-day, unemotional transactional encounters of modern urban existence'.[9] At the opposing extremes of this Bulge are two tapering ends: at one end we find the language of *intimacy*, that language we share with those closest to us; at the other end, we discover the language of naked *power and aggression*. In the Bulge, language is being used to create the relationship, whereas at the tapering ends the relationship is already established, hence the language has the space to become more creative and playful. The interactions at the tapering ends of the Bulge – those which feature the language of intimacy and of power – dominate in drama and fiction as they are the forms of language and relationship that are of most human interest. Conversely, it is the staid, unemotive, relatively uninteresting 'public' language of the Bulge that often exclusively dominates the daily interactions of the typical classroom, including the Shakespeare classroom – question and answering, analytical discussion and so on. It goes without saying that they are a necessary part of any pedagogy, but they are unlikely on their own to arouse the kind of interest in young people that playful uses of language will.

Shakespeare's poetic language is, of course, particularly characterized by intimacy on the one hand and by power and aggression on the other. The unusualness and variety of his insults, for example, has long been recognized as appealing to young people and, although it is quite natural for teachers to be wary of allowing aggressive language into the classroom, through carefully structured play it can become distanced enough from the immediate situation to be used and enjoyed safely. Rex Gibson's *insult generator* game is an apt example of how this can be managed[10] but there are numerous examples of how approaches demonstrated by the RSC harness the vibrancy and power of Shakespeare's emotive uses of language in ways that allow young people to play with, enjoy and hence feel its intensity far more fully than if they were simply to read them. The game *Crossing the Circle*, for example, is sometimes played using emotive lines from the text for students to shout at one another as they cross. In his workshop on the second day, which focused on *The Taming of the Shrew*, Miles had players read an edited version of the first meeting between Kate and Petruchio asking them to flick their scripts hard every time they encountered the word 'you', which lent a controlled but highly enjoyable form of aggression to the exercise.

Cook's emphasis on the specific appeal of the formal level of language play is particularly illuminating for those aspects of RSC pedagogy derived directly from Cicely Berry's work as their stress on the rhythm and suggestive sensuality of the language precisely parallels what Cook sees as the strong attraction of nursery rhymes for young children. These, he suggests, appeal through their form rather than their meaning, through their accentuated rhythms and the co-ordinated physical movements which often accompany them and which help generate a feeling of togetherness and well-being. Furthermore, they make positive room for the bizarre and the unexpected, the surprising and the absurd, which are so much a part of the attraction of language play and so often absent from the rational planning of the ordinary classroom. We can see a similar process in play in a range of RSC activities: those that prioritize the rhythm and beat of Shakespeare's language as a guide to its meaning; that make space for the shared, physical responses of the players; that welcome the surprising and the unexpected, which often happens when players are asked to find physical gestures as they speak specific words. All of these approaches help make young people's experience of the language enjoyable and rewarding at the same time as they generate the positive, collective feelings of working together as a company.

Learning through experience

In the *Toolkit* the RSC refers to 'learning experiences' and its choice of the words is not made lightly. The philosophical founder of the idea of learning through experience was, of course, John Dewey. He is often unfairly seen as the father of the more vacuous, unstructured, 'touchy-feely' forms of progressive education but he was against neither structure nor rigour in his educational philosophy; and in advocating that experience be placed at the centre of learning he was making an argument with clear practical implications. Dewey believed that young people needed to be educated within an environment that would help them understand, interact with and adapt to an ever changing world. He did not deny that all education offered experiences of one kind or another but argued that too often the experiences afforded by 'traditional' schooling – where the ends of learning are given absolute priority over the means – had worked against the best interests of the young people who had to endure them.

How many came to associate the learning process with ennui and boredom? How many found what they did learn so foreign to the situations of life outside the school as to give them no power or control over the latter? How many came to associate books with dull drudgery, so that they were 'conditioned' to all but flashy reading matter?[11]

Although written in 1938, these words strongly resonate with the concerns that motivated *Stand up for Shakespeare* and for the same reasons. Like Dewey, the RSC prioritizes the *quality* of the learning experience and its future implications in terms of motivating students and encouraging their positive engagement with the world. As Dewey advocated, the Company's intention is to provide learning experiences that are 'more than immediately enjoyable since they promote having desirable future experiences'.[12] Its pedagogy is designed to respond to what Dewey saw as the central challenge of an education based upon experience, namely 'to select the kind of present experiences that live fruitfully and creatively in subsequent experiences'.[13]

In a jointly authored article published in the *Shakespeare Survey*, Jonothan Neelands and Jacqui O'Hanlon have made it clear that these experiences are intended to offer young people what they call a 'double entitlement':

> This double entitlement to Shakespeare is grounded in the desire to establish purpose and rewards in learning that may lead, by choice, to other life-long and life-wide outcomes, in particular giving a broader range of children and young people the choice of Shakespeare, now and in later life, as a source of pleasure and as a reference point for understanding the complexities of their own and other lives.[14]

This idea of a double entitlement – both curricular and cultural – is congruent with Dewey's argument that education should be integral to society and not isolated from it. Neelands and O'Hanlon explain how the RSC manages this through using rehearsal room approaches that mirror the authentic work of theatre, beginning with the following quote from Dewey to outline the model they exemplify.

> First that the pupil have a genuine situation of experience ... secondly that a genuine problem develop within this situation as a stimulus to thought; third that he possess the information and make the observations needed to deal with it; fourth, that suggested solutions occur to him which he shall be responsible for developing in an orderly way; fifth, that he have the opportunity and occasion to test his ideas by application, to make their meaning clear and to discover for himself their validity.[15]

With the model of theatre-making in mind, we can readily align the 'situation of experience' with the rehearsal room; the genuine problem with that of script interpretation and its realization in performance; the information and observations needed as those that come from the text itself and the young people's shared responses to it; and the solutions as the interpretive choices that they as players then proceed to make, which are then tested out, clarified and critically responded to communally.[16] It is a practical example of young people learning by 'direct encounter with the phenomenon being studied rather than merely thinking about the encounter or only considering the possibility of doing something with it'.[17] It is also illustrative of another of Dewey's influential ideas: that communal art-making can provide a shared, democratic space for young people and their teachers to learn together.[18] Thus the teacher, although always an authority, is careful not to impose her own prior interpretations on the players but works to guide them into exploring possibilities, into making and evaluating their own interpretive choices.

Examples of this abound in the account of the workshop given in Chapter 4. Miles constantly sets open-ended tasks after which he says simply 'Tell me about that', taking comments offered as discussion points rather than leading with his own pre-determined agenda. The *scene study* progresses through a series of activities that encourage players to experiment with different forms of vocal delivery and share their own discoveries. When Miles does place clear boundaries around interpretive choices, this is consciously done as an 'enabling constraint' that is designed to assist rather than limit creativity, as with the performance of the dumb show, where a particular kind of music framed the emotional content of the performance without in any sense determining its form.

Dewey's writings on the importance of the aesthetic as a fundamental feature of experiential learning are highly relevant here. Current educational practice still tends to be dominated by an emphasis on learning objectives and measurable outcomes and these can lead to the kind of overly simplified, means–ends lesson planning that, rather than engaging and intellectually energizing young people, can produce experiences that Dewey defined as 'infected with apathy, lassitude and stereotype'.[19] In his book *Art and Experience* he makes an important distinction between experience as we commonly live it and having *an* experience. Ordinary experience, he suggests, falls between two poles; those of 'utter caprice and sheer routine'.[20] The first kind is characterized by drift, aimless indulgence and no clear sense of purpose, the latter by mechanization, coerced submission and tight control. In educational terms, we can see that these two poles correspond with the worst excesses of so-called progressivism on the one hand and traditionalism on the other. Both kinds of experience, Dewey suggests, begin and end without any sense of initiation or purposeful conclusion and their progress is marked by disjuncture and incoherence, whether due to whimsy and lack of planning on the one hand or by coercion and overly rigid planning on the other. Either way their effect is *an*aesthetic; they are humdrum, ordinary, eminently forgetful. What turns *any* experience into *an* experience – into something memorable, intrinsically worthwhile, satisfying and rewarding in itself – is its aesthetic quality and this is true whether we deem the experience to be predominantly intellectual or practical rather than artistic. This quality of the aesthetic he sees as dependent upon achieving the kinds of satisfaction we find in a good work of art: a unity and coherence achieved by 'internal integration and fulfilment reached through ordered and organized movement'.[21] It is these features that provide the experience with the satisfying emotional quality by which we feel and recognize aesthetic pleasure and, because learning is necessarily organized in time, Dewey likens it to the narrative structure of a journey whose success is dependent upon the pace of our progress. 'If we move too rapidly', he writes, 'the experience is flustered, thin and confused. If we dawdle too long after having extracted net value, experience perishes of inanition.'[22]

The *Hamlet* workshop exemplifies how aesthetic rather than purely technical considerations shape the form as well as the content of the learning experience. The games and warm-up activities initiate the session by clearly and briskly establishing a playful and enjoyable atmosphere of working together. The individual activities not only take the players on an aesthetic journey through the narrative of the play but pay due attention to issues of rhythm and pace as well as sequential logic. Just as different scenes in a play will vary in intensity, in the number of actors on the stage at any one time, in their emotional dynamic and so on, so the activities of the workshop move from whole group work, to pair work, to group performances, and are interspersed with time for reflection, response, analysis and evaluation and with due attention being paid to varying the levels of physical and vocal energy, all of which is intrinsically purposeful and never incoherent. In other words, not only are sessions like this very well planned, they are also very well *plotted*, demonstrating the skills of a good storyteller as well as those of a good teacher.

The RSC education team consciously shapes and organizes its teaching with aesthetic as well as cognitive intentions, aiming to offer as far as possible a 'complete' experience to young people, one that will leave them with a feeling of culmination rather than mere cessation. It is well aware that the toolkit of activities it offers to teachers can be misused if applied without due attention to the rhythm, pattern and pacing of the lesson as well as to the logical progress of its unfolding. That is why they insist that the teacher should see herself as an 'artist or a craftsperson' – someone who will be able to select and choose the tools they offer carefully and purposefully.[23] These metaphors for the teacher do not chime readily with the dominant terminology of 'curriculum delivery' – of teacher as postie – that continues to dominate educational policy-making; rather it defines the teacher as someone highly skilful, artful and autonomous. Here Richard Sennett's idea of 'experience as a craft' is particularly apt if we are to appreciate the work the RSC does with teachers.[24] There is a danger, he argues, that in talking of experience we tend to emphasize the inner, subjective quality of feeling and divorce it from form and procedure, from what he calls the 'techniques of experience'. These techniques of experience, in the RSC's case, are embodied in the bank of activities it has developed from its rehearsal room and, more significantly, in the schemes of work that exemplify how these can be used. Sennett's words on the implications of this idea, of experience as a craft, are worth quoting at length for the way they illuminate how the Company shares its own professional knowledge through its developmental work with teachers:

> These (techniques of experience) could guide us ... by furnishing an envelope of tacit knowledge for our actions. We would want to shape the impress people and events have made on us so that these impressions are intelligible to others who do not know the same people we know or lived through the same events ... we would try to make the particular knowledge we possess transparent in order that others can understand and respond to it. The idea of experience as a craft contests the sort of subjectivity that dwells in the sheer process of feeling.

Their pedagogy, then, does not place skills, subjective feeling, craft and artistry in opposing camps but works pragmatically so that the one complements the other, just as it models the oppositions of play and work, and of the aesthetic and the intellectual, as false dichotomies.

Learning through the body

I must at once disclaim any implied opposition between active and intellectual responses to Shakespeare. A fundamental assumption of active pedagogy is that it harnesses thought and action. In school classrooms, as on stage, all human faculties are in symbiotic relation.

REX GIBSON[25]

We have already considered Kate McLuskie's mistrust of playful approaches to the teaching of Shakespeare, particularly at the level of higher education, where she fears that due attention to theoretical positions and critical practices in Shakespeare studies will suffer if they are adopted. In mounting her argument, she acknowledges the work of Rex Gibson – and by implication, that of the RSC – but does so with a number of reservations and not a little irony. In particular she sees the desire to demystify Shakespeare and make him accessible through the immediacy of his plays as anti-intellectual – as substituting 'dancing' for 'thinking'. She derives her metaphor from Beckett's play *Waiting for Godot*, where the character Lucky, we are told, is not able to dance and think at the same time. '*Pace* Gibson and all the other gifted educators who have made the experience of "doing Shakespeare" such a pleasure,' she concludes, 'working on Shakespeare at advanced levels requires that the dancing stalls and the thinking goes on.'[26]

This opposition between 'dancing' and 'thinking' is a rhetorical ploy, of course, by which she is proposing a critical, discursive study of Shakespeare through the lenses of new historicism, feminist criticism and the like as preferable to an approach which prioritizes generating enthusiasm through personal response and physical engagement, which she fears are likely to produce superficial, liberal humanist readings. Although our own concerns are not with Shakespeare at university level, it is still worth pointing out that, as a rhetorical ploy, the tragi-comic irony of Beckett rather undermines the seriousness of her argument. More fundamentally, it all too blithely opposes thinking to doing, working to playing, the cognitive to the aesthetic, with the former in each case being proposed as the more powerful of the pair. These, I have argued, are false dichotomies founded on cultural prejudices rather than on any facts about learning; and at their base is the most fundamental false opposition of all, that of the mind to the body.

Mind/body dualism is, of course, deeply rooted in western culture and has its origins in the Christian idea of a disembodied soul, with the flesh being the source of sinfulness and distraction. Such dualism was enshrined in western philosophy by Descartes, who established his argument upon the radical differentiation between body and mind, the former being the major locus of identity, of rational thought and moral reflection. Much contemporary schooling is organized on this dualism; the body is fixed behind a desk and must be disciplined to remain still and unobtrusive for long periods of time so that the brain can be allowed to concentrate and do its job effectively. Subjects such as Physical Education, Drama and Dance that focus on the body tend to be viewed as less significant than those that focus on the brain; after all, it is the brain that will be tested in the most important examinations. Recent scientific work on neurology and the biological workings of the brain have, in many ways, re-enforced this split. It is not unusual in British primary schools, for example, to witness activities known as 'brain gym', where children spend two minutes or so between hour-long sessions of maths and English rubbing their tummies and patting their heads, or performing other gestural actions intended to enable the left and right hemispheres of their brains to work more efficiently together. Physical activity of this kind divorces the body from the mind and reduces its function to the servicing of neurons rather than the making of meaning.

One contemporary philosopher who argues passionately against mind/ body dualism is Mark Johnson. In his book *The Meaning of the Body* he draws upon the work of cognitive neuroscientists, psychologists and the philosophy of John Dewey to propose an embodied theory that situates our capacity to make meaning within the flow of experience, experience which is dependent upon the body engaging with its environment. Johnson rejects the idea of a disembodied mind and situates bodily experience and higher propositional thinking along the same continuum rather than seeing them as fundamentally different.

> An embodied view of meaning ... sees meanings and all our higher functioning as growing out of and shaped by our abilities to perceive things, manipulate objects, move our bodies in space and evaluate our situation. Its principle of continuity is that the 'higher' develops from the 'lower' ... if we reduce meanings to words or sentences ... we miss or leave out where meaning really comes from.[27]

If there is no separate mind entity to serve as the sole locus of reason, Johnson argues, then reason itself cannot be understood as something pure and abstract, as coming to us from outside of ourselves, from the words of a teacher, for example. What we call reason, he insists, consists of 'embodied *processes* by which our experience is explored, criticized and transformed in inquiry'. He adds: 'Reason is more an accomplishment of inquiry than a pre-given fact or capacity.'[28] If reason is embodied rather than disembodied, then the idea of it being dispassionate and detached from our feelings and emotions also turns out to be illusory; rather, Johnson argues, feeling and reason are intimately related and our emotions 'lie at the heart of our capacity to conceptualize, reason and imagine'.[29] In other words, to adapt a quote from Gloucester in *King Lear*, we 'reason feelingly'.

To illustrate his argument, Johnson refers to the poem *Purity* by the American poet Billy Collins, in which the poet imagines himself taking off not only his clothes but also his flesh and his organs, so that when he comes to write he is 'entirely pure: nothing but a skeleton at a typewriter'. The problem is that as such, he can only imagine and write about death. Sometimes he succumbs to the temptation to keep his penis and then he finds that he can also imagine and write about sex. The point is wittily and tellingly made: our bodies, far from impeding our ability to make meaning, are the very condition through which we do so.

Johnson points out that, because reason is generally understood to be expressed only through language, words are assumed to be the exclusive bearers of meaning. As a result, those forms of non-verbal meaning-making that we find in the arts, such as in dance and music, are presumed to be not part of meaning proper. This of course is nonsense, as musicians, dancers and visual artists are perfectly capable of making rational choices that are independent of verbal language and that can be apprehended at a rational-feeling level by others who can relate their expressiveness to their own experience.[30] We can, for example, appreciate the abstract movements and gestures of a dance by relating them to the meaning and feeling of our own bodily gestures.

> We know how it feels when our bodies sway gracefully versus when we slip and fall or jump back in fright. We know intuitively what it means to 'be up' and happy, just as we know what it means to 'feel low' when we are depressed. Our bodily posture and openness to the world is upright and expansive when we are joyful, and it is drooping and contracting when we are sad.[31]

In other words, dancing, or physical expression in general, is intrinsically related to thinking through the fact that both are concerned with the making of meaning; and their shared embodiment means that the language of one – movement – can inform and give direction to the language of the other – words and speech. We commonly experience the patterns and textures of human movement and gesture in ways that inform reflection, judgement and propositional knowledge even when they are used in an abstract, non-representational manner.

These key points of embodiment chime readily with the constructivist theories of learning through experience that lie at the heart of the idea of a rehearsal room as classroom. Simple warm-up exercises, where players are asked to show grief and do so instinctively, and complex group performances, such as that of the dumb show, both demonstrate how the body communicates meaning in ways that are clearly rational and emotive at one and the same time. More subtly, all of the work derived from Cicely Berry's approaches, such as *punctuation shifts* and *scene studies*, specifically incorporates the body into the heart of the meaning making process, using such means as physical effort, resistance, breathing and movement pathways through space to help players find meaning in the words or, as the RSC puts it, to unlock their latent power.

Learning together

The German philosopher, Friedrich Schiller, was not alone in experiencing the hope and promise of the French Revolution and then the extreme disenchantment of watching it descend into chaos, tyranny and blood-letting. His response, however, was unique and surprising. In a lengthy and complex series of letters, he proposed education – in particular, an 'aesthetic education' – as a way of keeping alive the utopian promise of a better, more egalitarian world, the possible realization of which seemed to be constantly undermined by political enmities and social divisions. To this end, his vision of beauty did not pertain to the particular properties of objects or art works, but was conceived as a moral and social necessity, 'an ideal by which it is possible for us to be guided in reflection upon ourselves and our lives'.[32] At its base was an idea that he described as 'aesthetic necessity', a quality that he saw as evident in all good works of art – in the poem where every word seems to be in the right place, in a piece of music where the notes, rhythm and tonality seem to intermingle and progress effortlessly, as though no alternative could improve it. The importance of this for Schiller's political philosophy is that aesthetic necessity allows us to experience what a good and happy society actually feels like. The principle of the ensemble, as defined by the RSC under the leadership of Michael Boyd, was, I suggest, founded on a similar, utopian principle in which social and aesthetic ideals are brought together to create an environment in which art making is intended to embody a particular conception of the good society. In the classroom, this presents a model for learning that necessarily has social as well as cognitive and artistic intentions.

Michael Boyd defined his own approach to ensemble theatre making very much in terms of an artistic vision underpinned by, and inseparable from, a particular set of social principles.

> At the heart of our developing practice at the RSC, there's a set of values and behaviours which we have found are both required and enabled by ensemble working . . .
>
> **Cooperation**: the intense, unobstructed traffic between artists at play and the surrender of the self to a connection with others, even while making demands on ourselves. **Altruism**: the moral imagination and the social perception to realize that the whole is greater than the sum of its parts. The stronger help the weaker, rather than choreographing the weak to make the strong look good. **Trust**: the ability to be appallingly honest and to experiment without fear. **Empathy**: caring for others with a forensic curiosity that constantly seeks new ways of being together and creating together. **Imagination**: keeping ideas in the mind long enough to allow them to emerge from the alchemy of the imagination and not the factory of the will. **Compassion**: engaging with the world and each other, knowing there may be mutual pain in doing so. **Tolerance**: accommodating difference and allowing mistakes. **Forgiveness**: allowing and recovering from big and potentially damaging mistakes. **Humility**: the expert who has nothing to learn has no need for creativity, because the answer is already known. **Magnanimity**: the courage to give away ideas and love, with no thought of transaction or an exchange in return. **Rapport**: the magic language between individuals in tune with each other. **Patience**: this is only really possible over years. Art can be forced like rhubarb, but it tends to bend in the wind. **Rigour**: dancers and musicians take life-long daily training for granted, and theatre could do with catching up.[33]

It is hard to see Schiller disagreeing with this vision. He wrote for the theatre and would have appreciated how the social necessity of working constructively together is needed to produce the aesthetic achievement of a good performance.

Under the artistic directorship of Gregory Doran, this principle of collective, co-operative endeavour remains as one of the RSC's core values but is guided by the word 'Company' itself rather than by the political vision of the ensemble. As such, it still sees social and aesthetic values as very much inter-related. In speaking of his 2013 production of *Richard II*, for example, he says:

> What I want to do is to create the environment in which we can work on this play and decide what this play is about. That is how we will take

control of it, invest in it and ensure that the play becomes entirely the product of us, here, now.[34]

This emphasis on the social, on developing productive ways to work with one another, is particularly necessary in the classroom, where some young people are likely to feel vulnerable and self-conscious and possibly uncomfortable when working physically in groups, being watched and having their work commented on by their peers. Equally, it is risky for teachers as the process might well necessitate a shift in the way that they conceive of and enact their own authority. Neelands and O'Hanlon summarize these challenges as follows:

> The teacher/director is taking risks in seeking a shift in the normative power relations within the class/company and between the class/company and the teacher/director and even by moving back the desks in both cases, or by exploring the choices rather than dictating/directing them. Young people/actors must make themselves vulnerable and visible in order to participate and must know that there is protection and mutual respect for difference from within the group to match the personal and social challenges of taking a part in the action.[35]

Whether inspired by the utopian ideals of the ensemble or by the shared values of a company, the challenge is to make sure that words match deeds and are mirrored in the actual practice. Any experienced teacher knows that this is easier to achieve with some classes than others. Difficulties may emanate from the personal histories of the young people, the ways in which they are used to working, group dynamics, gender relationships, socio-cultural backgrounds and a range of myriad and diverse factors over which the teacher may have little control. These can be exacerbated by the very physicality of theatre-making. As Helen Nicholson points out, issues of personal space and physical contact need to be handled with sensitivity in the drama class:

> There is an intimacy about bodies and how people feel about touching each other or using their bodies expressively is fraught with complications, particularly as the body is representative of wider cultural and social values.[36]

The RSC is well aware of such sensitivities in its work with teachers and young people. Its practitioners recognize, for example, that trust has to be earned – and often learned – and that appropriate boundaries have to be established. In order to promote the values of working as an ensemble, or as a company, the education team does not preach its virtues but deploys a range of approaches to encourage its development, those 'forms and procedures' that Richard Sennett has equated with 'experience as technique'. The initial games described in Chapter 4 are most readily illustrative of this; they are played in a circle, a structure which levels off status and makes the teacher one of the players, albeit one who also 'referees' the game; they encourage interaction and sociability, mixing players up, allowing for personal displays of skill or flamboyance but clearly locating them within activities where co-operative endeavour is what is called for. The spirit of the games persists in the playful ways that groups and pairs are formed and re-formed for text exploration and performance work. The shift in the teacher's authority, from all-knowing pedagogue to facilitator, is illustrated in the ways that Miles offers feedback. He always begins this by asking players what they have learned or 'discovered' from tasks and always accepts their responses at face value, commenting on them seriously and supportively, never contradicting them even when his own, authoritative commentary takes the discussion in a different direction. Above all he receives their theatre-making with enthusiasm and evident pleasure and – just as importantly – frames the theatre-making activities in ways that push many of the participants beyond their comfort zones but always in such a way that they are able to complete the task with a real feeling of success. The praise he offers them is genuine, and players know it is. In these complex but interconnected ways, players learn to trust their teacher as an integral part of being able to trust one another.

Learning together as a company does more than develop important social attitudes, or what are often considered to be 'soft' learning objectives. It is not only the basis for but also the process through which 'harder' (i.e. more visible) learning objectives are achieved through active and actionable collaborative inquiry. This is a skilful rather than a 'touchy-feely' process, as Sennett has argued. Drawing from his own experiences as a professional orchestral musician, he makes the point that: 'Musicians with good rehearsal skills work forensically, investigating concrete problems.'[37] Individuals may well be opinionated about how a particular passage ought to be played. A dialogic exchange with someone who disagrees does not necessarily mean that one will give way to the other's point of view but a decision does need to be reached. It is in the process of playing itself that opinions will be tested out and evaluated. Mere assertion, therefore, is not enough and good ensemble musicians, however individually skilled they are, have learned how to interact and exchange for mutual benefit. 'They need to co-operate to make art,' as Sennett concludes.[38] In the rehearsal studio and in the classroom that seeks to emulate its processes, it is the making of art that remains paramount as it provides direction and purpose for the social techniques of experience being developed; but their development cannot be dissociated from the inquiry at its heart, which involves collaborative decision-making that is at once rational and aesthetic in its concerns.

This ensemble is a secure environment without ever being a comfort zone. All of us are continually challenging ourselves and being inspired by those around us to reach new levels in all aspects of our work.[39]

These comments were made by Geoffrey Streatfield and relate to his experience as a member of the RSC between 2007 and 2009. They point clearly to the central dynamic of the rehearsal room as a place where the satisfactions are not only those of working co-operatively but of being challenged and inspired to move beyond one's comfort zone.

This immediately recalls the Vygotskyan concept of the 'zone of proximal development' or the ZPD, where, with guidance and support, we are helped to perform a step higher than we are currently capable of or comfortable with. The ZPD, Vygostsky insisted, is the zone of learning itself. In the classroom that mirrors the rehearsal room, the support we need to move beyond our comfort zones in part lies with the group but it is the prime responsibility of the teacher to structure or 'scaffold' the process if learning is to take place.

Learning through beauty

Beauty is a word that we may readily accept as applicable to Shakespeare's verse but be rather more surprised at its being associated with pedagogy, yet this is precisely what I have argued in a number of writings.[40] In order to apprehend what this might mean, we must begin by understanding beauty as an experience rather than as the property of specific objects, experiences that we will often share in common with others and which we can describe and articulate perfectly clearly. I know exactly what you mean, for example, when you talk of a beautiful sunset, a beautiful day, a beautiful melody or a beautiful painting, even if I won't always agree with you – the paintings and melodies that move you may not be those that appeal to me. The Enlightenment philosopher Immanuel Kant, from whom we have inherited many deeply rooted ideas in western thought, tried to be more precise in defining different experiences of beauty and proposed that we divide them roughly into two types, which he described as the 'beautiful' and the 'sublime', distinguishable by the different effects they have upon us.[41] Experiences of the beautiful are those we equate with charm, cheerfulness, serenity and domesticity; they move us but also reassure us. The sound of a cuckoo in late spring, a melody by Mozart, a painting by Renoir, the poem *Adlestrop* by Edward Thomas – these could all be readily associated with experiences of the beautiful. The 'sublime', on the other hand, signifies a beauty that is powerful and overwhelming, that thrills and shocks rather than charms: the beauty of a storm at sea, or a painting by Hieronymous Bosch, or of Sarah Kane's play *Blasted* could all fall into the category of the sublime. Although we might reject the polarity of Kant's theory, as we have done with other binary oppositions throughout this chapter, the distinction is still a helpful one as we seek to articulate a 'pedagogy of beauty' and how it applies to the RSC's educational work.

We have inherited a much older theory of beauty than that provided by Kant from the Greeks and in particular from the writings of Plato. Plato argued in the *Symposium* that beauty attracts us through the qualities we perceive in it – harmony, balance and proportion, for example – qualities we yearn for as creatures of nature and that we see in nature at its best. He also saw beauty as inextricably associated with love, inspiring within us a desire not only to possess but also to know; for when we love someone or something, we see them as beautiful and want to spend time with them in order to get to know them better. Beauty, in other words, brings the passions and the intellect together as its desire to possess is also a desire to know better, and this relationship is also of fundamental importance to the RSC's pedagogy.

Another concept important to theorizing a 'pedagogy of beauty' comes from the philosopher Iris Murdoch, and it is that of 'unselfing'.[42] Unselfing occurs, she says, when we forget about our daily preoccupations and are drawn into a process of unpossessive contemplation which she illustrates with reference to nature – the vision of a kestrel, the sudden sight of which encourages her temporarily to stop brooding over her personal anxieties and to see them for the petty preoccupations they are. Such sentiments we find in the world of art in Matisse, who wished his paintings to be so serenely beautiful that the very sight of them would make our worldly problems seem trivial and so fall away.[43] But as we are concerned with the education of young people here, we need a more dynamic idea of unselfing, one that places less emphasis on serenity and more on energy, and here we can draw upon the Platonic ideas of passion and love as more active qualities in the experience of beauty. The experience will still involve a loosening of personal preoccupations, in particular those teenage anxieties about identity and self-image that can lead young people defensively to reject forms of beauty outside of their immediate experience and behave in ways deliberately intended to impede their engagement with them. The form of unselfing we seek here will be a process through which young people can both possess and be possessed by the beauty of Shakespeare, willingly allowing it to shape their desires and thus, even in some small way, to change how they perceive what matters to them in the world. Such is to underline once again the relationship between the experience of beauty and that of love. I am suggesting that this is a fundamental aspiration for RSC pedagogy: to inspire in young people a love for the works of Shakespeare that hitherto may well have meant nothing to them. In this sense the RSC is seeking to guide young people on to and along pathways they previously never imagined they might wish to explore.

Those principles of the Company intended to provide a sense of security and trust are complemented by those elements of a pedagogy of beauty that charm young people into what we might call a 'readiness to unself'. Playfulness and good hearted laughter – laughter *with*, not laughter *at*, as we saw in Chapter 4 – are central to this charm, a charm through which the teacher conjures up an atmosphere intended to put all players at their ease; for although the aim is to have players work beyond their comfort zone, we need to feel at ease with the zone we are in before we will feel secure enough to venture beyond it. Once again, the opening games are good examples of this charm in action, where young people are swept along and energized by the surprising and comical nature of what they and their fellow players do in the game playing circle. At its best, this form of play relaxes the pressure on vocal and physical involvement and reduces self-consciousness by quite literally encouraging in players a spontaneous willingness to unself in playful interactions that often require them to touch or get close to one another for periods of time that are marked yet too brief for self-consciousness.

If activities such as these introduce the charms of the beautiful into the classroom, those influenced by Cicely Berry are more closely aligned to the thrill of the sublime as they seek to help young people connect with the power of Shakespeare, what she has called 'the heat in the language, the coarseness, the violence, the passion, the sorrow'.[44] When Mary Johnson talks of 'working from the gut', this is the kind of response she is referring to, and a good example of such an experience of beauty is her own account of the Cicely Berry exercise in which she took on the role of Ophelia, described in Chapter 3, and ended up feeling 'absolutely desolate'. When Miles asks the groups working on the scene where Hamlet meets the ghost to use the language to create an atmosphere of terror, he is clearly appealing to the aesthetics of the sublime, something that has great appeal for many teenagers.

Rather than considering the beautiful and the sublime as experiential polarities we can see them as tendencies that inform the rhythm and tone of RSC planning, as do considerations of balancing physical activity with discussion; individual with group work; high energy with stillness and so on. This idea of a continuum from one extreme to another should also balance our perception of the aspiration of the RSC to guide young people into a life-long love of Shakespeare. It is not an aspiration whose success can be easily judged in absolute terms, nor is it intended to be; but this chapter has attempted to show how its teaching approaches, based as they are on best practice, work in theoretically complex yet coherent ways to lead young people step by step into a journey which they will hopefully wish to continue for the intellectual and aesthetic pleasures they derive from it. Research commissioned by the RSC tells us about the impact of their pedagogy on teaching and learning in schools and we will proceed to examine what it tells us in Chapters 7 and 8.

6

Tim Crouch Directing the Young People's Shakespeare

When the RSC first decided to set up the Young People's Shakespeare, a key idea was to invite interesting innovators in theatre-making with whom actors would be excited to work. The choice of Tim Crouch to direct the 2011 and 2012 productions certainly fitted this agenda. Crouch is best known for his adult work, which he writes, co-directs and in which he also performs. His plays are original in their non-figurative approach to performance and in the ways that they test the usual conventions of theatre. They have received many awards, with his 2010 production *The Author* in particular gaining widespread recognition for its controversial subject matter and the particularly powerful effect it has had on audiences.[1] The plays have not only been critically well received but have also intrigued university academics. In 2011 The *Contemporary Theatre Review* devoted an entire issue to *The Author* and its editor, Stephen Bottoms, has hailed Crouch's work as 'one of the most important bodies of English-language playwriting to have emerged so far in the twenty-first century'.[2]

Although Crouch had never directed a Shakespeare play before – or indeed any play professionally, other than those he had written himself – he did have experience early in his career of working with young people in educational theatre projects. He had also more recently written and performed a series of one-man shows intended to introduce young audiences to Shakespeare's works from the perspective of some of their minor or secondary characters. Of these, *I, Malvolio* has toured to great critical acclaim and been recognized as a work that appeals equally to 'restless teenagers' and to older audiences, being 'nothing less than fully adult' in its themes.[3] Central to its dynamic is the way Tim's clowning provokes hilarity in the audience while the text forces them to question why they are amused by it and, indeed, mirror the humiliation and misery inflicted on Malvolio by the characters of *Twelfth Night*. But Crouch also sees in Malvolio an archetype of pomposity and joyless authority that is as equally pertinent today as it was in Shakespeare's time, particularly with regard to cultural attitudes to Shakespeare, where pomposity abounds. 'It needs to be explored,' he told me, 'to defuse the more damaging aspects of how Shakespeare is regarded contemporarily.'[4] He believes that the plays are too important and too foundational to be ignored – 'Shakespeare should be central to our culture,' he has said[5] – and in his own work aspires to bring them into an immediate, intimate relationship with young audiences by making them 'super real and relevant to now'.

The Taming of the Shrew

When Jacqui O'Hanlon first approached Tim, he was initially offered *Henry V* but proposed *The Taming of the Shrew* instead.

> It was a play I felt very strongly about, a play that I think connects very forcefully with young people because of the common themes of sisters, families and siblings, relationships and love, abuse, exploring abuse, what a relationship is and what love looks like. This is not an inappropriate text for a young audience.

Why it might have been thought inappropriate, of course, is due to the controversy around the subservient role of women, specifically in marriage, that the play appears to be advocating – at least ostensibly. Kate is a spirited young woman with a violent temper who is famously tamed by her husband, Petruchio, through sense deprivation and starvation in a way that anticipates, as Jonathan Bate has pointed out, the tyranny at the heart of the taming of Winston Smith in George Orwell's *1984*. Bate sees its presentation of female subordination as presenting 'the same kind of awkwardness for liberal sensibilities that the representation of Shylock does in the post-Holocaust world'.[6] Nevertheless, the RSC demonstrated their trust in Tim by immediately agreeing to his suggestion and he proceeded to edit the text and slim it down to the necessary seventy-five minutes. His principle here was to keep the original language whilst ensuring that the end result would be a piece of theatre with vivid characters and a clear story. 'It is not my job to confuse anyone or to try out any fancy notions or concepts. My mission is to tell the story.'[7] As a result, sub-plots were cut, some minor characters eliminated and the role of others changed. The farcical complexity was concentrated into the main plot but here he made some original and highly significant adaptations by re-incorporating the role of Christopher Sly and by changing Baptista – Kate's father – into a female role as Kate's mother.

In the original text, Christopher Sly is an itinerant peddler who, at the start of the play, is ejected from an ale house and falls into a drunken slumber. As he sleeps, a passing lord decides to play a trick on him, disguising him as an aristocrat, providing him with a wife (a page boy in disguise) and mounting the play *The Taming of the Shrew* supposedly for his particular entertainment. In the surviving Folio edition of the play, Sly does not reappear. Modern commentaries, however, have seen his role as a framing device key to a non-sexist reading of the play, one that sets up the story of the 'taming' of a spirited young woman as a conscious deceit, a wish-fulfilment fantasy, staged as a trick in front of a coarse, male drunkard.[8] In this way, the audience is in effect being signalled not to take the play seriously and certainly not to mistake its portrayal of how to tame a strong-willed female as in any sense a reality. Tim too saw the role of Sly as a crucial way to frame the play but very differently. He conjectured that there were no scripted lines for him beyond the opening scene as his role would have been that of a clown, improvizing at different points of the action and relating directly to members of the audience, amongst whom he would be seated. So a space was made for some non-Shakespearean text in this production as Sly reappears during scene changes to comment on the play or try to influence the action. A notable example of this is when he urges the male characters to put a stop to Petruchio's mistreatment of Kate at the end of the wedding scene. 'Come on, there's five of us!' he exclaims with a bravado that is quickly deflated as his words are silently ignored. As the play was being performed in schools, Tim also switched the nature of Sly's disguise from aristocrat to teacher, a move that mirrored the two suitors in the play, both of whom disguise themselves as tutors in order to woo Kate's more conventionally desirable sister, Bianca. The donning of the same teacherly disguise, common to all three actors – pipe, tweed jacket and black, thick-rimmed glasses – took the form of a lively, comic, physical motif performed on each of the three occasions to music. When staged in schools the role of Sly's wife was taken – to the great amusement of the children – by one of the female teachers, who had agreed to this in advance.

The decision to give Sly the role of a teacher was also influenced by Tim's reading of the French philosopher, Jacques Rancière. In his book *The Emancipated Spectator*, Rancière argues that we can learn more from the ignorant schoolmaster than from the all-knowing teacher, as with the former we will learn *alongside* him whereas with the latter we will only learn *from* him what he knows already.[9] Defined by his ignorance, Sly was transformed into a comic embodiment of such a schoolmaster, whose confused questioning throughout the performance offered no answers but instead guided the young audience to think about what was happening in front of them.[10] It seemed only right, then, that the post-performance workshop should be led by Jamie Beamish, the actor who had played Sly, thus continuing his role as a teacher with 'a load of questions to ask' (his words to the children) beyond the play itself.

Tim was clear that changing Baptista from a father into a mother figure would be important and effective in a number of ways. It would first serve to make the play more contemporary in its feel, certainly for a young audience, as single mother units are nowadays far more common than single father units. Dramatically, it would provide Baptista's character with its own depth and complexity. 'Here is a woman,' he told me, 'who seems to have money, seems to have power but also hasn't understood women's liberation and so has been trying to groom her daughters to be suitable fodder for men.' The part was played with great conviction by Caroline Martin as a *nouveau riche*, middle-aged woman, who would not have looked out of place in the UK television programme *The Only Way is Essex*, in which such women are portrayed as very much at home when half-tipsy and with a glass of champagne in their hand. She brought poignancy as well as humour to the role. At the beginning of the final act, for example, when her supposedly 'good' daughter, Bianca, admits to having married in secret, without her permission, she is greatly saddened as well as angered. 'Bianca, Bianca. Daughter, daughter.' These simple words are uttered with a mixture of hurt, shock and despair, and the sense of abandonment she finds in the line 'Thus mothers may be hailed and abused', is all the more acute for her being a single mother.

Bianca was conceived very much as a younger version of Baptista, with actress Emily Plumtree speaking in the same tones as her mother, pouting, chewing gum and flirting outrageously with her tutor. Opposite her was Madeleine Appiah as Kate. The nature of their relationship was introduced with great clarity and comic energy in a scene that preceded the entrance of Sly at the start of the play. As the audience enters and are settling, the two sisters are already on stage, Kate quietly trying to read a book while Bianca preens herself, applying lipstick in front of a hand mirror, practising dance moves, leafing through teen magazines, all to a background of brash pop music that is evidently annoying her sister. Once the audience settles, Bianca turns up the volume of the music, glaring provocatively at Kate as she does so whereupon an exasperated Kate jumps up and turns it down. A squabble ensues. Bianca snatches Kate's book, Kate yanks Bianca's hair. Bianca screams whereupon their mother enters with other members of the cast. There ensues a melee of confusion, shouting and argument. The quarrel grows more violent and the music is cranked up again as Kate chases Bianca through the audience, leaving Sly on the stage alone and the play proper ready to begin.

The Bianca of this production was certainly portrayed as desirable to men but not for her submissive and gentle ways. She was physically attractive but shown to be subject to the pressures of modern teenage culture, conforming to contemporary fashions and patterns of behaviour that had sexualized her in a very conventional way. Kate, on the other hand, was immediately shown to be resistant to those pressures, evidently preferring a good book to a teen magazine. She was not interested in making herself appear attractive to men and wanted to be left in peace rather than be subjected to unwanted male attention. Her shrewishness was thus framed as rebellious but also reasonable, as a reaction to the provocations of her sister and to her mother's plans to marry her off. Her taming was portrayed less

FIGURE 6.1 *Madeleine Appiah as Katherine and Daniel Rose as Hortensio in the 2011 YPS production of* The Taming of the Shrew.

as a breaking of her will and more of her coming to a conscious realization that, in Petruchio, she had found a kindred spirit, someone whose quickness of wit, strength of will and unconventional behaviour was a fair match for her own. In this sense, Bianca's comments 'being mad herself she is madly mated' took on the more positive, contemporary sense of the word 'mad' as used by many young people – of being wild, daring, individual and outrageous. Madeleine Appiah spoke Kate's infamous final speech with a knowing smile and directed much of it at her mother.[11] In this way the exaggerated case she makes for a woman's subservience to her husband, as well as appearing ironically tongue-in-cheek when applied to herself, had a visibly cutting effect on Baptista, who, of course, had no husband to share a life with and was about to lose both of her daughters. There was also a strong hint in the tone of its delivery that Kate had learned to value kindness, something her mother had singularly failed to display to her throughout. To emphasize this, Baptista was left in silent reflection, alone on the stage when every other character had exited, creating a sad, surprising, rather beautiful moment to end the play.

'YPS productions are not just dropped into a school,' Tim insists. 'There's no sense of hit and run about them.'[12] When performed in the Swan Theatre, the audience were given the chance to hot seat the characters and to direct questions to members of the production team. In the schools, a more substantial educational workshop of forty-five minutes followed each performance. In addition to asking questions of the characters, children also engaged actively in text work and were led to reflect upon Kate's final speech. I was fortunate enough to see the production in a Warwickshire primary school while it was touring. During the break between play and performance, I managed to snatch a few quick words with a small group of nine-year-old children. They had evidently enjoyed the play and were particularly taken with the performances of Madeleine's Kate and Nikesh Patel's Petruchio. While recognizing that Baptista was sad at the end, they had little sympathy for her as a mother and were in no doubt that Kate's marriage would be much happier than Bianca's. The girls had lots to say about the sibling rivalry while the boys were very impressed by Petruchio's cool leather jacket.

Back in the workshop, such initial responses were given more space for articulation and reflection. Caroline Martin was particularly skilful when answering questions as Baptista, providing answers that fed rather than closed down possibilities. For example, when one boy asked 'Do your daughters take after you?' she replied that they both had different fathers, neither of whom was around any more, leaving children to consider how this made life difficult for her as a parent, despite the money left to her by her second husband. While hot seating Petruchio and Kate together, children wanted to know whether Kate would have married anyone else and if she really liked Petruchio. 'I like the way he argues,' she replied, 'no one else can match me when I argue' – clearly guiding children to recall the energetic give and take of their dialogue when the two first meet in Act 2. In a subsequent exercise, children were later invited actively and very physically to explore lines from this exchange together (*Come, come, you wasp, I'faith you are too angry / If I be waspish, best beware my sting*). Nikesh as Petruchio had to field a number of questions about his mistreatment of Kate. 'Well it was just part of my plan,' he responded and attempted to excuse himself a little by exclaiming, 'I didn't eat either!' 'In the end,' he offered, looking at Kate, 'I think she might have tamed me a bit, too.' 'What do you think?' replied Kate, turning to the children. And here there ensued some vigorous, vocal and contrasting opinions.

In order to reconsider Kate's final speech, the scene was staged again and a puzzled Jamie Beamish asked children to think about what she was trying to say in it. Most children emphasized the literal message, the duty she owed to her husband, although one did say, 'She means that they should be obedient to each other.' The scene would now be replayed, the children were told, and Kate would this time be addressing the words explicitly to her mother and sister. How should she do it? 'Strongly and proudly,' suggested one boy, an instruction to which Madeleine Appiah duly responded to great effect.

The overall response to the production was extremely positive. In statistical feedback gathered by the RSC from audiences at the Swan, which included a fair mix of adults as well as children, it received a 98 per cent approval rating, with 65 per cent considering it excellent and a further 25 per cent very good. Critically, too, the production was very well received. Dominic Cavendish of the *Daily Telegraph* heaped praise on Madeleine Appiah's Kate. 'A stud in her nose and a baleful look in her eye, she's everything Emily Plumtree's pink-loving, Barbie-brained Bianca, beset by three dopey suitors, isn't.' He saw Kate as 'both the product of a shouty, louty, bling culture and also enough of her own woman to be its saving grace'.[13] He also evidently admired the respect the production showed for its young audience.

> There's no dodging the fact that after enduring the cruelest privations, Kate advises 'head-strong women' at the play's close that 'Thy husband is thy Lord, thy life, thy keeper' and much more besides, but most kids of eight-plus 'get' irony, and the way Madeline Appiah plays the submission scenes exudes a deadpan, tongue-in-cheek quality that at once honours and subverts the sentiments.

Cavendish had intimate knowledge of how one child at least responded to the play as he took his own ten-year-old son to see it and he, we are informed, remained 'fidget-free' throughout the entire performance. 'I'm sure he emerged beaming from ear to ear,' he adds, 'not because he'd been handed a primer in chauvinism but because he'd seen for the first time how uproariously fun Shakespearean comedy can be.' Cynics might remark that this is hardly surprising for the son of a cultural commentator who works for one of the country's elite newspapers; but the evidence from schools, from other members of the Swan audience and from my own observations suggest that its appeal to the young audiences who saw it was far broader and more general than that; and that this production of the play, at least, could hardly be described as a primer in chauvinism or anti-chauvinism, or as didactic in any sense of the word.

The directing and rehearsal process

> I think a bad teacher is someone who stands in front of a class and pontificates and delivers the summation of their pedagogical knowledge. A good teacher is someone who looks at the class, reads what the class wants, where the class is, what the class needs and doesn't need, and responds accordingly. Open to improvisation, open to a sense of dialogue. That is a teacher model I would ascribe to and it is also a director model I would ascribe to. To try not to go into a rehearsal process with a hard and fast pattern of how I want this production to be; to be open minded, to see what's in the room, to see what's in the people in the room, the qualities of the people in the room.

This approach to direction and rehearsal that Tim Crouch brought to both of his productions for the YPS was effortlessly in tune with the definition of ensemble at the heart of the RSC's artistic and educational philosophy at the time. 'From my experience as an actor,' he told me, 'I think a lot of directors come with a very hard and fast process of how to approach the play and apply that process to it.' This was something he particularly wished to avoid. Of course he had to take responsibility for the editing process, which in itself determined an overall concept and vision behind both plays, but from then on he strove to keep the rehearsal process as open as possible, actively seeking to incorporate the ideas of the actors themselves into the staging decisions. He also made conscious efforts to present the language of the rehearsal room as 'open to fallibility, to reverse, to all those things that will work against the idea of the director as an autocratic presence'.

As a playwright who has placed the imaginative responses of audiences at the heart of his artistic concerns, it was unsurprising that Tim should similarly prioritize audience response in his role as a YPS director. 'For me, as a director, I feel that I speak on behalf of the audience. I am their representative in the rehearsal room.' His practice goes beyond this, however, as he likes to conduct a number of open rehearsals; as he puts it, 'theatre is a public form and when you rehearse you are rehearsing for a public moment'. The Company and the actors were initially resistant but were won over by the way in which the vision was conceived. It would provide a chance for anyone in the Company – people from the box office and the Estates department as well as from the marketing and the artistic teams – to come and see what a rehearsal process was like. For some of them, this would be their first opportunity to do so. A 'table of love' was placed at the back of the room, close to where these public guests sat and upon which they were asked to contribute a gift for the play, the actors or the space. Usually this consisted of food and drink and various treats of some kind. It was made clear that they were invited there to watch and nothing else – not to pass comment, or pass notes to the actors, or intrude in the process in any way. 'I would always give little ground rules when people came into rehearsals. You are not here to be directors but we do really value your presence in the room.'

I myself was able to take advantage of this offer early on in the rehearsal process for *Shrew*.[14] One of the scenes being worked on was a short one from Act 4 of the edited script, in which the attraction between Bianca and Lucentio, disguised as her tutor, Cambio, becomes evident and is secretly witnessed by Hortensio and Gremio, both rivals for her hand. The actors Emily Plumtree and David McGranaghan first of all sat down with Tim and explored the context together: how old the two were (sixteen and nineteen respectively, they speculated), what they saw in each other, when they had first fallen in love and so on. Emily proposed that perhaps Bianca had not seen many attractive young men in her life and so was suddenly swept off her feet by the charm of Lucentio. They then looked specifically at the first few lines of the scene:

Enter BIANCA and LUCENTIO (as Cambio). They court.
Enter HORTENSIO and GREMIO
LUCENTIO
Now, mistress, profit you in what you read?
BIANCA
What, master, read you? First resolve me that.
LUCENTIO
I read that I profess the Art to Love.
They kiss.

Ten minutes of discussion now ensued as to where the two might be positioned on the stage, what they each might be reading, whether they were really reading or just pretending and so on. Various props were positioned about the studio and Tim suggested they select something they felt to be appropriate. David chose a heavy book, Emily a magazine. They now began to work spontaneously, choosing to enter from opposite sides of the stage and to play the lines as a kind of foreplay as they slowly approached one another, neither paying any attention to their reading matter. On the words 'the Art to Love' David dropped the book and Emily leapt into his arms. For me watching, the result was immediately sexually charged and extremely funny. But nothing was fixed as they discussed specific details and new possibilities and played the scene again, differently this time, before moving on to explore in a similarly open and improvised manner Hortensio and Gremio; where they might be hiding, why they were there together and how they might physically respond to what they were witnessing. I was interested to see in the final production that these initial experiments had been completely reworked and significantly changed. However, the obvious sense of ownership and the dynamic energy of the ensemble that such an open approach to directing fosters had clearly left its imprint on the sparkling quality of the final performance.

King Lear

With the success of Tarell Alvin McCraney's *Hamlet* in 2010, the RSC felt it had proved that even primary-school-aged children could be enthralled by one of the most complex of Shakespeare's tragedies and wondered if the same could be true of *Lear*, considered by many to be his bleakest and most moving work. For his part, Tim was once again drawn to the play by the theme of families and siblings; in this case two families in break down, two sets of siblings in crisis and two fathers, Lear and Gloucester, each in their different ways sympathetic but far from perfect. 'And then,' he adds, 'there is the rich landscape of the play, a play that encompasses all sorts of things, from death to madness, to passion, to lust, to envy, to jealousy, to disguise, to loyalty, to love. And, as in any Shakespeare play, all of these things co-exist in a really exciting story.'[15] As with *Shrew*, Tim wanted to avoid any over-simplification of the story in the edit and, as far as possible, to intensify its potential impact on a young audience. In reducing the text by more than half, however, he had to lose some favourite speeches, including most of Lear's reflections late on in the play on society, injustice and government. 'I mourned for a lot of what I had to cut,' he explains, 'but I had to push forward with the idea of family, the domestic situation, fathers and daughters, fathers and sons. That was the motor of my edit.'

Once again, as with *Shrew*, the editing process was also driven by some strikingly original conceptual ideas for framing the play and for how certain key characters were to be represented. Tim chose to compress the action into seven days over the Christmas period, beginning it on Christmas Day and ending it as the chimes of Big Ben bring in the New Year. For a young audience, this presented a tidy, understandable timeline for the play's action. More significantly, the Christmas week provided a context with certain clear, dramatic reference points. It is a time when families come together, to celebrate and have a good time, but it is also a time when tensions or hidden resentments often break to the surface. It is a time, too, when homelessness is often in the news and when it is particularly cold on the streets, so not a good time for an old man or a beggar to be out there alone. All these references are secular rather than religious and hence understandable to young audiences from diverse cultures and religious traditions. In rehearsals, he worked with the cast to consider what happens on Christmas Day so that these ideas could come alive in the opening scenes of the play. As with *Shrew*, there is action on the stage as the audience enters. There are people standing around smiling, chatting, playing charades. There is a Christmas tree and presents around it; evidently everyone is waiting for these to be opened. There is also a servant dressed in a ridiculous reindeer outfit with a red nose, who is carrying around a tray of drinks, often looking balefully at the audience as he is treated like a skivvy. Once the play begins, this servant is quickly identified by Gloucester as Edmund, his bastard son, whose murderous resentment at his treatment has thus been graphically, if somewhat comically, explained from the outset. When Lear makes his entrance, he does so in a Santa hat as his three daughters line up and play 'We Wish You a Merry Christmas' on the recorder. Recorders present an instant cultural connection for UK children – they are ubiquitous in primary school assemblies – and it is quite evident that only one of the sisters is enjoying this and is actually playing in tune. That she is the king's favourite is further made clear as she sits on the floor beside her father and is offered the biggest present from beneath the tree as her part of the kingdom. Lear's laughter throughout this scene is childlike and genuine enough, whereas for the family and guests we sense that they are forced to go through this performance every year, feigning good humour, laughing at his tired jokes – only this time, of course, he explodes and everything begins to go terribly wrong.

Setting the play during the Christmas period, then, rather than imposing awkwardly on its dramatic texture, actually manages to achieve what all good directorial decisions do: in Tim's words, 'to bring out the flavours that are already there'. Christmas is a time when young people 'meet the oldsters' in their family, 'and they are suffering from their age-related issues and can be really annoying and difficult'. In this production, Lear's mood swings and sudden anger are clearly signalled from the outset as a sign of creeping dementia. His throne is, in fact, a wheelchair. He confuses Goneril with Regan when initiating the test of who loves him most. Christmas clearly delights him as it would a child and when Cordelia refuses to tell him what he wants to hear, he has an irrational tantrum as a child would, but with devastating consequences – he is a king not a child. The moment of his irascible explosion is all the more theatrically powerful as it is deliberately delayed to contrast with the avuncular, fun-loving, rather cuddly figure that the actor Paul Copley had been playing up to that moment. From then on the tone is set for a man who is losing his mental capacities, and whose mood may swing at any moment. He is fascinated by a snow globe given to him as a present and loves playing with tinsel, using it laughingly to 'whip' his servants. But he is demanding and difficult, irascible as well as playful. He clearly needs the kind of care that comes not only from a sense of duty but also from love, from true 'charity', to use Poor Tom's word. Neither of these does he receive from two of his daughters, Goneril and Regan, but instead from Kent, the loyal servant he insults and banishes in the opening scene.

A key change to the original text introduced by Tim was to have Kent disguise himself as the Fool rather than as Caius as in the original, and to incorporate lines from both parts into his script. He recognized the Fool's important dramatic function to 'prick Lear's conscience and debunk his actions', the problem being that he does this through riddles and in the kind of language that is impossible for a modern audience to understand without prior study. Kent disguised as Caius does the same, though in blunter, more straightforward terms. In this production, Edmund abandons his reindeer costume at the end of the opening scene and it is later rediscovered and used by Kent as his Fool's disguise. In this role, as well as warning and scolding Lear, he greatly amuses him and the audience alike and is largely responsible for bringing the necessary moments of lightness into the play. When Lear first sees him, the 'Fool' farts loudly and theatrically, helps him reprimand and beat the rude servant, Oswald, gives him the present of a snow globe and quite literally takes on the role of a reindeer in one delightful image, leaping and harnessed to the wheelchair, pulling Lear to his daughter's castle to the rhythm of the old Christmas hit 'Sleigh Ride', as it plays in the background. Kent in this disguise also allowed Tim to solve the riddle of the cryptic disappearance of the Fool from the play near the end of Act 3. In this production, we see Kent discard his disguise and reappear as himself when Lear is close to death, thus removing a possible confusion in the storyline. There was, moreover, the added theatrical excitement of watching a character transform on the stage, as we see the actor Matt Sutton experiment with accents and physicality in front of the audience before deciding on the voice and gait of the Fool he will play. Similarly, when Gloucester's good son, Edgar, later disguises himself as Poor Tom, the beggar, this is not done offstage (as in the original play) but in front of the audience, who see the actor Dharmesh Patel deliberately adopting the accent specific to British South Asian Londoners as he begs them for 'charity'.

The key character whom we see openly and self-consciously play a part in *Lear* is, of course, Edmund, the bastard son of Gloucester. Tim knew that he risked some negative reactions from primary school audiences by retaining the potentially offensive word 'bastard', particularly in Edmund's famous line 'Now Gods stand up for bastards' which he describes as 'like a little bomb'. He goes on: 'I couldn't afford to lose that as it gives a kick-start to his character and if people are shocked, that's a good thing because he is so honest to the audience and to himself about what he wants and who he is.' His merciless and murderous behaviour to his brother and his father is, of course, bred from his sense of resentment for the social prejudice and lack of rights associated with illegitimacy; but Tim was keen to maintain Edmund as a seductive figure, who charms the audience as he confides in them, much as he seduces Goneril and Regan while deceiving them. The opening of *Lear*, as has been well noted, is very like certain old versions of Cinderella.[16] Here, however, it is Edmund rather than Cordelia who brings to mind the skivvy, Cinderella; and, deprived and despised as he is, we cannot help but sympathize with him. Later there is a small dumb show in which, to the tune of 'I Saw Mummy Kissing Santa Claus', Edmund kisses both Regan and Goneril in quick succession, glancing knowingly at the audience, as if inviting them to admire his wicked charm and share in the success of his deceit. Certainly the small group of young people I spoke to after one school performance were drawn to Edmund as a dramatic figure, relishing and deploring his wickedness at one and the same time.

Another key choice made by Tim was to enhance the subplot so that the overall balance between Lear and his daughters and Gloucester and his sons became quite even. This was achieved through the edit but also through staging decisions. In particular Gloucester's death, instead of being merely reported as in the original text, was given a particularly moving intensity on stage. Blinded and in the arms of Edgar, his hands move tentatively over the face of his son and he recognizes him. As Judy Garland sings 'Have yourself a merry little Christmas', his heart bursts in a sudden moment of happiness and he dies. If anything, this was a more moving scene than the later death of Lear, whose heart similarly breaks at the very moment he thinks he detects life in the body of the dead Cordelia.

The decision to use old Christmas hits from the 50s and 60s as the soundtrack for the play was taken early on. As this production was due to tour in the late summer it would be an instant way of setting up and maintaining a Christmas atmosphere, one that was rooted in popular culture rather than in any religious setting. The use of these songs was inevitably ironic and all the more effective for that: 'Let it Snow, Let it Snow, Let it Snow' plays as Lear is banished into the storm, 'Santa Claus Is Coming to Town', with the lyric *He's going to find out who's naughty and who's nice* is sung as a counterpoint to the blinding of Gloucester. The play was due to tour in New York and almost all of these songs were American, sung by artists such as Bing Crosby, Perry Como and the Ronettes. I first saw the production at a dress rehearsal along with a group of American teachers and theatre educators, and one woman in particular spoke eloquently of how the Judy Garland song had moved her to tears because its cultural connections were so powerful for her but she wondered if the same would be true of a young British audience. Another expressed some concern about bringing a show into schools where knives are used. 'Do we feel okay with the violence?' she asked. Tim appreciated her point but stressed the evident staginess of the violence in this production; that the knives were clearly wobbly and that there was no 'vile jelly' in the scene of the blinding of Gloucester. As a writer whose play *The Author* is explicitly concerned with issues relating to the representation of violent abuse on stage, Tim's thoughts here are particularly pertinent.

> There's an aspect of *Lear* that is hard to ignore, which is the brutality of the play. I've explored in my own work what our responsibilities are as theatre-makers and what our responsibilities are as audience members as to what we choose to look at. There is this gross act of violence, the blinding of Gloucester, which is most shocking. But if I can keep that action in the imagination then I think the audience can believe it much more than if they were actually to see the action itself. Gloucester is bound to Lear's wheelchair in our production and we stop it just at the moment before the knife connects. We then hand over the authority of that action to the audience's imagination. That is, I think, where theatre exists most successfully.[17]

Audience responses to the YPS *King Lear*

The YPS production of *King Lear* toured hub schools and partner theatres throughout the UK in the autumn of 2012. Statistics gathered by the RSC show that of the 10,000 people who saw the production while on tour, almost half were school students. The audiences were significantly more diverse ethnically and socially than those who normally attend the Stratford theatres. 13 per cent had never seen a Shakespeare play before and for 30 per cent this was their first RSC production. Overall approval ratings were very high at 95 per cent, with 49 per cent judging the play to be excellent and a further 30 per cent describing it as very good. Some younger children felt that the play was confusing and were intimidated by the language, and some adults also judged the play as either too difficult for a younger audience or too simplified for A-level students. None thought the subject matter inappropriate or too violent, however, and overwhelmingly the comments were positive. The selection below is a typical sample.[18]

> *'I really liked it but in some bits I didn't understand what was going on. I liked meeting the actors at the end!'* **8-year-old**

> *'I liked the singing and the recorder playing. But we didn't like the swearing and we loved the play. We also liked the scenery.'* **10-year-old**

> *'I really enjoyed King Lear and got to slap Edmund in the face.'* **12-year-old**

> *'Remembered and understood the plot. Loved the actors – especially how approachable they were afterwards.'* **13-year-old**

> *'It is difficult to find fault in the production. I never saw the people on stage as actors – I was so drawn in by the story that I always thought I was there with the characters. This is the greatest thing an actor can do. Fantastic.'* **17-year-old**

And from adults:

> *'My 9-year-old said, on leaving the theatre, "I thought it was going to be boring, boring, boring but it was brilliant! Can we watch Shakespeare again Mum?" A very positive first "contact" with Shakespeare.'*

> *'I felt that it was a good introduction to Shakespeare for children and young adults. However, if people didn't bear this in mind I believe they would have thought it was too simple (a comment I heard as I left the theatre).'*

> *'Very original adaptation. Although it was an abridged version, it didn't feel as if anything had been left out. I never thought a tragedy could make me laugh in places!'*

These comments gathered by the RSC are nicely complemented by a series of reviews that were written by young people who saw the play at York Theatre Royal and published online on the theatre's website.[19] They are disarmingly honest and engaging, filtered as they are through a quirky imitation of the style of a theatre review and no doubt written in English lessons back at school. They reveal with charming naivety the initial, untutored responses of a set of secondary-school children to their first encounter with a great Shakespearean tragedy in performance, what has impressed them and gripped their interest. 'Wonderfully acted,' writes one Year 7 girl, 'portraying many different emotions, most of them at once.' She is here struggling to capture the deep emotional texture of the play but has evidently felt its intensity. 'Shakespeare tragedy with a modern twist!' comments another Year 7 girl. 'They all spoke Shakespearean and even though I couldn't understand them half the time I knew exactly what was going on.' A Year 9 boy appreciated some key directorial decisions, given that this was a play for children, many of whom were younger than himself. 'Despite small amounts of bad language, this play was well child-proofed.' For one girl, this was a new experience and she offers quite a neat summary of the production. 'I have always wanted to see a Shakespeare play. It lasted about ninety minutes. There was a mixture of witty comedy plus lots of tragic moments with some deaths.' Most of the reviewers were greatly impressed by the quality of the acting and one girl was particularly taken by the way different actors changed their accents throughout the production. She only had one point of criticism. 'Overall I would give this play 9 out of 10. It wasn't a 10 because there was no interval.'

I managed to catch a performance in an inner-city secondary school in the West Midlands, which had a large majority of black and minority ethnic (BME) children, about 300 of whom from across the year groups were packed into a large, grim hall with uncomfortable seating.[20] Despite their evident discomfort, most of the young audience remained focused throughout, although the concentration of a substantial minority did appear to falter in the final fifteen minutes, when the comic elements that lighten the rhythm of the action had given way to sustained tragic intensity and when it was easy to lose key moments in the plot development. As I watched from the side, several things were apparent. The lighter moments, particularly those provided by the clowning of the Fool, worked extremely well, especially for younger students, who were amused and delighted by his antics. The audience clearly connected with the family rivalries being played out in front of them, the plotting, the nastiness, the quarrelling and the fighting – all elements one might find in a popular TV soap. They enjoyed Edmund a lot, greeting the scene where he kisses one sister then the other with appreciative cheering and laughter and particularly enjoying the moment when he invites a member of the audience to slap him so that he can better convince his father he has been struck by his brother, Edgar. They also enjoyed other moments of evident theatricality, such as when Edgar donned his filthy costume (moans of disgust from the younger students here) and transformed himself in front of their eyes into Poor Tom, begging them for charity. This was clearly an honest audience so there was little doubt that the generous applause they gave at the end of the play was genuine enough.

Some days before coming to the school, I had tried to organize half an hour to talk with a group of children after the play. In the event, I was given ten minutes to discuss the play inside a cramped storeroom with eight Year 8 students, who reflected the ethnic make-up of the school. As well as seeing the production, they had also experienced a pre-performance workshop with the RSC education team. There was not enough space for us to sit down and they were slightly anarchic and over-excited, but I was nonetheless

FIGURE 6.2 *Paul Copley as Lear and Dharmesh Patel as Edgar in the 2012 YPS production of* King Lear.

able to glean a number of things from them. They had very little trouble with the plot and had clearly grasped its complexities, although they struggled at times to articulate them. 'It's about betrayal in families,' said one girl. She went on: 'The two sisters, their only interest was money and power and both of them say they love the king very much but it was all like a plan.' As for Edmund, they offered a variety of comments: 'He is playing a game.' 'He can't have land because he is a bastard. His brother Edgar could so he wants to fight against him and take it.' 'He was a proper mean dude. He had good tactics.' They were indeed charmed by Edmund's cool manner and cleverness but keenly aware of the moral distance between this enacted fiction and real life. 'That actor, I think he enjoyed being the bad guy,' said one boy, 'because on stage you can be as bad as you want. But in real life you can't be that bad or you'd be straight off to prison.'

In previous studies on young people's responses to theatre in schools, I have pointed to the thrill they feel when the normal, strictly moral codes of school behaviour are playfully transgressed in live performance. This was certainly true of their responses to Edmund and also helps explain why the scene in which he kisses Goneril and Regan in turn was their favourite moment of the play.[21] Another key finding of my previous research was the importance of liveness, the magnetic appeal of good, live acting for young people and its power to hold their attention. The first thing this group talked about with me was the quality of the acting and comments about individual performances peppered the discussion. 'They actually did some real acting and they wasn't nervous.' 'Edgar was filthy. He pretended to be filthy. He was a good actor, though.' 'The man playing the father acted like he had dementia really well.' Shakespeare, of course, is fascinated by performance and play-acting, deception and honesty, themes constantly at the heart of his work, and one girl saw this as something to be learned from the play. 'One of the morals that I thought it's trying to make you understand is that at the end of the day there are real people and there are fake people out there.'

Interestingly, the group equated enjoying the play with seeing a modern production of it. 'In the olden days it was supposed to be all serious and boring but now they've improved it and they've put all those funny things in.' Both the humorous elements and the contemporary setting had evidently helped them connect to its themes and, although cultural materialists might rail against finding universal, humanistic themes in the plays, it was clear that the perennial human issues embedded in family conflict had helped these young people see the play as relevant. 'I know that it's a play,' said one girl, 'but some families are like that. I see some families out there and, well, loads of dads don't do what they're supposed to.' 'The father should know who loves him,' another girl added, 'because obviously it's his daughters so he should know without asking.' 'He wanted to be flattered,' a boy commented. It is precisely upon such shared, human understandings that Shakespeare fashions his dramatic irony and so lures us into the play.

'It was a good play,' said one boy as we concluded our brief talk, 'I'm not going to lie.' And this seemed to be the general consensus as they rather boisterously made their exit. As they left, another boy, it turned out, had a final question for me. 'Sir,' he asked, quite seriously and with genuine curiosity, 'If you do a kiss on stage, do you get more money?'

7

The Impact of the Learning and Performance Network on the Practice of Teachers

Introduction: rhetoric or research?

Not everyone with a passionate interest in the teaching of Shakespeare has been impressed by the RSC's work with teachers and students. Kate McLuskie's recognition of their achievements, as we have seen, has been tempered with scepticism and a sense that its approaches are uncritical and anti-intellectual. A former student of McLuskie's, Sarah Olive, has taken this criticism further, mounting a sustained rhetorical attack on *Stand up for Shakespeare* and the work of the Learning and Performance Network in an article published in the *Shakespeare Review* in 2011. As this is a prestigious journal in the world of Shakespeare studies, and because she raises a number of significant points, I wish to address her arguments directly before looking at evidence from research, some of this conducted by teachers themselves, as to the actual impact of the RSC's education work on teaching and learning. This will be spread over two chapters, the first concentrating on teachers, the second on students. Readers will themselves decide whether it is the rhetoric or the research that impresses them most.

Sarah Olive makes a number of accusations in her article. First and foremost she accuses the RSC of appropriating Shakespeare and consciously substituting values and practices that pertain to the Company itself and foisting these on Shakespeare. These values – of the ensemble, of the journey of the actor, of Shakespeare as playwright as opposed to poet – are so integral to their practices that teachers and students internalize them and equate them with Shakespeare rather than with the RSC.[1] Thus when the RSC proclaims that it is giving ownership of Shakespeare to students and teachers, she criticizes it not only for presuming that ownership is its to give but also for constructing him 'not as a wide range of knowledges and practices on which students will be assessed through coursework or examination, but primarily as performance and rehearsal'.[2] The fact that many teachers and students report back on how they have appreciated the RSC rehearsal techniques is seen as further evidence of this. 'Shakespeare is notably absent from many of the teachers' quotations,' she comments and sees this as a confusion between the intrinsic value of Shakespeare and the instrumental value of the methods used to teach him.[3] Furthermore, she accuses the Company of deliberately choosing the feedback it receives to confirm its own narrative of 'desk-based, literary criticism as "the bad old days"'.[4]

The pedagogy itself she attacks as being covertly prescriptive whilst promoted in the warm language of progressivism. Here she refers back to an earlier article by the cultural materialist scholar, Richard Wilson, who had criticized Rex Gibson's work as politically kow-towing to the conservative establishment, rather than critiquing the elitist values of a national curriculum which had imposed the compulsory study of Shakespeare. Gibson, he proposed, was advocating an anti-intellectual pedagogical approach, exhorting joy at the expense of critical thought, his instructions to students sounding like 'matron's most muscular instructions to swallow the medicine whole'.[5] Olive is, in fact, a great admirer of Gibson's work and she sees little difference between his pedagogy and that of the RSC, as both claim to promote active, physical approaches and aspire to make the classroom more like a rehearsal room.[6] In fact, she accuses the Company of effectively rebranding Gibson's methods and discourse as its own and of going much further in proscribing what she considers to be valid forms of pedagogy – critical and literary study – from a curriculum for Shakespeare. Moreover, she sees a gap between the acknowledged values of the RSC – the warm progressive tones of playfulness and interpretive choices – and how they go about implementing them. As Wilson attacked Gibson, so she attacks the RSC, for being covertly prescriptive in the methods it proposes, accusing *Stand up for Shakespeare* of 'faux-progressivism' – prescriptive practices couched within progressive language.

Two final criticisms are worthy of our attention here: that the Company makes uncritical use of the government's language of curriculum to proclaim what its work can achieve; and that it commissions research principally to validate itself in order to justify the huge subsidies it receives from the government.

The best way to judge the validity of these criticisms, as I have suggested, is through evidence from research but nonetheless there is enough in Olive's argument that needs to be challenged before we move on. First of all, as noted, much of it is rhetorical and based upon uses of language rather than actual substance. In criticizing the RSC for using the term 'ownership', for example, it is the current pervasiveness of the term that ought to be questioned, common and uncritically deployed throughout educational discourse as it is, rather than the RSC's use of it. When the Company talks of helping young people gain ownership of Shakespeare, common usage suggests that it wants to help them feel and appreciate the power of Shakespeare's language for themselves rather than simply be told or made to feel that they *should* appreciate it. And while it is true, of course, that nobody owns Shakespeare, the RSC does at least have a substantial history of exploring, producing, examining and performing Shakespeare, and has developed a set of rehearsal room practices to do so. It does, therefore, have some established *authority* when it talks about making Shakespeare accessible to a wider public.

To suggest that because Gibson uses the terms 'rehearsal room' and 'active approaches' the RSC is rebranding his work as its own, is an argument similarly based on vocabulary rather than substance. I have shown in Chapter 3 that, despite some similarity in terminology, there are substantial differences between his work and the work of the Company; his rehearsal room is a lot less like a Company rehearsal room and his active approaches a lot less active.

To accuse the RSC of uncritically using the government's language of curriculum to describe what it achieves is to confuse the discourse of marketing and publicity – a discourse common to all arts companies that seek to encourage schools to buy into their services – with that used between practitioners when discussing the value of its practices. If the Company did not relate its education programmes to the demands that teachers face in terms of learning objectives, attainment targets, problem-solving, cross-curricular skills and the like, then schools could be forgiven for ignoring them. If the RSC actually thought about, rationalized and discussed the nature and value of its work in these terms, then the criticism would be valid. But it is clear that it doesn't, as even a quick reading of the introduction to the *Toolkit* would evidence, never mind a full day's immersion in practical workshop activities such as those described in Chapter 4.[7] The content of this chapter, as well as the entire content of the *Toolkit*, should also put paid to any accusation of faux progressivism on the part of the RSC, as it neither aspires to progressivism nor practises prescriptiveness in the ways that Olive implies. It is true that Michael Boyd's words, as I have already pointed out, echo the Romantic vision of childhood and play that inspired the likes of Rousseau and Froebel, but the educational strategies themselves emanate from the practical demands of the rehearsal room, not the Romantic theories of progressivism as practised in classrooms in the 1960s and 1970s. When the RSC talks of the importance of play, enjoyment and togetherness, it does so in terms of establishing work practices necessary to unlock Shakespeare's language and to make theatre, not in the touchy-feely rhetoric of personal development. It offers its strategies not as prescriptive – a term which deliberately echoes the metaphor of medicine, which we will come to shortly – but, as it makes explicit in the *Toolkit*, as the tools of an artist or a craftsperson that enable teachers to make choices, not follow prescriptions. To talk of such a provision as prescriptive is rather like criticizing a course in car mechanics for introducing apprentices to how they might choose a spanner suitable for a particular job; or a course in oil painting for advising students on effective ways to mix colours and how to select appropriate brushes for particular tasks. Such advice enables good craftsmanship and creative judgement; it does not close them down through overprescriptiveness.

Olive's borrowing of Wilson's metaphor of medicine to describe active approaches could possibly be applied to some uses of drama in schools but it is surely flawed when applied to RSC pedagogy. In those schools where drama is understood solely in instrumental terms – for example, as a means to combat bullying, or to tackle racist attitudes – then it is perhaps being used for 'socio-medicinal' purposes, so to speak: as a means to purge or cure young people of perceived social or moral ills. However, a far better metaphor for the kind of experience that the RSC brings to the classroom is that of inviting young people to share in a good meal, to derive some cultural nourishment from a communal, convivial experience from which they will hopefully leave with a feeling of satisfaction and a desire to return, to feast on Shakespeare again in the future. This is at the heart of the RSC's educational vision: to help young people and teachers enjoy Shakespeare together, to derive something intrinsically valuable from studying his plays. The Company has never attacked 'desk-bound *literary criticism*' but has instead sought to counter 'desk-bound *ineffective teaching*'. As we shall see when we look at the work of lead teachers in the LPN who followed the PG Certificate, they were not discouraged from making use of these strategies to feed into analysis and criticism, to complement active approaches with the 'table work' of the rehearsal room. The Company recognizes the demands of examination and coursework but seeks to counter the negative effects of teaching solely to the test, effects that many secondary-school English teachers testify to.[8]

As Olive points out, values are at the heart of the issue, but not, I think, in the way she suggests. Effectively she is arguing that the RSC elides the instrumental value of its own rehearsal room strategies with the intrinsic value of Shakespeare himself, to such an extent that teachers are unable to distinguish one from the other. But this is surely not the case. The RSC does, indeed, see its approaches as instrumental, as ways to help students and teachers engage with Shakespeare, but it advocates them because it believes in the intrinsic value of such an engagement. Experience in rehearsal rooms and classrooms informs them that the open-ended, interpretive choices they promote are particularly effective in enabling young people to find that personal connection with Shakespeare which helps them enjoy and appreciate him as opposed to seeing him merely as an examination hurdle to cross. And if teachers' comments often focus on the effectiveness of the rehearsal room strategies it is because, as teachers, they are interested in effective pedagogy; and, as published research demonstrates, they judge it as effective because it helps their students enjoy and appreciate Shakespeare.[9] In ignoring such comments Sarah Olive risks being seen as guilty of that which she accuses the RSC – of being selective with her examples in order to support her own partial narrative.

Perhaps Olive is irritated by the rather evangelical tones of the *Stand up for Shakespeare* manifesto and this has stirred her antagonism. Perhaps, despite her admiration for Gibson, she shares with eminent literary critics such as Harold Bloom a penchant to teach Shakespeare as an object of literary study.[10] There is, of course, nothing intrinsically wrong in such an approach and the following comment by Jonathan Bate is, I think, most apt:

> A theatre person's starting point with Shakespeare is always: Shakespeare wrote for the theatre. Well, yes, Shakespeare did write for the theatre but there is good evidence that he also wrote to be read and that he was happy when his plays went into print. Certainly if you think of the first folio, his fellow actors who edited it, Hemmings and Condell, say *read* him, again and again. The danger for *Stand up for Shakespeare* is if it substitutes for sit down with Shakespeare and read him. You've got to have both.[11]

This is the key point: students should have access to both, certainly at secondary school level, and I have heard teachers of English *and* teachers of drama say precisely this. The RSC is clear that, although it naturally argues for the effectiveness of its own rehearsal room approaches, what matters above all is that Shakespeare be taught in ways that enlighten and enthuse students. As Jacqui O'Hanlon comments:

> There are many other ways of approaching these plays that another practitioner or organisation might promote and they are all absolutely entitled to have their own distinctive and unique approaches. I know that there are brilliant teachers of Shakespeare out there who don't want to use our approaches. And that's fine.[12]

I have throughout this book tried to avoid either/or thinking and my purpose in this chapter is not to attack literary approaches but rather to analyse the nature and the effects of an education programme that concentrates on theatrical approaches, as this is what the RSC quite naturally does. The effects of these are best considered, I would hazard, through research evidence rather than through rhetoric – research commissioned to create a knowledge base to inform future development and not, as Sarah Olive suggests, solely to validate the Company's practices. Two of the major research reports we shall look at were not, in fact, commissioned by the RSC but by outside agencies interested in whether the Learning and Performance Network offered a more general model for the professional development of teachers.

The rest of this chapter, then, will concentrate on research and what it tells us about the impact on their practice of teacher involvement in the LPN. To do this I will be drawing on a range of sources:

- an article written by Tracy Irish for the journal *English in Education*;
- meta-analyses of the research reports written by lead teachers as part of their accredited work;
- a 2009 report on research commissioned by the Teacher Development Agency (TDA) and carried out by the Centre for Educational Development, Appraisal and Research (CEDAR) at the University of Warwick, which examined the impact of the PG Cert training and the effectiveness of the hub-cluster relationship. The methodology consisted of two postal surveys to teachers in hub and cluster schools; a meta-analysis of twenty-seven action research assignments; and interviews and observations completed in five of the clusters;
- a subsequent report (Thomson *et al*, 2010) commissioned by Creativity, Culture and Education (CCE) to evaluate the comparative impact of involvement in the LPN for teachers from hub schools and cluster schools. This research was carried out by academics from the Universities of Nottingham and London. The methodology was qualitative in nature, consisting of interviews with teachers and students; observations of lessons, rehearsals and planning meetings; and documentary analysis;
- an interview I conducted in October 2013, with a head of English who had been involved with the LPN as a lead teacher in one of its hub schools.

Some of these sources will legitimately be seen as rather close to the LPN, in particular the words of those teachers who were involved in it; but I believe to exclude their voices would be to omit a range of illuminating, qualitative detail and readers will judge for themselves how convincing they find what these teachers have to say. The two personal stories that bookend the chapter are intended to provide readable, narrative accounts to complement evidence drawn from the more general research reports that inform the rest of the chapter. My use of these reports is far from exhaustive and necessarily selective. For the interested reader, they are readily accessible from the RSC's website.

Karen's story

In her article 'Would you risk it for Shakespeare?', Tracy Irish presents a detailed case study of one teacher's journey as she strives to incorporate rehearsal room strategies into her teaching of Shakespeare. The article draws from the teacher's own research assignment, written for her postgraduate accreditation; from a Master's thesis which tracked this particular teacher as part of its research; and from interviews conducted by Irish herself with the teacher at the end of her three-year association with the LPN.

'Karen' is described as a mature entrant to the teaching profession, working as an English teacher in an ethnically diverse comprehensive girls' school in London, where 60 per cent of students speak English as an additional language and an above average number have special educational needs and/or disabilities.[13] The school's involvement in the LPN was instigated by the drama department but, unlike the rest of her more experienced colleagues in English, Karen was immediately interested in this initiative, having had a taste of active approaches during her teacher training. Despite their scepticism, her colleagues were, in fact, quickly enthused by an initial day's INSET training with an RSC practitioner. One teacher of thirty years' standing immediately saw the potential to use the strategies in her poetry teaching, while another commented on what she had learned about the plays themselves through these active approaches – plays she had actually taught before. Despite this initial enthusiasm, however, many of Karen's colleagues quickly found the realities of classroom and school organization as impediments to any real change in their teaching approach. Irish identifies the issues here as fourfold: those of space, commitment, time and confidence.

Issues of space and time are practical. The need to move back the desks within a classroom can be seen as cumbersome and time-consuming if access to a drama studio or hall is limited; and, if the classroom is small, space can be cramped even when the desks are moved back. Time, too, is tightly structured and precious in a secondary school timetable and, when students are unused to them, active approaches can be time-consuming in themselves as they depend upon a suitable atmosphere of trust and co-operation being established before they will work efficiently. Issues to do with commitment and confidence are clearly attitudinal and inter-related: for teachers unused to this way of working, the risks can be intimidating and the inevitable initial setbacks can discourage them into falling back on the more traditional methods they are used to.

Irish's account of Karen's journey is honest about failures as well as successes, failures that Karen was able to learn from because she had the commitment and courage needed to take risks, buoyed as she was by the support she could receive as a PG Cert student from mentors and tutors. Her research focused on the implementation of a six week scheme of work on *A Midsummer Night's Dream* with her class of GCSE Year 10 students.[14] As Irish describes it:

In this six week unit, Karen wanted to combat the feelings of boredom and dread that she found invariably accompanied her announcement to a class that they would be studying Shakespeare: 'a resounding dread that ripples through the class in the form of an agonised groan.'[15]

One student went so far as to say that she 'didn't do Shakespeare', having had such a dreadful three-month experience the previous year studying *Much Ado About Nothing*. Karen's intentions were therefore pro-social as well as exam-related, Irish explains; she wanted her students' attainment to improve but through a shared, co-operative and enjoyable experience of Shakespeare.

Karen describes how two simple activities were immediately energizing for the students; firstly, how the actual clearing of the classroom to create a space for active work became in itself the kind of co-operative, physical activity that encouraged ensemble working; and how using edited scripts rather than the whole play text had an instant effect. In her words:

> The advantage of this was two-fold: firstly with sections of the play photocopied as scripts, they would only need to focus on one section of the play at any one time, thereby reducing any anxiety of tackling the whole text . . .; secondly the script became personal – it would be their own working document to annotate with their ideas, responses, questions and in planning activities.[16]

But initial success was accompanied by setbacks. Three sessions spent on having her students create their own settings and scenarios as a context for the first scene of the play were a struggle until one girl – the same girl who had hated Shakespeare in Year 9 – began to take a lead in directing others in the class and, in so doing, inspired a more general air of confidence. Another setback occurred when Karen introduced the form of ensemble reading to study the opening dialogue of the play between Theseus and Hippolyta. The girls felt impeded by not knowing the meaning of all the words and found it difficult to engage in the spirit of the exercise. So Karen made the decision to switch to a different exercise, one used by Cicely Berry, explaining the context of the scene and asking the girls to read it aloud together but emphasizing the long vowel sounds 'oo' and 'ee'. This led to exaggeration and laughter but also to students connecting with the meaning carried by the sounds within the words – that Theseus is in anguish and impatient to be married, an understanding that carried across into their written homework, the quality of which delighted Karen. Irish makes the point that a less committed teacher would have doubtless resorted to the more traditional methods she was comfortable with; it was only Karen's commitment and determination that made her resourceful enough to continue and make progress.

It is clear from her account and from the words of her students that Karen's efforts to make her classroom more like a rehearsal room did indeed achieve positive overall effects with regard to student engagement and learning. She describes a particular example using the punctuation shift to explore Egeus's first long speech, when the girls were quickly able to identify moments where the chaotic intensity of his anger is breaking through as well as those moments when he is forcing himself to calm down, no doubt because he is in the presence of Theseus, his king. In the words of one student in response to this exercise: 'learning has become more fun' and 'we are analysing without realizing it'. Karen explains that this became a common feeling throughout the class and quotes the words of the following student as equally typical.

> I enjoy all of us being together in the circle; the exercises have helped us to identify with the characters' feelings. When you are reading at your desk or just watching the film version, I have no interest because you are being told everything. This way I feel better about myself because I am learning things for myself.[17]

Karen was struck by how the girls' writing became more individual and detailed, revealing 'a better understanding of how Shakespeare crafted his writing to reflect emotions. In this respect,' she adds, 'I would say that my expectations for them were exceeded and most students achieved grades better than expected.'[18]

Irish visited Karen in her school two years later. By this time she had been promoted to Head of English and was more confident and authoritative in her use of rehearsal room approaches. Her students, she commented, invariably produced high-quality writing from this particular scheme of work, helped by the way she encouraged them to annotate their scripts and write ongoing responses to the active work. In this way the scripts became journals, personalized records or, as she puts it, a key part of their 'three-dimensional literary criticism'. This was achieved, she said, by believing that the time spent was worthwhile:

> . . . time not just to reflect on their own experience but to reflect on the language – how they'd understood character reactions, thoughts and feelings, motivations, injustices, complications – and that's why I think they've written the essays that they have. I've never had such perceptive comments and sensitive comments and confident comments as well. They know what they're talking about. They can talk about metaphor. They can write about pace and tone and the choice of words and rhythm very confidently because they have done the exercises. It's like watching little light bulbs go on every time we do it.[19]

Beyond the personal story: surveying the impact of the LPN on teaching

Karen's story brings to mind Deborah Britzman's classic critical text on teacher education *Practice Makes Practice*, specifically in the way it reminds us that learning to teach is 'not a mere matter of applying decontextualized skills or of mirroring predetermined images'. Rather it is 'the process of becoming: a time of formation and transformation, of scrutiny into what one is doing, and who one can become'.[20] Of course Karen was fully trained but Britzman makes the point that one should never stop learning as an educator; and throughout her account, we see Karen striving to transform her Shakespeare classroom by transforming her practice. She cannot do this by merely applying the RSC strategies willy-nilly; she needs to appreciate and understand their principles as well as their techniques, reflect upon and critique her failures as well as her successes, and have a clear vision in mind of what kind of teacher she is aspiring to be. The PG Certificate that was an integral part of the LPN programme for lead teachers was instrumental in helping her do this.

Personal stories such as Karen's are important as they privilege the voices of practitioners themselves, thus following the insistence of Madeleine Grumet that teachers need to be the authors of their own experience, articulating and formulating questions and responses to the experience of teaching for themselves.[21] It was indeed one of the key drivers of the PG Cert that teachers be encouraged to reflect critically on their practice, that is, to think beyond 'commonly used and officially approved pedagogical approaches'.[22] Stories such as Karen's help convey the vicissitudes, details and key markers of a journey to transform practice, but can nonetheless be susceptible to the accusation of being selective not only in the details they choose to recount but also because of those stories that remain untold. For this reason, we will turn to other sources to gain insight into evidence of the general impact on teaching, principally on the lead teachers in 'hub' schools who followed the PG Cert, but also on others involved in 'cluster' schools, who did not pursue the certificate but who were involved in the performance festival and also in some more limited RSC input.[23]

Thomson *et al*, in their report, detail the qualitative richness of the experience for lead teachers such as Karen:

> In addition to the undoubted expertise and craft knowledge amongst the trainers, there are a range of other factors that make the lead practitioner INSET particularly powerful: it is residential; it involves commitment to the group; there is a chance to see and discuss a high quality production of the play the group is working on. Above all, it exposes teachers to the work of a company who believe that Shakespeare's plays have contemporary relevance and meaning.[24]

The report by CEDAR commissioned by the Teacher Development Agency provides quantitative evidence to support this, in the form of a survey of the twenty-seven lead teachers in the 2006 and 2007 cohorts. Nineteen (70 per cent) completed the survey which made a series of statements to which teachers could respond in the form of a Likert scale – strongly agreeing, agreeing, disagreeing or strongly disagreeing. The following are composites solely of those statements which solicited either agreement or strong agreement from all respondents:[25]

- Particularly effective aspects of their experience were: having access to the professional expertise of the RSC practitioners; having these practitioners work alongside University of Warwick tutors in the teaching of the PG Cert; being required to research the impact of RSC rehearsal approaches on their own practice.
- Particularly effective interventions were: the training days in Stratford, including the practical workshops led by RSC education practitioners and by RSC artists; seeing an RSC production; the workshops led by RSC practitioners with pupils in hub schools.
- Completing an action research project was personally rewarding and impacted both on lead teachers' own practice and on the practice elsewhere in their departments or key stages.

In addition, CEDAR undertook 'before' and 'after' surveys of lead teachers over a range of performance indicators and found significant differences ($p < 0.0005$) in mean before and after scores in all of them. These indicated that teachers felt that students in their classrooms were now significantly more likely:

- to work with a broader range of Shakespeare texts;
- to be given the skills and opportunities to make their own interpretive choices;
- to speak and understand Shakespeare's language;
- to see a Shakespeare performance live;
- to take part in performing Shakespeare in school.

Similar statistically significant responses were found in before and after surveys that included teachers in cluster schools. Responses from cluster teachers amounted to only 22 per cent (sixty-three teachers out of a possible 290) but all indicated significant increases in confidence in the following areas:

- in engaging children in Shakespeare's language;
- in using a range of drama approaches;
- in setting the pace and challenge of learning;
- in managing pupil behaviour;
- in their uses of questioning and group work;
- in their ability to teach in innovative and creative ways.

They also indicated that classroom furniture was regularly being moved to create an open space for learning; that students had more positive responses to Shakespeare and were more able to find contemporary relevance in his plays; and that the active drama approaches were being applied more frequently in lessons devoted to content other than Shakespeare.

In their report for the CCE, Thomson *et al* are clear that 'involvement in the LPN has a significant effect on the ways in which teachers approach the teaching of Shakespeare, and in some cases, other texts'. They put this down to three key factors: the 'substantive intellectual resources and enhanced repertoires of practice' made available to the lead teachers; the regular opportunities they had for discussion with RSC practitioners; and – very significantly – the way that the participation in RSC workshops led them to appreciate what the co-operative atmosphere in such classes actually feels like, an experience that for some led them 'to see themselves and their work differently'.[26]

The research project at the heart of the PG Cert was, as we have seen, conceived of as a key driver in helping lead teachers achieve such a change by encouraging them to critique and transform their practice in ways that went beyond a superficial adoption of rehearsal room approaches. Although all respondents recognized its value and testified to finding it personally rewarding, 30 per cent did not respond and it would be highly unlikely that all would feel so positive about it. Thomson *et al* add a useful gloss to these statistics, impressive as they are. Unsurprisingly, they found that teachers were 'not quite as enthusiastic about the formal academic requirements as they were about other aspects of the programme'.[27] They appreciated the support they received from Warwick tutors, the way the programme was organized, and many did find keeping a research journal practically useful and completing the project both valuable and rewarding. But a few teachers admitted that they would not have done the work if it had been an optional part of the programme. This is only to be expected given the current pressures on teachers' time and energies and arguably serves to make the actual completion rates of the PG Cert all the more impressive; all but one of the teachers failed to complete in the initial cohort and, based on current rates, the RSC estimates that by 2016, 116 teachers will have received the award.

Transforming practice through action research

In this section I will draw from two meta-analyses of the research assignments submitted by teachers in the initial two cohorts of the PG Cert. Twenty-eight teachers enrolled on the programme and, of the twenty-seven who completed it successfully, eighteen worked in secondary schools and nine in primary schools. Of these, eight achieved grades A or A* and eighteen grade B, so all but one of the assignments were judged to be good or better at Master's level. The report by Tracy Irish conducted for the RSC concentrates on the first cohort of sixteen assignments, whereas the CEDAR report looks at both cohorts. Both of these provide qualitative insights that complement the personal details of Karen's story and the data cited in the last section.

From the CEDAR report we can see that teachers focused on a broad range of research topics. These were often framed in terms of student engagement and/or achievement, their understanding of Shakespeare, and the originality of their interpretive analyses. Some addressed specific concerns – a group of high achievers were under-performing on the GCSE Shakespeare paper, for example, or a specific top set was overly preoccupied with 'getting the right answer' as opposed to exploring their own interpretive responses – while others addressed more general concerns, such as a primary school teacher who explored how this work could impact on children's oracy.[28] As part of their final report, all gave clear accounts of their own starting points and specific contexts, and were encouraged to see the research process in critical, problematic terms and not just to concentrate on issues such as measuring student attainment. Of course, this created a tension for many teachers; as one wrote: '(In my school) active approaches to Shakespeare have to have a statistical improvement in order to change departmental practice as there is sadly no time within the syllabus to engage in activities purely for the enjoyment they offer.'[29] We will look specifically at the effects on student learning in the next chapter and concentrate squarely here on summarizing what they reveal about changes in teachers' own understandings and practice. In doing this, I will draw simultaneously from the analyses offered by both CEDAR and the RSC before tempering them with comments by Thomson *et al.*

Teachers began from different starting points. Some felt they knew a lot about Shakespeare but were aware that their students did not enjoy studying him, while many, including English specialists, displayed a lack of confidence. One young secondary school teacher, for example, admits to having spent very little time on Shakespeare during her degree and teacher training, having only her own unsatisfactory school experience to draw upon. 'We studied Macbeth', she writes. 'We only focused on key scenes. We therefore did not read the whole play and I never actually knew what happened in the end.'[30] 'Whilst I have studied Shakespeare at degree level', writes another, 'it has been some time since I have experienced any Shakespeare at all and I did not feel entirely confident of my knowledge and understanding of the plays.'[31]

Another recurrent concern, especially for the secondary English teachers, was the testing and examination system, described as restrictive and limiting on teacher choices and student experience.[32] 'Typically students from all sets will be given a paper copy of the SATs scenes', writes one secondary school teacher about the teaching in her own department, 'with the Shakespearean text on the left and a modern version on the right. The text will then be annotated.' This might get results, she comments, but it was no way to ensure that her students actually appreciated or enjoyed their study of Shakespeare.[33] Far from avoiding or by-passing issues of assessment, however, the assignments show teachers using rehearsal room approaches as a means to motivate students.[34] There is clear evidence of teachers genuinely perceiving a need to change their practice, with the research project providing a framework for them to take the necessary risks in order to do so.

Teachers report a variety of different contextual factors that had to be negotiated in order to effect such change. Many felt acute pressures on time and space, as noted in Karen's story; some lacked the support of their colleagues, including one teacher whose head of department seems to have been openly hostile to any change of approach.[35] Others actually benefited from their local context, such as the teacher whose local school network was already investigating the potential of drama to impact on children's writing.[36] But in most cases the discoveries teachers made from doggedly pursuing their research led not only to new understandings but also to a renewed excitement in their teaching. Irish demonstrates this by pointing to examples of those teachers who experienced but triumphed over what she calls 'the fear factor'. One teacher was fearful that rehearsal room approaches might weaken classroom discipline. He writes of the 'safety, predictability and control offered by close textual analysis'. By the end of his research, however, he has discovered that it is by 'loosening our hold on a particular interpretation that we permit our students to reach their own understandings of Shakespeare'.[37] Another problem for teachers is identified by Irish as the fear of 'not being the expert, not knowing it all, or looking silly by taking part in active work'.[38] In actual fact, she informs us, they discovered the opposite to be true, reporting that this way of working 'improved relationships with their classes, as students of all abilities responded in kind to the trust and respect that the active approaches required of everyone in the group'.[39] Then there is the concern that teaching to the tests might not be enjoyable but is actually what students need. One teacher's research focused on this fear of letting go, of trusting students to find their own interpretations. The emotional impact of her discoveries, of how changing her practice served to transform her understanding of herself as a teacher, is clearly evoked in the comment below.

> Somehow in the space of only seven years, I had gone from enjoying Shakespeare's plays to doing them in order to cover a part of the exam. The freedom to come out of the classroom and really practise my teaching was at times terrifying but also rewarding. I found that I could do all kinds of things I didn't think I could. The working space was different. The activities were different. The timings were different. The expectations were different. And so I had to be different.[40]

As in Karen's story, pupil enjoyment appears as a key marker of change in practically every assignment, often identified in better teamwork and sometimes expressed using the term 'ensemble'.[41] And the accompanying improvements in students' communication and social skills that emanate from the process of co-operative learning is something noted by all teachers in their assignments.[42]

Both reports, then, are very clear about the transformative effects on lead teachers' classroom practice. The CEDAR report concludes by commenting on the 'refreshed and enthused approach they have developed, and the new confidence they feel about working with active approaches in teaching Shakespeare'. The action research reports, it says, show a high level of professional curiosity and reflection[43] but Thomson *et al* offer a more measured response. They describe the RSC pedagogy as a challenging one to internalize and see the key markers of change not only in teachers adopting the principles of the ensemble but principally in their ability carefully to select and edit text and successfully apply the pedagogic resources offered by the RSC to encourage close reading by their students.[44] They present evidence that not even all the lead teachers were able to achieve this and point to the example of two whom they observed from the 2008 cohort, a year after those analysed by CEDAR. One of these, a primary teacher, clearly saw the development of literacy as far more important than the children understanding or knowing the play they were studying; another is quoted as speaking of Shakespeare as a 'great leveller as no one can really understand him'.[45] Such responses, they suggest, are often accompanied by strong emotional reactions and feelings of success at how well students engage with the Shakespeare work. They add:

> These teachers were being moved by the feeling that something difficult was being conquered, something boring was being made interesting. These feelings did not necessarily encourage them to emphasise meaning-making and interpretation in their lessons with young people.[46]

These observations are usefully cautionary. They indicate that the emotional nature of some of the teachers' comments offered by a few lead teachers in their assignments and, in particular, by other teachers involved in the LPN clusters, will not necessarily be accompanied by an understanding of the pedagogy's key purpose, namely to achieve a deeper understanding of interpreting Shakespeare's plays through rehearsal room approaches. They propose that the Action Research projects did not always manage to move the teachers into the level of critique and understanding they were intended to and see the number of teachers concentrating on issues of student attainment, or tangential issues such as literacy levels, as evidence of this, of still having their educational visions pre-determined by narrow, instrumental criteria rather than of concentrating on the key agenda of the LPN. In their report, they propose some changes to the organization of the school-based research in order to address this.[47] However, despite these reservations, their key findings are positive. As noted earlier, they see genuine evidence that lead teachers' involvement in the LPN did, in most cases, bring about the transformation in practice that the RSC was aspiring towards, a transformation enabled by the quality and directness of the relationship over a sustained period of time.[48]

Impact beyond lead teachers:
a 'diluted' effect?

In being part of the LPN, teachers in hub schools and cluster schools other than the lead teachers profited from a range of interventions. Cluster schools received two half-day INSET sessions from RSC practitioners in their first year and further training with hub and cluster colleagues, focused on creating a Shakespeare production, in the second year, including two visits by RSC practitioners to support the rehearsal process. The CEDAR report contains a long section in which it evaluates the effectiveness of the cluster model of working, chiefly by reporting the comments of twenty-five teachers from five different clusters, all of which had different geographical and socio-economic characteristics. Comment after comment reflects the enthusiasm and excitement of teachers with regard to their involvement in the LPN. The INSET sessions taught by RSC practitioners, both to teachers and to pupils, evidently made a huge impression on many of those interviewed. 'The INSET for staff has been amazing', reports one head teacher. 'We used that INSET in a writing task across the school and the writing was absolutely amazing.'[49] 'She was brilliant', comments another about a session taught to her class. 'She was absolutely brilliant. She came in for a morning and she got the children really enthused.'[50] Teachers testify to having gained both in confidence and in subject knowledge, and to using more active approaches generally in their teaching as a result. 'It is telling', the report comments, 'that the high quality training takes in people who are at the periphery just as much as the core postgraduate lead teachers.'[51]

Once again Thomson *et al* provide a useful cautionary gloss on these findings. Such strong emotional responses do not necessarily indicate that the teachers interviewed had taken on board the central agenda of the LPN nor are they indicative of the quality of their understandings or of the subsequent changes in their practice. In fact, their report points to a 'dilution effect' beyond the lead teachers, progressing through to other teachers in the hub schools and further into the cluster primary school. They conclude:

> As the circles get more distant from the RSC centre, the belief in the relevance and value of Shakespeare is diluted. Many of the teachers have had negative experiences of Shakespeare and they often lack the confidence that accompanies strong subject knowledge or previous lesson successes. They accept Shakespeare's standing in the canon and want to make a good job of teaching a mandatory and highly visible part of the curriculum. Improving students' knowledge of the plots, their performance skills, their facility in articulating Shakespearean language and their enjoyment of lessons constitute marked progress. The work of developing their own readings of the plays and organising ideas to create particular interpretations is a step further.[52]

This conclusion is realistic rather than disappointing. It indicates that there are visible signs of marked progress that go beyond the impact on lead teachers, but that these are neither of the same quality nor of the same depth. Despite this overall tendency, however, there are nonetheless examples of lead teachers bringing about substantial changes in the teaching of Shakespeare that reached beyond their own classrooms. This could be particularly effective when they had leadership responsibilities in their schools, as in the case of Michelle, whose story will conclude this chapter.

I spoke to Michelle some three years after her involvement with the LPN had ceased.[53] Unlike Karen, she was a Head of English when she became involved in it and was already experienced in using drama strategies as part of her teaching. She worked in one of two large, mixed comprehensive schools in a Midlands town which she described as 'quite insular in its outlook'.[54] The majority of the school's intake was white working class or lower middle class. At the time when her school become one of the hubs, practically none of her Year 8 students had been introduced to Shakespeare in their primary schools and very few had ever attended live theatre. She saw her key task as one of leadership, of helping to embed the rehearsal room approaches in schemes of work that teachers across the English department would co-develop and make use of in the future. In a series of staff meetings that focused on rehearsal room approaches, she attempted to move her team into a deeper understanding of the pedagogy's purpose, the kind that Thomson *et al* see as often lacking beyond the practice of the lead teachers themselves.

Michelle recalled initial resistance. 'The idea for them of changing an English classroom into a rehearsal space was an alien concept, so they needed some convincing.' This came about through a number of small steps, with teachers gradually coming to appreciate the value of these new approaches, particularly those which explored nuances of language in ways they saw as having immediate relevance to the assessed curriculum. A few began by using the 'punctuation shift' exercise, with students on their feet by their desks; some then started to move back just a few of the desks and, as they gained in confidence, more began to move the desks aside completely or book space in the drama studio or hall for the more physical activities. What convinced them that these efforts were worthwhile were student responses. 'Our students used to see the language of Shakespeare as alien, the storylines as irrelevant,' Michelle told me, 'and some would refuse to get involved in the work at all.' It was a big shift, then, when teachers not only noticed deeper analytical engagement in class but also started to be approached by students in the playground asking if they would be doing Shakespeare that day during English, and being excited when told that they were.

As with Karen, teachers noted positive, pro-social outcomes emanating from the initial ensemble building activities, from working with edited 'chunks of text' as opposed to the textbook, and from the emphasis being placed explicitly on interpretive choices, rather than right or wrong answers. In other words, teachers in Michelle's department were engaging with the processes of meaning-making at the heart of the LPN agenda. Teachers also noted the inclusiveness of these approaches, with all students being able to benefit, from those with special needs through to the most academically able. 'Because the rehearsal room approach allowed all students to contribute, we found we were getting a wider variety of interpretations and that they were all more willing to contribute. So verbally it was quite quick, the change in our students. But,' she adds, 'the challenge for us as an English team was to get them from talk to writing.'

The true benefits of the rehearsal room approaches for writing at GCSE level, like the true benefits of being part of the LPN, accrued over time and were most noticeable in those students who began working on them in the first three years of the school (Key Stage 3). 'Because we'd seen that shift at Key Stage 3, by the time we hit Shakespeare in Year 10 coursework, students were really confident at approaching the text. The language wasn't a barrier; the barrier for us actually was that they wanted to do more drama work.' She described how her team organized the coursework for *Romeo and Juliet,* beginning with rehearsal room approaches, interspersing them with moments for reflection and note-taking, culminating in a final three-week process devoted to the necessary analytical writing. The results in this case were significantly better than those of students in previous years, with all forty-five students who had also chosen to take part in the performance festival attaining either grade A or grade A*, a remarkable achievement.

Perhaps more remarkable, however, have been the long-term effects on those students who volunteered to set up a Shakespeare ensemble group in the first year of the school's involvement with the LPN. Calling themselves the 'Slings and Arrows' ensemble, they rehearsed and performed their own Shakespeare productions using the RSC approaches; were core to the school's involvement in the festival year; and became RSC ambassadors, leading Shakespeare workshops in local primary schools during the third and final year of the project, with two of them being invited to speak at the RSC's Annual General Meeting. Of the original twenty who set up the ensemble in Year 8, many still go regularly to the theatre, often specifically to see a Shakespeare play, and sixteen have gone on to study either drama or English at degree level, some specifically choosing courses with a strong emphasis on Shakespeare studies. Michelle recalled how these students made Shakespeare a key part of their school identities, high-fiving one another for Shakespeare, and inventing their own names for certain approaches to studying his plays. One of these that they called 'the Peverley method' was named after the actor Peter Peverley, who was at the time working for the RSC (he played Polonius in the YPS *Hamlet*) and taking his Postgraduate Award. He led a workshop on *Romeo and Juliet,* starting with the bodies at the end of the play, arousing curiosity and tension through his careful questioning in the style of a 'whodunnit'. The students were very taken with this and liked to discuss with their teacher which other plays could be tackled using 'the Peverley method.' This workshop had been a highlight of their association with the LPN, taking place in a purpose-built rehearsal space in Stratford on a day that included a communal lunch by the river. 'This was a lovely experience for them and they raved about it for days,' Michelle recalls.

The life-changing legacy for this group of students was identified by Michelle as chief among the many benefits for the school of their involvement in the LPN. There was also a memorable community event in the second year in the form of the performance festival, which she led and which involved her working with five of its feeder primary schools. 'We had 200 performers from ages five to fourteen. That's a big community effort, and we had a lot of positive feedback from parents and grandparents. I would go into town on a Saturday morning and, for a few months, people would still be stopping me, telling me what a fantastic time they'd had, and how great it had been to see that amount of school children come together on something like Shakespeare.' However, it had been a huge amount of work and had involved Michelle in a great deal of fund-raising. So when the support of the RSC went away, so did the incentive to continue with a large-scale festival such as this.

Michelle did voice some nostalgia as she reflected back on the three years. 'You have this wonderful three-year process, you see all the benefits in school, and then it just ends, and the students find that quite hard to cope with because they've had this amazing experience and then they go back to their relationship just with you as the sole teacher doing Shakespeare. And that's quite hard for them to navigate, actually.'

Schools are, in many ways, fragile places and change is constant despite the stability they try to offer to young people; good teachers often get promoted and leave, curriculum demands alter according to government initiatives. In the short time since Michelle's involvement in the LPN, there have been major announcements regarding changes to GCSE examinations that have tightened the written demands and abolished coursework in English. Michelle herself has left to take on new responsibilities in a school in a different geographical district with no prior relationship with the RSC. She has taken her knowledge with her, of course, and spoke enthusiastically of how she continues to apply their approaches in her own teaching. And she knows that this is the case for those English teachers, part of the team in her previous school, who remain working there. But she spoke with more than a hint of regret that her association with the RSC had ended and that her current school never benefited from it. 'I think what you've got are hubs and communities that have really benefited, without a shadow of a doubt. But the question is how you sustain that and further the spread of good practice.'

Conclusion

The evidence is demonstrable that involvement in the LPN did, indeed, impact on how teachers taught Shakespeare and, in some cases, other aspects of the curriculum; and that this impact was particularly marked on lead teachers at the centre of this involvement. Teachers new to these approaches needed time and commitment to bed them into their practice and the Action Research project was, in most cases, an effective means to help them achieve this. For other teachers in hub and cluster schools, the impact was variable and dependent upon local leadership and the adoption of a suitably rigorous model to cascade the approaches that did not simply rely on the few INSET days provided by the RSC team. In those schools which benefited from such leadership, as Michelle's account exemplifies, the transformation could be profound both on teachers and on students; whether they will be sustained over the long term, as good teachers depart for new opportunities and as governments continue to impose changes on curriculum and examinations, is still open to question.

As the LPN approaches the end of its eleven-year lifespan, the RSC has been well aware of the issues of access and sustainability voiced by Michelle. It is currently working in partnership with ten regional theatres, training theatre artists alongside teachers, in a positive indicator of the evolutionary nature of the LPN and of the dynamic way in which the Company is planning for a sustainable future that can build upon its legacy.[55] However, rather than look here at organizational issues best left to the conclusion of the book, I wish to end this particular chapter by suggesting that Michelle's recollections and regrets point to something deeply significant in the achievements of the LPN, even though it is unlikely ever to be discussed in any evaluation report. I am referring once again to the idea of beauty and to its neglected importance as an educational value.

If beauty is rarely discussed in issues of curriculum, it is seldom if ever dreamt of as relevant to teacher development. Yet I contend that its concerns are pervasive throughout both of the personal stories recounted in this chapter, particularly so in the case of Michelle's. In her seminal text *On Beauty and Being Just*, Elaine Scarry points to a number of aspects of beauty that resonate with her account: that it energizes; that it is an urge to creativity; that it moves us to see the world differently; that it is life-changing.[56] In a previous study, I have argued that we should see beauty as an uplifting source of cognitive-emotional learning from which 'we enthuse, admire and empathize at the same time as we observe, evaluate, attend and respond'.[57] In this sense, beauty does not only refer to the language and artistry of Shakespeare but more particularly to the aesthetic achievement of the LPN itself. I interpret Michelle's recollections of her association with the LPN as her recalling it as a particularly beautiful time in her professional life – beautiful as it is a high point marked by pleasure and creativity, a time of joy and togetherness as well as hard work and concrete achievement. It is a time, I would hazard, which re-invigorated and re-enforced her love of teaching. The transformative impact on her students, the inter-school performance well loved by her local community, and the fact that she and her students missed their involvement with the RSC so much all mark this out as a profoundly significant period, the kind of significance we associate with beauty. Her regrets also remind us of another, more poignant and unavoidable aspect of beauty signalled by Scarry; that is, its fragility. Like many experiences we value in our lives, beauty is fragile as it is time-bound; it must inevitably pass. If this will necessarily leave us with some regret, it can also, however, leave us with memories to sustain us, to help us recall 'feelingly' how rewarding the profession of teaching at its best can be; it can remind us why we became teachers in the first place and help us rediscover, as one lead teacher put it, 'the teacher I always wanted to be'.

This, for the RSC, constitutes no mean achievement.

8

The Impact of Rehearsal Room Pedagogy on Students: What Research Shows

(co-authored with Steve Strand)

Introduction

From the outset of the Learning and Performance Network, the RSC has been keen to see whether its sustained relationship with schools has a measurable effect on students' attitudes to studying Shakespeare. To this end it commissioned a series of quantitative surveys between 2007 and 2011 from CEDAR at the University of Warwick that attempted to measure any such change over time. I shall begin this chapter with a summary of the findings of this complex and large-scale study, much of which will be presented in the words of Professor Steve Strand, now of Oxford University, who designed, developed and analysed the attitudinal surveys. I shall then consider two case studies, one conducted by a lead teacher in the LPN that used both qualitative and quantitative measures to gauge the impact on children's writing of teaching Shakespeare through rehearsal room pedagogy; and another, especially commissioned by the RSC, to look at the impact of this pedagogy on the language of a class of early years children. This latter will include a lengthy theoretical analysis which revisits and expands aspects of the theory discussed in Chapter 5. Although concentrating on the work of very young children, I hope to show that this analysis is relevant to our understanding of how and why Shakespeare taught in an active, theatrically vibrant way can be so appealing and linguistically nourishing for young people of all ages, not just for those of the age range involved in this particular study.[1]

Student attitude to Shakespeare: the initial surveys

The first Shakespeare survey commissioned by the RSC was completed by over 1,500 students beginning their Year 10 GCSE studies in September 2007. These students were drawn from the ten secondary schools that constituted the second cohort of the LPN, spread across urban and rural areas in England and broadly representative nationally in terms of gender and ethnic mix. The questionnaire was designed to develop a reliable and robust measure of student attitude to Shakespeare and to examine the relationship between this measure and other student and school factors.[2] It was then repeated two years later in the same schools with the new cohort of 1,250 Year 10 students in order to gauge the extent to which the schools' involvement in the LPN had impacted on teaching approaches and subsequent attitudes to Shakespeare. In the light of these findings, the survey was revisited for students in the 2010 cohort but this time in a more focused and targeted manner. Steve Strand reported the findings of this new survey to the RSC in 2011 and the rest of this section is comprised of his summary report.

****

The initial 2007 Attitude to Shakespeare (ATS) survey produced some key findings in terms of overall attitudes to Shakespeare. The majority of students held negative attitudes vis-à-vis the following:

- Only 18 per cent agreed that 'Shakespeare is fun' (and 50 per cent disagreed).
- Almost half (46 per cent) agreed with the statement 'Studying Shakespeare is boring'.
- Only 30 per cent agreed with the statement 'I would be happy to watch a Shakespeare play/film in my own time' (and 51 per cent disagreed).
- Almost half (49 per cent) agreed with the statement 'I find Shakespeare's plays difficult to understand'.

Students did not see the usefulness or relevance of Shakespeare:

- Only 35 per cent agreed with the statement 'It is important to study Shakespeare's plays'.
- Only 33 per cent disagreed with the statement 'Shakespeare's characters and situations are not relevant to life today'.
- Only 27 per cent agreed that 'Studying Shakespeare is useful for other subjects, not just English or drama'.

- Only 23 per cent agreed that 'Shakespeare's plays are relevant to events in the modern world'.
- Only 20 per cent agreed that 'Shakespeare's plays help us to understand ourselves and others better'.
- Only 17 per cent agreed with the statement 'I have learnt something about myself by studying Shakespeare' (and 60 per cent disagreed).

The initial survey also pointed to a number of pertinent factors.

- Attitude to Shakespeare was not simply a reflection of a more global attitude to school. There was a moderate correlation between school engagement and attitude to Shakespeare, but the correlation was far from perfect, indicating that attitude to Shakespeare is more than just a reflection of general attitude to school.
- Attitude to Shakespeare did not correlate significantly with students' reported Key Stage 3 English level. Thus students could be high attaining but still be 'turned off' from Shakespeare, or low attaining but with positive attitudes towards Shakespeare.
- There was a highly significant gender difference in attitude to Shakespeare, with the mean score for boys being significantly lower than the mean score for girls.
- There was significant variation between schools in attitude to Shakespeare. However, variation between classes was four times greater than the variation between schools, which suggests that classroom practices might be particularly important in accounting for variation in attitudes to Shakespeare.
- There was evidence of an association between aspects of the teaching of Shakespeare, as reported by students, and their attitude to him. Pupils who reported that they did not often act out scenes from Shakespeare plays, did not often read aloud from the plays and did not cover Shakespeare in drama classes as well as in English had less positive attitudes to Shakespeare than other students. Furthermore, those students who reported that there had been a whole school production of a Shakespeare play or a visit to a performance at a theatre had more positive attitudes than those who did not report these experiences.

These results for the Year 10 group in September 2007 were compared with the results for the Year 10 group in 2009, two years after the start of the schools' involvement in the LPN, in an attempt to evaluate its impact. This comparison revealed no significant change in overall attitude to Shakespeare between 2007 and 2009, although striking changes were noted for two questions: students in 2009 were significantly more likely than their peers in 2007 to report that they agreed/strongly agreed that 'Shakespeare was fun'

(Q2), and significantly less likely to agree/strongly agree that they 'found Shakespeare's plays difficult to understand' (Q6).

However, this design, focused on a 'whole school' effect, may have been too generalized to detect the specific and more localized impact associated with the LPN. A new project was therefore designed more directly to evaluate change in attitudes to Shakespeare by asking each school to select a specific year group to focus on, identifying more closely the level of input received by different classes (by identifying target vs control classes), and by testing the same group of students at the beginning and end of the academic year.

Attitude to Shakespeare: the revised student survey

The new study involved the six secondary schools and five primary schools that joined the RSC Learning & Performance Network in 2010 and attempted a more focused evaluation. At the start of the year in September 2010, the LPN schools:

- Identified the year group that would be the focus of the school's work in the coming year.
- Identified target classes in the year group with whom the lead practitioner would be working directly. 'Lead practitioners' would be taking the Postgraduate Certificate in the Teaching of Shakespeare and, as usual, were to receive five days' training at the RSC in Stratford and an additional two to three days' assistance when an RSC practitioner would work with them in school.
- Identified other classes in the same school and year group as 'control' classes that would not be directly taught by the lead practitioner.

Students completed the ATS scale (and associated measures) at the start of the year in September, 2010. The same classes completed the ATS scale again at the end of the year in July, 2011. The main focus of the analysis was a comparison of changes in attitude to Shakespeare in the targeted classes, compared to control classes.

Measures

The Attitude to Shakespeare scale for secondary school students consists of thirteen questions assessing a range of attitudes, beliefs and behaviours in relation to studying Shakespeare, as presented in Table 8.1. The scores across the items can be summed to create a total ATS score. A version for primary

TABLE 8.1 *The Attitude to Shakespeare scale – secondary school version*

What I think about Shakespeare	Strongly disagree	Disagree	Neither agree nor disagree	Agree	Strongly agree
Shakespeare is for everyone not just posh people	❑	❑	❑	❑	❑
Shakespeare is fun	❑	❑	❑	❑	❑
Shakespeare's characters and situations are not relevant to life today	❑	❑	❑	❑	❑
Shakespeare's plays help us to understand ourselves and others better	❑	❑	❑	❑	❑
I would be happy to watch a Shakespeare play/film in my own time	❑	❑	❑	❑	❑
I find Shakespeare's plays difficult to understand	❑	❑	❑	❑	❑
My friends laugh at those who enjoy Shakespeare	❑	❑	❑	❑	❑
It is important to study Shakespeare's plays	❑	❑	❑	❑	❑
Shakespeare is only for old people	❑	❑	❑	❑	❑
Shakespeare's plays are relevant to events in the modern world	❑	❑	❑	❑	❑
Studying Shakespeare is useful for other subjects, not just English or drama	❑	❑	❑	❑	❑
Studying Shakespeare is boring	❑	❑	❑	❑	❑
I have learnt something about myself by studying Shakespeare	❑	❑	❑	❑	❑

TABLE 8.2 *The Attitude to Shakespeare scale – primary school version*

What I think about Shakespeare	Yes	Don't know	No
Shakespeare is for everyone	❑	❑	❑
Shakespeare is fun	❑	❑	❑
I find Shakespeare's plays difficult to understand	❑	❑	❑
Shakespeare's plays help us to understand each other better	❑	❑	❑
I would like to do more Shakespeare	❑	❑	❑
People in Shakespeare's plays are like people you meet today	❑	❑	❑
My friends don't like Shakespeare	❑	❑	❑
It is important to study Shakespeare's plays	❑	❑	❑
Shakespeare is only for old people	❑	❑	❑
Things that happen in Shakespeare's plays can happen in real life	❑	❑	❑
Shakespeare is boring	❑	❑	❑
I have learnt something about myself by learning about Shakespeare	❑	❑	❑

schools (Year 4 – Year 6) was also developed for this project, in which the language of the items was simplified and the five choice options for each question were reduced to three, as shown in Table 8.2.

General attitudes to school were also assessed, using the questions given below.

- I like coming to school
- I get on well with my teachers
- I often get bored in class
- I always attend school unless I'm ill
- I am good at most subjects at school
- I am good at working with other students
- I feel confident in explaining my ideas to other people
- I find a lot of schoolwork difficult
- I want to leave school as soon as possible and get a job (Secondary school version only)

Scores across these items can again be summed to create an 'attitude to school' or 'school engagement' score.

Results: primary schools

Pre-test questionnaires were returned from 270 pupils in ten classes in five schools. Classes were drawn across the range Year 4 to Year 6. This represented all pupils present in class on the administration date in September 2010. Seventeen pupils (5.9 per cent) absent on the administration day were not included. Post-test questionnaires (July 2011) were returned for all classes. There were seven targeted classes and three control classes.

Table 8.3 and Figure 8.1 below show the mean scores, with 90 per cent confidence intervals, for the pre-test and post-test measures for both the target and the control classes.[3]

The results show that attitude to Shakespeare improved significantly in the target classes. The 'effect size' for the target classes was 0.20 SD and was highly statistically significant. In contrast, there was no significant change in score in the control classes. The target classes initially had significantly lower scores on ATS than the control classes but by the end of the year there was no significant difference in ATS between the two groups. The target classes also showed greater improvement in general attitude to school, with an 'effect size' (ES) for the target group of 0.18 SD. The improvement for the control classes was smaller (ES = 0.07 S) and was not statistically significant. Again the target classes initially had significantly lower scores than the control classes; however, by the end of the year, there was no difference in general attitude to school between the two groups.

TABLE 8.3 *Change from pre-test to post-test for primary schools (target and control classes)*

Measure	Treatment	2010			2011			Change	Effect size
		Mean	SD	N	Mean	SD	N		
Attitude to Shakespeare	Control	27.6	4.2	87	27.3	4.8	71	–0.3	–0.08
	Targeted	26.0	4.1	179	26.8	4.8	187	0.9	0.20**
General attitude to school	Control	19.7	3.0	89	19.9	3.1	72	0.2	0.07
	Targeted	18.6	3.0	181	19.2	3.0	188	0.5	0.18**

Notes
** *indicates a statistically significant change at $p < 0.01$. Individual pupils could not be matched over time so a conventional related t-test could not be computed. The post-test means were compared using a one-sample t-test against the pre-test mean score.[4]*
SD = Standard deviation

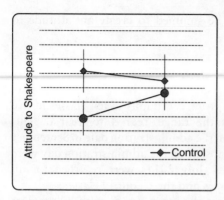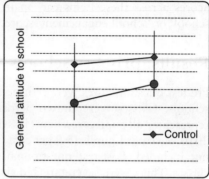

FIGURE 8.1 *Change from pre-test to post-test for primary schools (target and control classes)*

Results: secondary schools

Pre-test questionnaires were returned from 1,135 pupils in fifty-seven classes in six schools. Classes were drawn from Year 9 and Year 10. This represented all pupils present in class on the administration date in September 2010. Post-test questionnaires (July 2011) were returned by four schools. However, for one of these schools the classes were re-grouped shortly after the baseline was administered so it was not possible to match classes at pre- and post-test. Additionally, data for three control classes were not returned for one school and these classes were removed from the pre-test. The achieved sample was therefore composed of five target classes and twenty control classes.

The results show that attitude to Shakespeare improved substantially in the target classes. The 'effect size' for the target classes was 0.56 SD and was highly statistically significant. There was no significant change in attitude to Shakespeare in the control classes. The target and control classes did not

TABLE 8.4 *Change from pre-test to post-test for secondary schools (target and control classes)*

Measure	Treatment	2010			2011			Change	Effect size
		Mean	SD	N	Mean	SD	N		
Attitude to Shakespeare	Control	35.8	7.6	461	35.6	8.3	453	−0.2	−0.02
	Targeted	35.1	8.6	111	39.8	7.9	110	4.7	0.56**
General attitude to school	Control	17.1	3.6	460	17.0	3.6	449	−0.1	−0.02
	Targeted	16.7	3.9	111	17.5	3.8	109	0.8	0.20**

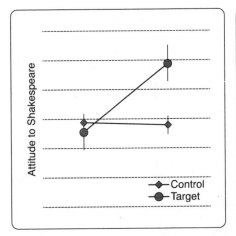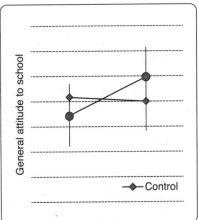

FIGURE 8.2 *Change from pre-test to post-test for secondary schools (target and control classes)*

differ significantly at baseline but by the end of the year the target classes had significantly higher ATS scores. The target classes also showed significant improvement in general attitude to school, with an ES for the target group of 0.20 SD. There was no significant change in attitude to school in the control classes. There was no significant difference between target and control classes at either pre- or post-test, but the greater improvement for the targeted classes is clearly evident.

Conclusion

There is strong evidence of substantially greater improvement in Attitude to Shakespeare in the target classes where the teacher was actively involved in the LPN compared to control classes. This was evident in both the primary and secondary schools, but was particularly marked in secondary schools with an ES of 0.56 SD, a large effect. There are also significant improvements in general attitude to school for target classes, compared to no change in control classes. This was noted in both the primary and secondary schools to about the same degree (ES = 0.20 SD). While we should be suitably cautious in drawing causal connections, this may well indicate that the benefits of the involvement with the LPN are more generalized than just in attitudes to Shakespeare.

* * * * * * * *

Strand concludes his report by suggesting that these results are highly suggestive of the benefits of the LPN for schools and students, but that further research is needed. There is a good case, he argues, for a truly randomized study, using a larger sample and tracking individual students, to evaluate robustly the impact of the RSC rehearsal room approaches. As yet no such study has been undertaken but the evidence collected from these surveys is striking in itself. The results of the more recent survey, as contrasted with the 2009 report, are congruent with the conclusions of Thomson *et al*, that the impact of the LPN on the practice of lead teachers was far more marked than on other teachers within the network. Similarly, the 2007–09 survey, concentrating as it did on whole-school impact, showed only minor evidence of attitudinal change in students, whereas the later survey, concentrating as it did on those students taught by lead teachers, showed clear evidence of significant attitudinal change. Particularly striking is the corresponding effect on these students' attitudes to school. We can only speculate here as to why that might be the case. Perhaps Michael Boyd was right in pointing to the knock-on effect on students' overall confidence that can result from their coping with and enjoying something they know to be high status and difficult; perhaps there is something in working co-operatively on Shakespeare's language and stories that is culturally nourishing for young people; perhaps, as Jonothan Neelands believes, the pro-social as opposed to the pro-technical emphasis of RSC approaches lead to marked improvements in young people's communal sense of well-being.[5] Or perhaps it is a combination of all these effects.

The following two case studies offer data particular to two specific school contexts and age ranges that, whilst pointing clearly to changes in levels of attainment, nonetheless resonate strongly with the themes of general attitudinal change indicated in Strand's report. For in both it is clear that those feelings of confidence, positivity and well-being at the heart of attitudinal change are inextricably inter-related with improved levels of learning. The first of these studies is drawn from a strong research assignment, carried out by a primary school teacher whose class was part of the 2010 cohort included in Strand's survey. As such it presents both statistical and qualitative data that help illustrate just how the changes in attitude noted in the survey findings were brought about in one particular school. The second, based in an early-years classroom, provides a close analysis of practice that demonstrates how the artistry and co-operative playfulness at the centre of rehearsal room pedagogy drew children into a pleasurable engagement with Shakespeare's language and story. Whilst they evidently hugely enjoyed the experience, at the same time they were drawn and encouraged into advanced levels of language play.

How Shakespeare can impact on children's writing

Jackie is a teacher of some twenty-five years' experience who works in a sizeable Roman Catholic primary school in a small industrial town in

Lancashire. The school itself serves a challenging catchment area, identified as one of the most deprived areas of the country, with multiple levels of deprivation and neglect and high levels of unemployment.[6] When children enter the school at reception level, baseline assessment shows that they are 'significantly below the national average'. When they leave at the end of Year 6, test results show that they are performing at above the national average. Recent reports (2009, 2011) by the national inspectorate, OFSTED, judge the school as good overall with some outstanding characteristics. Statistics evidently suggest that the school is doing a lot of things right, with or without Shakespeare.

Jackie herself is very experienced in using drama and the school has received wide recognition in the form of two national awards for best practice in the teaching of speaking and listening. She was already aware of the RSC's approaches before joining the LPN along with Nicola, one of her co-teachers in the upper primary years. Despite her prior experience, she writes vividly in her assignment about the initial INSET days at Stratford, in particular, how struck she was by the variety of interpretive choices the strategies encouraged and by the imaginative engagement she personally experienced. Here she felt the thrill of powerful theatre and was inspired to adapt and use these new strategies in her own teaching. Her research focus turned out to be far more specific than this, however, and was determined by a particular challenge that the school was currently facing.

Despite the progress made by children in their language work throughout their years at the school, and despite the evidence of good SATS results, the school had identified a significant group of boys persistently under-achieving in their written work at the end of their final year at the school. In addition, the number of pupils achieving Level 5 – judged nationally to be a good overall level of writing – had fallen off over the previous two years. A survey she conducted with her own class of Year 5 pupils indicated writing as a valid area of concern, with well over half the class responding that they did not like writing and three-quarters feeling that they were not good at it. In meetings with school leaders and governors, Jackie argued the case for a significant change in the teaching of literacy in Years 5 and 6. There was already an hour a week set aside for drama; this would in future be devoted to Shakespeare. At the same time, one of the weekly literacy lessons would be devoted to writing emanating from the drama sessions and would be taught immediately afterwards. The curriculum change, called 'Shakespeare for Drama' and 'Shakespeare for Writing', was agreed and would continue to run throughout Years 5 and 6, dependent upon whether Jackie's research project could show that it produced results. Pupils would have eight sessions of each per term – almost fifty hours of Shakespeare a year. In each term they would study a different play. During the first year, these were *The Tempest*, *Macbeth* and *Romeo and Juliet*.

Although the curriculum change would involve all the children, Jackie focused much of her research on four boys. One was potentially a good writer but had suffered traumatic family circumstances and was described by his previous teacher as 'an elective mute with no self-confidence'. The other three were identified as having special needs or specific behavioural issues, and had all achieved only Level 2c in writing – well below average – in the national tests they had taken at the age of seven. She organized the research in order to achieve maximum objectivity in the eyes of the head teacher, staff and school governors. Three pieces of writing – one derived from the study of each play – would be independently assessed by a validation group of twelve teachers from across the school who would work independently in pairs. As well as a piece of 'Shakespeare for writing', teachers would be given another example from the normal literacy programme. In each case, both would be written under the same classroom conditions and follow the same writing frame: a diary account in round 1; a character description in round 2; and a letter of complaint in round 3. In the context of Shakespeare, these consisted of three entries in Miranda's diary in Term 1; a description of one of the weird sisters in Term 2; and a letter of complaint to the Prince from the people of Verona in Term 3.

The validation groups were asked to level each piece according to national writing assessment guidelines and to compare them, stating which they judged as better and why. The findings were significant. In round 1, 80 per cent of the validation group preferred the 'Shakespeare for writing' piece; in rounds 2 and 3, 100 per cent preferred it. On each occasion, reasons were specific to the demands of the differing criteria. So, for example, reasons given by teachers for preferring the character description from Shakespeare included a range of indicators demonstrating more creativity and imagination; more variation in sentence structures, including use of subordinate clauses; better use of vocabulary to produce more descriptive imagery; more attention to detail; wider variety of punctuation; better structure and content. The letter of complaint, on the other hand, demonstrated better appreciation of the reader and stronger vocabulary choices; a stronger use of both emotive and formal language; better variations in sentence length and structure; better use of connectives to shape the text; and more persuasive arguments, with clearer viewpoints established and maintained. I list these in detail as they each indicate that technical effects, such as grammar, punctuation and use of connectives, feature strongly as well as imaginative quality and use of vocabulary.

The long-term improvement in the overall level of the four boys' writing *beyond* 'Writing for Shakespeare' was nonetheless substantial. Progress in writing is measured in sub-levels (4c, 4b, 4a etc) and an improvement of two sub-levels over the year is anticipated; the four boys did much better than this, two of them improving by three sub-levels and two by four. When interviewed by a member of the local authority's support services, all four boys spoke extremely positively and with pride about their writing, about the progress they had made and about how much they enjoyed the Shakespeare sessions.[7]

The effect was evidently common across the whole of Years 5 and 6. At the end of the year, when Jackie repeated her questionnaire, attitudes to writing in her class showed a marked improvement. No child now either disliked writing or felt they were a poor writer. All but four children, in fact – over 80 per cent of the class – answered that they liked writing and that they were a good writer; the other four answered that they sometimes liked it. SATS results at the end of Year 6 confirmed that the marked improvement in overall attainment in writing was general. In 2011 the school achieved its best ever writing results, with the overall percentage achieving level 5 (up 13 per cent from the previous year) and, notably, a number of boys reaching this level who would in previous years not have been expected to do so. In a formal report written to the governors at the end of the year, the Year 6 teachers note these improvements and point to the only significant difference between their teaching this year and in the previous seven as being the introduction of 'Shakespeare for Writing'. 'Children always enjoyed and were engaged during "Shakespeare for Writing" lessons,' they state. They comment on 'how attentive the children were during these lessons', 'how well they wanted to achieve' and 'how they began to use more adventurous vocabulary'. They conclude: 'We feel that the stimulus and build-up prior to writing allowed the children, including lower ability pupils, to have a thorough understanding of the text, making it easy for them to apply this knowledge to their writing.'[8]

Jackie considers a range of possible variables that might have influenced these results but agrees with the Year 6 teachers: it is the nature of the engagement with Shakespeare that has made the difference. SATS results in the following year, in which pupils had by now had two years of Shakespeare, demonstrated a continuing upward trajectory in writing attainment, with 94 per cent achieving Level 4 or above (up from 78 per cent) and 35 per cent achieving level 5 (up from 34 per cent). Most remarkably, 20 per cent of boys who had achieved only Level 2c at the end of Key Stage 1 were now assessed at level 5. The latest national figure for this improvement is just 7 per cent for both boys and girls – for boys alone it is below this.

Shakespeare has now become a key fixture in the whole school, Jackie told me:

> Even if you go down to the foundation Key Stage you can't open a door without there being a poster of a Shakespeare production, so he is very visible and high profile throughout the school. We do assemblies so the rest of the school see and want to be there, too. Shakespeare has become a rite of passage when children come into Years 5 and 6. They are eager for it and they tell their mums and dads this.

Perhaps similarly improved results could have been achieved through active drama strategies feeding into writing using different textual stimuli; there is certainly evidence that drama can improve writing when implemented in a carefully structured manner.[9] But the very high profile of Shakespeare throughout the school indicates that there is something more in play here, akin to Michael Boyd's suggestion but also once more, I feel, to the metaphor of Shakespeare as food, as nourishment. Of course served badly, children can find any food unpalatable, no matter how good for them they are told it will be. But when prepared and offered in the convivial, enjoyable, communal experience of a good meal, the healthy nourishment it offers has a wider effect on our overall health and well-being. Similarly, the cultural and imaginative nourishment of Shakespeare's language and his stories appears to have had a broader long-term impact on how these children felt about themselves as writers.

Our final case study offers some theoretical insight into why this might be the case. Although the age range is different, and the pedagogy adapted to suit very young children, its underlying principles remain true to the artistic practices that underpin the RSC's rehearsal room approaches at all levels of schooling. As such it illustrates how the pedagogy, at its best, activates the power latent within Shakespeare's language and his stories in a way that helps explain how and why it is so potent for language learning. It will lead us to revisit the playfulness at the heart of both rehearsal room pedagogy and of Shakespeare himself and offers some potent metaphors for the teacher who is able to make good use of both.

Shakespeare, language play and rehearsal room pedagogy in the early years: a case study

The project centred on *The Tempest* and was taught in November 2010, to a reception class of thirty-one four- to five-year-old children in a small Warwickshire market town. Eight children in the class had English as an additional language (EAL), and seven were on free school meals. The teaching was planned and led by Miles Tandy, then working for Warwickshire Local Education Authority, along with Jamie Luck, a creative associate of the RSC at the time, and Rachel Gartside, who also conducted the fieldwork for the research and presented a report of the findings to the Company in February 2011. The research was commissioned as a special project to explore the potential effects of adapting rehearsal room pedagogy for very young children and was jointly funded by the RSC and the University of Warwick.

The report stretched to sixty-six pages and drew evidence from detailed observations of the class, in particular, from a focus group of eight pupils, four of whom had EAL. Interviews were conducted with the head of the foundation stage, the class teacher, and the teaching assistant, all of whom observed the sessions, and with the practitioners themselves. Video recordings were analysed for evidence of specific moments when children could be seen to engage with language in specific target areas drawn from the document *Every Child a Talker* (*ECAT*), part of the then current National Strategy for English, which the school used for guidance. These included twelve general categories such as 'extends use of vocabulary/syntax' and 'engages verbally with ideas introduced', as well as some categories that were more specific to this project, such as 'uses words/expressions drawn from Shakespeare' and 'interprets Shakespeare's words either verbally or nonverbally'. The *ECAT* tracking sheets were used to assess the levels and extent of language engagement demonstrated during the sessions by children in the focus group, and these were then compared with previous assessments.[10]

The overall evidence was remarkably positive. Not only did children display great levels of enthusiasm and interest and show evidence of enjoying, making sense of, and using those elements of Shakespeare's language that they were introduced to, but they also demonstrated measured improvement across all four of the categories specified on the *ECAT* tracking sheets. For the more linguistically developed children, this was evidenced in the broader range of language they were observed to be using, while for others there were jumps of up to twelve months in their developmental levels. In the transcribed interview with the reception teacher (graded 'good' by OFSTED), she uses the word 'amazing' seven times and talks of children making 'huge steps' on three separate occasions.

Rather than summarize the report here I will present a theoretical explanation as to *why* these very young children were able to engage so readily with this project and why it had such an immediate and noticeable effect on their language use. For this I will revisit the work of Guy Cook, who helps explain why Shakespeare's language and stories can be accessible and enjoyable for young children;[11] then I will examine the particular form of playful pedagogy deployed during this project. First, I provide a brief summary of the teaching scheme itself.

The Tempest, as it was taught

The scheme was taught over six sessions of sixty minutes each.[12] Inbetween sessions the class teacher did additional follow-up work, including story writing and character descriptions, but it is the drama work I concentrate on here. The children were introduced to the play through a form of active storytelling, in which they had the chance to physicalize characters and events. They began with the backstory, learning how Prospero, the Duke of Milan, was betrayed by his brother, Antonio, and set adrift on a boat with his young daughter, Miranda; and how they were saved when a storm tossed them on to an island, which the children then explored imaginatively and created through drawings in the form of an image carpet. The story continued with their discovery of a strange young creature, Caliban, who befriended the two castaways and learned English from them but later became Prospero's slave after unintentionally frightening Miranda one night while she was sleeping. The children then played games that explored the harsh ways Prospero now treated Caliban and the tiring jobs he gave him to do. Later they learned how Prospero saw a ship sailing close to the island and knew the ship was carrying his brother and enemies. The children now took on the roles of Ariel and the spirits of the air that inhabited the island and helped Prospero make a magic potion that he would pour into the sea, causing a great storm to bring the ship to the island. The storm was created communally through sound and music and through tossing a small paper ship together on a large, blue cloth. The children then physically enacted it as the sailors being tossed and battered in the ship while calling out phrases from the opening scene of the play. Later, collectively in role as Miranda, they tried to convince Prospero to halt the storm. Then, portraying the spirits of the air, they were called upon to advise him on the kind of tricks he could play on his enemies now that they were on the island in order to teach them a lesson they would never forget. These and their effects they acted out in small groups. As an ending to the story, the children were called upon to talk to both brothers and get them to resolve their differences.

All in all the children were introduced to twenty-five extracts from the text of the play ('text scraps'). All were complete sentences, some short – as when the sailors call out *We split! We split! We split!* as the ship breaks up in the storm – others more complex, such as Caliban's reminder to Prospero *'Thou strok'st me and made much of me; would give me water with berries in't.'* The teachers introduced these as integral to Prospero's telling of the backstory; as phrases used to describe characters and the island; and as emotive expressions exchanged in dialogue between the characters. Active, physicalized storytelling was the main way in which children were introduced to both the play's narrative and to Shakespeare's language, but there were other pedagogic strategies deployed. Some of these were games involving language; so, for example, a version of grandmother's footsteps ('Caliban's footsteps') had the teacher as Prospero trying to spot the children in role as Caliban as they crept up behind him. If he saw a child moving, the whole class had to return to their initial positions unless they could call out a slightly edited version of Caliban's famous curse: *'This island's mine! . . . toads, beetles, bats light on you!'* There were in-role discussions, in which children collectively played one character and the teacher another; there were games such as 'Go, stop, show me' in which children moved through the space and were asked to freeze into physical depictions of a character, described in Shakespeare's words ('Show me *the Duke of Milan, a prince of power*' for Prospero; 'show me *a freckled whelp, hag-born, not honoured with a human shape*' for Caliban).

The experienced drama teacher may well note that many of these activities are practices shared by primary drama specialists who are not using

Shakespeare but their particular application here, especially with the inclusion of Shakespeare's language, makes of them something more akin to rehearsal room strategies. As we saw in Chapter 4, Tandy's use of games and image-making, of exploring the backstory to help the group co-create the world of the play, and of improvising around the play's given circumstances relate directly to authentic artistic practices and the kind of work that happens in the early stage of a rehearsal period. More of these activities will be described later, but first we need to revisit the relationship between such structured forms of playful pedagogy, language learning and the work of Shakespeare himself.

Language play and language learning: revisiting Guy Cook

Theories of play and language learning have long been influential in the early years. Some twenty-seven years ago, Ann Levy reviewed the literature on the role of play and its benefit to language and suggested five categories: stimulating language development; introducing and clarifying new words and concepts; motivating language use and practice; developing metalinguistic awareness; and encouraging verbal thinking. Jerome Bruner and Lev Vygotsky remain seminal to this understanding, of course, but these theories are dominated by psychological approaches and tend to concentrate on the kind of language that emanates from various forms of improvised play.[13] While disputing neither their validity nor indeed their relevance to aspects of this project, I wish to return to Guy Cook's work, previously discussed in Chapter 5, because it draws from less influential *cultural* theories of play, notably the work of Roger Caillois, who in turn was influenced by Johan Huizinga.[14] These theories are particularly enlightening, as they provide a perspective on the appeal and value of language play driven by form and repetition as well as by improvisation, and they also address the value to young children's language of some of the darker elements of play.

Cook begins his study by looking at the language of nursery rhymes, common across languages and cultures, and argues that such rhymes inspire both attention and affection in children, not because they are *meaning*-driven but, rather, because they are *form*-driven; that is to say, they are shaped primarily around a patterned use of sound and rhythm whose unusual and often absurd meanings result from, rather than shape, the form. Young children enjoy the co-ordinated actions that often accompany the accentuated rhythms of such rhymes (as with, for example, 'This little piggy went to market'), as they create a sense of fellowship, a feeling of togetherness and well-being that constitutes the key social purpose of the language exchange. But these rhymes, he suggests, have their own imaginative drive, plunging children into the middle of unexplained stories, set in vanished worlds, using archaic vocabulary that children not only tolerate but also enjoy repeating and making their own sense of. Moreover, such uses of language persist in children's own culture in the form of playground chants, such as skipping rhymes, jokes, puns, and the darker, more aggressive forms of play – taunts, verbal duelling, and the kind of transgressive rhymes that I certainly recall from my own childhood, such as 'Buffalo Billy had a ten-foot willy'.[15] As children grow up, this kind of language play becomes socially and aesthetically ritualized not only into intimate but also aggressive forms that provide a sense of identity and belonging, such as praying and singing and the kind of chanting exchanged between rival groups of fans at football matches.

Two key points made by Cook are that when presented within the spirit of play, children can tolerate, and indeed enjoy, ambiguous or unusual language from texts that are principally driven by form rather than meaning; and that it is therefore an educational error to assume that language is learned best when approached for functional rather than playful purposes. Here, as we saw in Chapter 5, he draws from Wolfson's Bulge theory of social relations that emphasize the human appeal of the kind of playful language that we find in intimate exchanges on the one hand and aggressive exchanges on the other.[16] It is the staid, relatively uninteresting 'public' language of the Bulge that often dominates the daily interactions of the classroom. In early-years settings, of course, the language of intimacy, as well as the language of the Bulge, is given a space in role-play corners where home settings as well as public venues such as cafes and post offices are set up for children to play in. The language of power and aggression, however, is seen as far more problematic, in imaginative play as well as in reality, as can be seen by the negative ways in which boys' propensity for aggressive forms of play has often been viewed.[17] Yet we only have to return to the seminal work of Iona and Peter Opie to remind ourselves that it is quite natural for young children to find pleasure in such language and interrelationships.[18]

Based on the practices they discovered in school playgrounds in a variety of primary schools across the UK, most of which were accompanied by various forms of language play expressed through rhythm and rhyme, the Opies classified children's uses of language into eighteen chapters. Chapter headings such as 'Wit and Repartee', 'Guile', 'Nicknames and Epithets', 'Jeers and Torments', 'Partisanship', and 'Pranks' do not fit readily with the more Romantic visions of play, derived from figures such as Rousseau and Froebel, that still influence early-years discourse. We can, however, find numerous examples of language used for precisely these purposes in any play by Shakespeare, including *The Tempest*, and it is to him that we now turn and to a direct consideration of the theories of Caillois that shape much of the rest of this case study.

Shakespeare the player

The human proclivity for play, far from disappearing with childhood, is actually at its most sophisticated in what are commonly appreciated as supreme works of art.[19] Indeed, as Shakespeare understood it, it is not only artists and actors who play but all of us throughout our daily lives. This point is commonly made and is usually referenced to Jacques' famous monologue recounting the seven ages of man in *As You Like It* ('*All the world's a stage / And all the men and women merely players*').[20] However, the categories of play theorized by Roger Caillois help us understand how Shakespeare's portrayal of humans at play stretches beyond representing them merely as players of social roles. They also enable us to appreciate how Shakespeare's characters, as well as Shakespeare himself, play games with and through language.

Caillois classified play into four main rubrics according to the underlying characteristics of the game involved: these he called (i) *agon*, where the spirit of competition is dominant, as in competitive sports; (ii) *alea*, where chance dominates, as in gambling and in games such as roulette; (iii) *mimicry*, characterized by simulation and typified by games of illusion, including theatre itself; and (iv) *ilinx*, where the play is intended to produce sensations of dizziness or vertigo, such as the helter-skelter or skiing. In addition to these four 'horizontal' categories, Caillois proposed two 'vertical' categories, to be viewed as either ends of a continuum: *paidia*, for improvised, unstructured, spontaneous play; and *ludus* for play in its more structured forms, such as games of chess and football, where there are detailed sets of rules.

There are examples of play as *ludus* in *The Tempest*, most typically in the theatrical masque arranged by Prospero (Act 4 Scene 1) to celebrate the betrothal of Miranda and Ferdinand. Mostly, however, Prospero, the key playmaker, plays in a less rule-bound form closer to *paidia*. We can also see that much of the way in which he plays with his enemies falls into the category of *mimicry* rather than *agon*, characterized as it is not so much by the spirit of competition but more by various acts of deceit and illusion. For example, he makes Ferdinand believe that his father is dead, and he uses Ariel and the spirits to conjure up all manner of images and sounds to mystify his enemies as they wander lost across the island. There is, however, more than an element of *alea* in his play, as he cannot control, for example, how Miranda and Ferdinand will feel about each other when they meet, nor what Caliban will do when stumbled upon by the drunken crew of the ship. The tempest he conjures up can also be seen as a form of *ilinx*, in which those on the ship are tossed and tumbled about by his magic, a dark form of play in which Prospero alone knows that they are safe.

These categories of play – *mimicry, alea* and *ilinx* – are actualized through the language as well as the action of *The Tempest*. The competitive spirit of agonistic play, on the other hand, which typifies the master–slave relationship between Prospero and Caliban, is really *only* actualized through the language, as exemplified in their opening exchange in Act 1 Scene 2:

> **PROSPERO** Thou poisonous slave, got by the devil
> Himself, upon thy wicked dam, come forth!
> **CALIBAN** As wicked dew as e'er my mother brushed
> With raven's feather from unwholesome fen
> Drop on you both!

Here, as they aggressively trade insults, the language *is* the *agon*, a form of play well appreciated by young children, particularly when it does what Caliban manages here: to take the form of the insult and turn it back on his adversary. Children appreciate how such repartee calls for quick thinking and a sure linguistic touch, as in numerous examples provided by the Opies, my personal favourite being:

> If I had a face like yours, I'd put it on a wall and throw a brick at it.
> If I had a face like yours, I'd put it on a brick and throw a wall at it.[21]

With typical Shakespearean ambiguity, throughout the play it is Caliban, rather than Prospero, who wins the verbal battles if not the actual contest. It is he who speaks the more colourful, poetic language; who comes out with the most telling insults and curses; and who is often more appealing to children as a character.

The play's playful spirit, then, is very broad and also rather dark, and I argue that it is this as much as anything else that captures its potential appeal for young children, those 'geniuses at playing', as Michael Boyd has described them. Furthermore, this spirit is not only conveyed through the language but is also often expressed in its very form – its sounds, rhythms, imagery, and patterning. Rehearsal room pedagogy has the potential to match the extent of this playful spirit, to activate both the imaginative power of the story and the formal appeal of the language. It is also, crucially, able to harness its darker elements in ways that do not undermine the atmosphere of warmth, security, and togetherness that characterizes the best of early-years practice – and, indeed, the spirit of ensemble.

Drama, play, and language learning: looking closely at rehearsal room pedagogy through the lens of Caillois's theory

Cook is particularly interested in what he calls the 'affinity' between games and language. In both, he argues, we create relationships, collaborate and compete, take turns, and are offered opportunities for both individual display and communal enjoyment – a list that also offers a neat summary of the kind of artistic play that goes on in a rehearsal room. Furthermore, both language and games – brought together in the kind of theatrical improvisation we saw demonstrated in Chapter 4 – offer us opportunities not only to co-operate but also to manipulate, deceive, and actively play with what we think others may be thinking so that we can use this for our own purposes. A skilful actor can be very good at this, but it is a skill ignored or mistrusted by those educational drama practitioners who uncritically adopt a discourse of 'ownership', mistakenly conflating it with a belief that children's ideas must shape the unfolding drama at the expense of all other considerations. It is exactly this kind of deceptive artistry, however, that skilful storytellers and magicians use to weave their spells upon their audience – and we know how readily children respond to stories and to magic. 'Like the unfolding of a fairy tale . . .', Cook suggests, 'the playing of a particular game follows predictable patterns and stages, but with infinite variations. There is a "games competence" involving knowledge of particular games, in the same sense that there is "literary competence."'[22] Working as a game – actively, experientially, and in the present – but doing so with a story, a theatre-based pedagogy can be used to bring both of these competences particularly close together.

Caillois, understandably, classified traditional theatre such as Shakespeare's as a form of *ludus*, tightly governed as it is by rules and conventions. Participatory forms of theatre, on the other hand, necessarily loosen these rules to become more open and interactive, hence moving along the continuum toward the improvisatory nature of *paidia*. The trick here is not for very young children to actually shape the story – it is, after all, Shakespeare's, and he was pretty good at stories – but for them to *feel* that they are experiencing it live within the patterns, stages, and variations that they experience when they play a good game; and, in this case, a game that is being played with and through language. A close look at some of the activities used in this scheme of work, classified according to Caillois's rubric, shows us precisely how the RSC practitioners skilfully managed this in ways that parallel how Shakespeare and his characters are playing in key parts of the play. In the process, given the close affinity between play and language expounded above, it helps explain why the work had such noticeably positive effects on children's language use.

We begin with the dark, aggressive form of play in *The Tempest*, the *agon* that we have seen manifested in the insults and curses exchanged between Prospero and Caliban. Such language games, as we have seen, can be highly creative and enjoyable to children, but they can, of course, be hurtful to the child subjected to them and can also be the precursor to actual violence; hence, understandably, early-years teachers tend to mistrust such play. The key to harnessing their playful energy and making them safe is, for the teacher, to ensure that the fictional frame is very strong and that the play is firmly within the rule-bound territory of *ludus*. In other words, it must be clearly framed as a theatrical game, one that includes the language of the insults, and this was exactly the case in the example of 'Caliban's footsteps'. As previously explained, this game had the teacher take on the role of Prospero with the children collectively in role as Caliban trying to creep out of his cave without being seen. If Prospero turned around and called out *'Hag seed, abhorred slave'*, the children were to respond with *'This island's mine! Toads, beetles, bats light on you!'* As with a nursery rhyme – and as is common in RSC rehearsal room practice – the speaking of the language had specific hand gestures added to it and strongly accentuated the rhythm to help children recall it. The video shows children playing this game with absolute delight, relishing the insult that they call out with great gusto and stabbing the air viciously with their fingers as they point at Prospero on the word 'you'. Yet the more aggressive they pretend to be, the bigger the grins on their faces. And, interestingly, their teachers can be seen to join in the game happily and freely, evidently feeling no discomfort with the simulated aggression being shown by the children in their charge.

The spirit of competitiveness in drama need not be so aggressive, however, and in activities much closer to the play of *paidia* than *ludus* there was a gentler agonistic tension in the form of children being set a challenge. One of these challenges was to represent the storm in a highly theatrical fashion by tossing the paper model of a ship together on a large, blue cloth without letting it ever fall on to the floor. Another took the form of a dialogue with Prospero in which the children were given the challenge of persuading him to stop the storm. In both of these examples, a strong spirit of co-operation was called for, the kind we have seen at the heart of rehearsal room pedagogy. Children needed to work together, watch and listen to one another, in order to be successful; and in both cases the teacher was quick to praise them afterward for having played so well together.

The *agon* of drama/theatre has an imaginative dimension to it that other games lack, inasmuch as it is set within a fictional framework, within the boundaries of a good story. So in the examples above, the play is, in effect, deepened as it is working on two levels at once, with the agonistic play being framed within the play of *mimicry*. Mimicry is, of course, the form of play most pervasive in drama, as it involves pretence, spectacle, and illusion, the very substance of theatre. Throughout the entire scheme, the children were called upon to 'mimic' with their voices and with their bodies, to pretend and engage in games of illusion in a variety of ways common to the artistic practices of the rehearsal room. Different activities had them pretending to be different characters. The game 'Go, stop, show me', for example, involved them responding to language through physical representation; work in collective role, on the other hand, in which they all took on simultaneously the role of either Ariel or Miranda, was an entirely verbal form of play, calling upon them to sit, listen, talk, and maybe argue with Prospero. Whenever the story was being narrated, the children sat in a circle and had the opportunity to enter the circle with the teacher/storyteller to help enact a particular scene, such as Miranda and Prospero being cast adrift in the boat.[23]

The boat is a particularly interesting example, as the teacher used Shakespeare's own words to describe it: '*a rotten carcass of a butt, not rigged, nor tackle, sail, nor mast: the very rats instinctively have quit it*'. Children were invited not only to represent this scene with their bodies but also, as with a nursery rhyme, to repeat the phrase accompanied by stylized gestures, one of which involved bringing their hands to their cheeks and wriggling their fingers to represent both the rats' whiskers and their scurrying off the boat. The children evidently relished this, and some of their laughter centred on the word 'instinctively', more particularly the syllable 'stinc', which suggests that they imagined this meant that the rats were incredibly smelly! Rather than see this as an unfortunate, childish misunderstanding, we need to remember Cook's argument about the formal appeal of such playful uses of language to young children's imaginations (a playfulness emphasized by the gesturing), their tolerance of ambiguity and their ability to make their own sense of it.[24]

The teachers' own use of mimicry went beyond their taking on the role of Prospero themselves; it included adopting particular formal patterns of language use to capture the ritualistic potential of specific exchanges. A good example of this was in the spell-making exercise, in which children in role as the spirits were invited to read what was needed in an imaginary book of spells, fetch it and drop it into Prospero's cauldron. The following observation is drawn directly from the report:

> Jacey has an idea for 'carrots'. Miles asks: 'just carrots?' Jacey adds, 'mouldy carrots'. Miles extends her idea into a line that can be chanted: 'Mouldy carrots they need no more.' Now Alice approaches and suggests 'onions'. Miles asks: 'what are they like, these onions?' She says, 'white and short'. Miles extends: 'Mix in onion, white and short.' Alice goes to get the 'onions' from an imaginary location on the island on the other side of the room. As she puts them in the cauldron, she clearly and exactly repeats the line: 'Mix in onions, white and short.'[25]

What is particularly interesting here is how the teacher uses the 4/4 stress verse pattern that is so common in nursery rhymes such as *Georgy Porgy* and *Little Miss Muffet*, to extend the children's language by adding to it the kind of rhythmic pattern typical of formal ritual and enunciated with suitable gravitas. 'Mouldy carrots they need no more'; 'Mix in onions, white and short.' Alice's spontaneous repetition of the phrase is indicative of the formal appeal of such language, argued earlier. The use of this 4/4 stress characterized other language games – for example, one played in pairs that centred on Prospero's and Miranda's efforts to teach Caliban English by naming things on the island. This took the form of call and response: 'Caliban, Caliban **what** do you see?' 'I see a ___, **that's** what I see!' The blank, of course, was to be filled in by the second child naming something that Caliban could see – a tree, a crab, a cave – taken from the image carpet of the island that the children had already drawn.

The *ludic* structure of these language games provides a strong pattern that controls their improvisatory nature, yet their appeal and their energy nonetheless lie in the potential for variation and surprise that they embrace. In this sense, games like this are games of chance that move us into the territory of *alea,* and the looser their structure, the chancier they become. Like Prospero, teachers who open up stories and invite children to contribute ideas must be willing to incorporate them skilfully into their overall plan without abandoning the story in their head. There are times, then, when enjoyment of the game, for both children and teachers, lies in this willingness to take a risk, to surrender to chance and trust that any surprising results can be used artistically to enrich the experience. This, of course, elides with the playful approaches the RSC uses to encourage young people to make interpretive choices and helps explain why the process can be energizing and enjoyable. For younger children, it is best achieved through whole group participatory interaction.

A good example of this occurred with one child, Hussein, a recent arrival to the country and an elective mute, who never spoke in the classroom. As Miles was telling the story of how Miranda and Prospero first met Caliban, he said, 'Here's what happened', approaching Hussein. 'They stroked him on the head and said. . .'. Whereupon, before Miles could continue, Hussein let out a raspberry, the first sound he had ever uttered at school. Grasping rather than rejecting this response, Miles continued: 'Which is exactly what he did! But then they said "Hello, Caliban",' to which Hussein uttered another, slightly different raspberry sound, which allowed Miles to point this out to the children. After a couple more exchanges, in which Caliban/Hussein was offered a drink *'with berries in't'* by Miranda and Prospero, Miles was able to announce that they suddenly realized that Caliban could speak, 'but that he just didn't speak the same way that they did'. The class teachers were convinced that this exchange was extremely significant for Hussein, but the rest of the children were gripped throughout too. They found it hugely funny, listening silently and intently to Miles's improvised narrative and laughing wildly each time Hussein/Caliban responded. They were doubtless experiencing here what Cook calls 'the sheer delight that seems to arise from surrender to chance and unpredictability' and the way in which the storyteller/teacher was able to use it as a valid, interpretive choice and pattern it into the unfolding drama.[26] Needless to say, when the teacher asked the children to recall how Caliban had greeted Prospero and Miranda in the following session, she was met with a huge chorus of raspberries!

Play that falls into the category of *ilinx* implies an even greater surrender of the self than *alea*; it involves players in a game in which they feel they are abandoning themselves to a force other than luck that is greater than or beyond themselves. At first it might appear that such forms of play have little to do with rehearsal room pedagogy, but in fact that is not the case. Cicely Berry makes great use of this kind of play in her work with actors, in the form of what she calls 'displacement strategies'.[27] These strategies are designed to help actors connect in deep, subliminal ways with the inherent power of Shakespeare's language by releasing them from the tyranny of always trying to make literal sense of the words. They are intended to help the actors connect with 'the surprise, the anarchy, in the language' through a variety of intensely physical activities.[28] For example, in one speech from *Hamlet* (Act 2 Scene 2) she has actors bounce on the floor as they speak it, then kneel on all fours speaking it into the floor, and, finally, having chosen a favourite line, they are asked to roll together around the floor, 'feeling the vibrations in their bodies as they speak'. 'It is great to do this', she comments, 'because it gives each actor a feeling of freedom with the language.'[29] This forgoing of rationality is akin to the theory of 'unselfing', which Iris Murdoch understands to be at the heart of the experience of beauty, in which we forget about ourselves, our anxieties, and immediate preoccupations.[30] It is a physical way of surrendering to the beauty of Shakespeare's language.

Young children, of course, generally love games in which they consciously seek dizziness, rolling on the floor or being physically swung about by an adult they trust. One of the exercises to evoke the storm involved these children tossing themselves about through the space of the room, as both the waves and the sailors, following the teacher, periodically stopping and calling out text scraps drawn from the sailors' shouts at the opening of the play, one of which was 'We split! We split! We split!' This observation was made during the recap at the beginning of the following session:

> Miles asks: 'what was happening when "*we cried to the wind that sighed to us*"?' and as soon as he hears that phrase of Shakespeare's language, one boy remembers and spontaneously starts being the wave in the sea that he was during that part of the story, crashing against the side of the boat. He is grinning all over his face. His action encourages the rest of the group to join in, and there is a spontaneous re-enactment of the moment when the boat was rocked by a storm. Caleb instantly recognizes the phrase and suggests: 'Let's make the boat again, it broked apart.' A girl rolls on to the floor and says, 'I'm broke, I'm broke!' embodying the moment which she connects with Shakespeare's words 'We *split! We split!*'

The children's exuberance here, in both the exercise and their recall of it, is, I would argue, on a continuum with the kind of controlled anarchy Berry sees as so advantageous for connecting actors to the text. Their willingness to make themselves dizzy with the language is a way for them to physically connect with it. But the relevance of *ilinx* to this scheme goes beyond this isolated exercise, for it is at the heart of the power of theatrical storytelling itself. When we are enthralled by theatre, we do indeed abandon ourselves to it, allowing ourselves willingly to lose our sense of equilibrium and be swept along by the language and the spectacle. Good stories told in the theatre can embody the playful spirit of *ilinx* as they deliberately create worlds in which the balance of ordinary life is disrupted and turned upside down before being resolved at the conclusion.[31] This sensation, so loved by children in its physical manifestation, has its psychic twin in the very real sensations we experience when captivated by a good story and by good theatre. If Shakespeare can provide us with the language and the substance of such a story, skilful uses of rehearsal room pedagogy can actualize this playful spirit and bring it to life in the classroom.

Conclusion

In drawing upon the work of Cook and Caillois, I have attempted to demonstrate that an expansive, cultural theory of play can help us appreciate the intimate connection between language development and the aesthetics of play, and how this can in turn be enhanced by a skilful use of rehearsal room pedagogy, one that harnesses the broad spectrum of human playfulness in much the same way that Shakespeare did. Many educators might still pose the question: '*Why* teach Shakespeare in the early years?' The success of the project described above suggests that the answer is the same for very young children as it is for all young people of school age: if Shakespeare is globally recognized as one of the best dramatists, poets, and storytellers to have ever lived, why deprive them, whatever their age or background, of the very best when there are demonstrable ways of making him accessible, and if there is evidence that it can directly benefit their learning and well-being?

Key to this accessibility, as we have seen, is skilful, knowledgeable and aesthetically aware teaching as exemplified by the practitioners who have featured throughout this book. Cook helps us appreciate the nature of their skill by finding analogies for it in the different cultural forms of play. From these he identifies three key figures: the storyteller, the referee, and the magician, all of which have been in evidence both in this example and in others described in earlier chapters. All three are figures, Cook writes, 'whose power rests upon special skills and knowledge rather than coercion, and whose authority is accepted voluntarily by the players. Perhaps it is to such models as these, rather than those of the manager or facilitator, that the modern teacher should aspire.'[32] In aspiring to such models, teachers would need to strive to become, like young children, 'geniuses at playing'. This remains a foundational principle to rehearsal room pedagogy, and the RSC believes it offers a particularly effective and enjoyable way of enticing young people into a potentially lifelong relationship; for surely no serious person who might blithely argue that children need to grow up and leave the world of playing behind them would also argue that they do the same with Shakespeare.

9

Looking Forward

Since the planning and implementation of the Learning and Performance Network, much has changed in the cultural and educational climate of the UK. The political ramifications of the 2008 global financial crisis are still being felt in austerity measures that have drastically reduced the funding available to cultural institutions and arts organizations and many smaller companies have been forced to close. The well-known economic commentator, Robert Peston, himself very supportive of the arts, has indicated that, the scale of the downturn being so enormous, there can be little expectation of any significant improvement to public funding even in the event of an economic recovery.[1] Arts education, too, is feeling the shockwaves. Universities are no longer provided with subsidies to support the teaching of the arts and humanities; and in schools, the arts have not been included as core subjects in planned examination reforms in England and have had to fight hard to maintain their status as examination subjects. Furthermore, with the accelerated drive towards the privatization of schooling in the form of increased provision for academies and free schools, local authority in-service programmes for teachers have all but disappeared. As a result, schools increasingly need to turn to external agencies for their continuing professional development. Within this context, the educational role of large, prestigious and influential arts organizations such as the RSC is bound to become increasingly significant. The LPN is therefore being reconceived in a form intended not only to ensure sustainability but also to allow for development and expansion; and, internally, it is in a strong position to do this as education remains a key part of the Company's overall vision and continues to be valued at its highest levels.

In September, 2012, Michael Boyd and Vikki Heyward officially stepped down from their positions, to be succeeded by Gregory Doran as artistic director and Catherine Mallyon as executive director. Despite her previous considerable experience running major arts organizations, Catherine admits to being surprised by the range, quality and scale of the Company's education work when she first took up her post and has been particularly impressed by the LPN and its work with teachers. She told me:

> Educational activity is now such a part of our organization, it is so integral to it, that I cannot conceive of the RSC without it. That is probably a change that has come about over the past ten years. The nature of the challenge now is to keep this work energised and of a consistently high quality.[2]

This recognition and firm support at the top of the organization also comes from the artistic director. 'Michael and Greg are completely different people,' she said, 'but in terms of understanding what our education team is doing, Greg has the same commitment that Michael had.' And she defined his educational vision in terms of the rehearsal room:

> We have to lead with the text and find ways of exploring and understanding it as we do in the rehearsal room. It is absolutely about the work of the rehearsal room being part of education, absolutely aligned with the view that, taught well and in the right context, Shakespeare isn't this mystical figure who is incapable of being understood.

Doran has, in fact, voiced this vision in a foreword to the revised *Shakespeare Toolkit* sent out to all state-maintained primary schools in England in March 2014. Here he affirms his support for the current practices of the education team, pointing to the seminal influence of Cicely Berry, expressing his full commitment to the *Stand up for Shakespeare* manifesto and its vision of young people as 'active, capable agents in the artistic process' and acknowledges the centrality of rehearsal room pedagogy. He writes:

> Over many years of working with young people we have found that engaging students directly and physically with the sound, shapes and rhythms of the text allows them deeper access to it and invites personal responses from them about it. . . . The lesson plans we've devised here are inspired by the rehearsal room, which is really just another kind of classroom.[3]

To argue that Doran is here re-affirming the core traditions of RSC educational practice implies neither reification nor stagnation, however, and the Company's intent to move further with its education work has been demonstrated by recent developments in the 'See it Live' strand of the SUFS manifesto.

We saw in Chapter 1 how the *Young People's Shakespeare* evolved into *First Encounter*, becoming integrated more closely into the LPN in ways that have brought teachers, actors, directors and young audiences closer together. Taking live theatre into schools and regional theatres remains a core commitment of the Company, with *The Famous Victories of Henry V* scheduled to tour in 2015. The title is derived from an earlier play that toured and played in Stratford in 1587. 'It is a pretty sure bet', writes Doran, 'that in the audience was a 23-year old William Shakespeare.'[4] The plot of this play spans his own, later version of the story comprising the three plays *Henry IV Parts 1 and 2* and *Henry V*. In the 2015 production, the text will be Shakespeare's, edited from all three plays, but the structure will be that of the sixteenth-century play. It will thus introduce audiences to a key influence on Shakespeare's work, something that Doran sees as part of his artistic remit.

In order to reach wider audiences, the education team is currently exploring ways that schools can benefit from a recent innovation within the Company, the live streaming of performances from the Royal Shakespeare Theatre to cinemas around the world, begun in November 2013 with *Richard II,* which featured the popular television actor David Tennant in the title role. A package for schools was built around this event, created in partnership with students from Ravensbourne College, a higher education institution in London that specializes in vocational courses in digital media and design. Two days after the broadcast to cinemas, a recording of the live performance was streamed into schools across the country, wrapped around a live studio interaction. Ravensbourne students had built an interactive, online platform that could receive comments and questions from students watching the broadcast, followed by a session where David Tennant and Gregory Doran offered their responses, filmed live and streamed directly into classrooms. A total of 460 schools in all took part in the broadcast, 83 per cent of these being state-run, with roughly three-quarters overall being secondary and one quarter primary schools. More than 31,000 young people saw the broadcast, with over half of the audiences including students with special needs. For 57 per cent of those viewing, it was the first time they had attended a Shakespeare play.

The Company gathered detailed feedback from schools and this was overwhelmingly positive. Sixty-five per cent rated the production as excellent, 24 per cent as very good and only 1 per cent as less than good. Eighty-four per cent responded that they would definitely like to progress their students to seeing a live theatre performance, 80 per cent a Shakespeare play and 82 per cent an RSC production. Education packs were provided to support the broadcast, differentiated for primary and secondary schools. Of those schools that made use of them, over 40 per cent rated them as excellent with a further 30+ per cent rating them as very good. A range of comments were made by teachers that testified to the strong impact the broadcast had had on them and their students. In particular, many teachers expressed the opinion that the broadcast successfully captured the feel of a live theatre event. 'The theatre felt very intimate', commented one, 'even from the other side of a computer screen!' Another wrote of how this was a 'fantastic opportunity for those from less privileged backgrounds to see a live piece of theatre'. 'While I would always prefer to see a live performance', one teacher reported, 'this came a close second best.'[5]

As with any experience of Shakespeare, it was evident that those schools that had prepared their students well had benefited most and teachers testify to the usefulness of the resource packs in helping them do this. Primary schools had been encouraged to allow their children to watch just the opening thirty minutes of the play, up to and including the jousting scene in Act 1 Scene 3, and the subsequent banishment of Bullingbrook. They had been provided with ideas for activities for the remainder of the broadcast, when it was suggested they return to watch David Tennant being interviewed live. Teachers from some primary schools, however – those that had done the preparatory work – reported that their children had been enthralled and wanted to continue watching. A few teachers reported difficulties, principally technical in nature due to problems with local servers, and some technical suggestions were made to improve future broadcasts.

An informal feedback session with teachers in the current LPN cohort was very much reflective of this broader evaluation.[6] They were asked in particular to contribute ideas as to what the RSC could do to enhance this sense of 'liveness', of an audience watching together, simultaneously, and many were voiced. Could there be a pre- as well as a post-performance experience? For example, with webcams in all the schools and students being invited to call out a greeting in turn, to create that sense of excitement and enjoyment of a live, simultaneous, online audience? Could some young students from a network school be invited to Stratford to see the play beforehand and then interview some of the younger actors live themselves, so that school audiences would feel a closer connection with the production? These and other suggestions were listened to and welcomed. It remains to be seen as to how they will inform future developments but the process did provide just a small example of how the LPN can act structurally as a sounding board for the Company's educational strategy.[7]

The current funding stream from the Paul Hamlyn Foundation is due to end in 2016 but financial considerations have not been the driver behind plans for the future evolution and sustainability of the network; rather these plans are an attempt to respond to the changing cultural and educational climate and to recognize and build upon the achievements of the last ten years, those of the LPN and of other organizations intent on transforming the teaching of Shakespeare. Plans for the sustainability of the LPN are already partially implemented, in fact. In 2011–12, recruitment was paused to give the Company time to review the programme and to revise its structure. In the new format, the number of hub schools for each cohort was reduced from ten to six and, crucially, regional theatres were included as partners.[8] Formal and informal consultation has continued with teachers, partner theatres, funders and stakeholders and has resulted in a paper circulated in April 2014, which outlined the projected future shape and direction of the network. Many concrete ideas were expressed in the paper but at the time of writing they are still speculative and, as the current framework has some years still to run, it would be premature to set them down here. The current accreditation programmes for teachers and theatre artists are set to end in 2015 but the paper voices the RSC's commitment to furthering and expanding the work of the LPN, with school and theatre partners continuing to offer 'support, advice and inspiration to teachers and young people at a local level, connecting them to a wider national community of practice'.

The phrase 'community of practice' is worth lingering over as it echoes the title of a CEDAR report evaluating the LPN in 2010 that actually defined its work as 'Creating a Community of Practice'.[9] The phrase, taken from Lave and Wenger's work on situated learning, also informed the theoretical work of the PG Certificate, with relevant extracts included in the core reading.[10] It is important as it helps theorize the grossly over-used term 'community' in ways that point to how cultural institutions such as the RSC can nonetheless foster a climate of shared values and purpose amongst a group of diverse practitioners. It also, intriguingly, reflects the processes of community-building that are part of the rehearsal room, part of the creation of theatre itself; specifically, it can stimulate some final reflections on the achievements of the LPN and the challenges it now faces.

Wenger sees three integrated features as constituting a community of practice: mutual engagement; participation in a joint enterprise; and the process of developing a shared repertoire.[11] Such a community is not realized in abstract terms, nor by geographical proximity, but through the process of an actual, shared activity. Community maintenance is a crucial part of any practice but diversity as much as homogeneity is necessary for it to remain productive. 'Mutual engagement involves not only our competence but the competence of others', comments Wenger, and what matters is not that those involved agree on everything but that the enterprise is communally negotiated. Over time, such processes of mutual engagement and negotiation create a history, a repertoire of shared resources, through which a community of practice can become a 'privileged context for creating meaning'. So, although it needs to operate with specific resources and within a range of practical, political and financial constraints, the joint enterprise shared by community members is nevertheless *their* enterprise.

This definition provides, I think, a ready if speculative theoretical template for the continuation of the LPN. Following this notion, the RSC will have the central role of fostering and maintaining the community, which will take on diverse forms in different regions. It will continue to draw on the competences of different practitioners – theatre artists and teachers – and, although it will necessarily operate within a climate of constraints determined not only by financial resources but also by government policies and school priorities, its repertoire of shared meanings nonetheless will make it robust and independent enough to persist and thrive in its central quest to make Shakespeare accessible to as many young people as possible. But Wenger's theoretical framework is realistic, not romantic. He warns that the balance within such communities between reification and the ability to think creatively and move forward is a delicate one. They are not per se, he warns, emancipatory forces, yet they will always be a force to be reckoned with:

As a locus of engagement in action, interpersonal relationships, shared knowledge, and negotiation of enterprises, such communities hold the key to real transformation, the kind that has real effects on people's lives.[12]

The RSC believes it has shown, through its Learning and Performance Network, that it holds such a key, a key to unlocking Shakespeare's dramatic language and to removing the barriers that prevent many teachers and students from experiencing its particular power. Time will tell just how far this transformation will extend.

NOTES

Introduction

1   See Fiona Banks, *Creative Shakespeare: the Globe Education Guide to Practical Shakespeare*, London: Bloomsbury, 2014. In the US, the Folger Shakespeare Library has published a number of educational texts. See, for example, *Shakespeare Set Free Toolkit: Resources for Teaching and Learning*, published in 2009.

Chapter 1

1   There has, in fact, been a company devoted to the performance of Shakespeare's plays in Stratford since 1879. In the words of Colin Chambers: 'When the Royal Shakespeare Company was founded in 1961, it was not conjured out of the sky. The Shakespeare Memorial Theatre at Stratford-upon-Avon already enjoyed a national and international presence, with its own eighty years of history, culture, values and internal arrangements.' See Colin Chambers, *Inside the Royal Shakespeare Company: Creativity and the Institution*, London and New York: Routledge, 2004, p.3.

2   No mention of this was made, for example, in the final *South Bank Show* on the UK's ITV channel, broadcast on 28 December 2009, which was entirely devoted to Boyd's work at the RSC. By contrast, when given the opportunity, Boyd would readily refer to the company's work with young people. In an interview with Charlie Rose in the US in 2010, when asked about the current RSC visit to the country, he immediately enthused about the Young People's Shakespeare production of *Hamlet*. See www.theatrevoice.com/2173/shakespeare [accessed May 2013].

3   The quote is from a paper entitled 'Report on Educational Activities' written in November 1948. I have taken it from p.12 of Patricia Milsom's unpublished MPhil dissertation *The History and Development of the Royal Shakespeare Education Department: Glorious Hybrids*, awarded by the University of Birmingham in 2003, from which I derive most of the details in this brief history.

4   See 'On Safari with the RSC', originally published in *Flourish*, 1967, vol.1, no. 9, cited in Patricia Milsom (unpublished MPhil dissertation), *The History and Development of the Royal Shakespeare Education Department: Glorious Hybrids*, 2003, p.18.

5 Michael Boyd in an interview with the author, 25 April 2013. All subsequent quotes from Michael Boyd in this chapter are from this interview.

6 See Patricia Milsom (unpublished MPhil dissertation), *The History and Development of the Royal Shakespeare Education Department: Glorious Hybrids*, 2003, pp.106–107.

7 Maria Evans in an interview with the author, 8 June 2013. The observation about directors being reluctant to allow members of the education department into rehearsals is a point also made by Patricia Milsom (unpublished MPhil dissertation), *The History and Development of the Royal Shakespeare Education Department: Glorious Hybrids*, 2003, p.90.

8 See for example Graeme Paton's article 'Why all is not well in the world of Shakespeare' published in the *Times Educational Supplement*, 15 September 2006.

9 See Nicholas Monk *et al*, *Open Space Learning: a Study in Trans-disciplinary Pedagogy*, London: Bloomsbury, 2011, p.60.

10 Jonathan Bate in an interview with the author, 29 April 2013.

11 For a substantial and theorised account of the Postgraduate Certificate work and its link with the Learning and Performance Network, see Chapter 3, 'Learning to Play with Shakespeare', by Jonothan Neelands, in Nicholas Monk *et al*, *Open Space Learning: a Study in Trans-disciplinary Pedagogy*, London: Bloomsbury, 2011.

12 *Stand up for Shakespeare Manifesto*, p.1. This can be accessed on the RSC's website. http://www.rsc.org.uk/education/how-our-work-makes-a-difference/stand-up-for-shakespeare/

13 *Stand up for Shakespeare Manifesto*, p.3

14 *Stand up for Shakespeare Manifesto*, p.6

15 *Stand up for Shakespeare Manifesto*, p.7

16 *Stand up for Shakespeare Manifesto*, p.4

17 Jacqui O'Hanlon in an interview with the author, 23 May 2013.

18 Lyn Gardner, reviewing the play for the *Guardian* from White Hall Junior School in Walsall, 20 May 2009.

19 Details from an interview with Jacqui O'Hanlon, 26 September 2013.

20 See, for example, Nosheen Iqbal's review in the *Guardian*, 5 February 2010, from which I have taken the subsequent quote from McCraney. I happened to be in a West Midlands primary school researching a different project at this time. When interviewing the children, I found that all they wanted to talk to me about was this production of *Hamlet*, which they had seen the previous week.

21 Nicholas Monk *et al*, *Open Space Learning: a Study in Trans-disciplinary Pedagogy*, London: Bloomsbury, 2011, p.86

22 Jacqui O'Hanlon, in an email to the author, August 2013.

23 See, for example, Dave O' Brien, *Measuring the Value of Culture: a Report to the Department of Culture, Media and Sport*, December 2010; David Throsby, 'Determining the value of cultural goods: How much (or little) does contingent valuation tell us?' *Journal of Cultural Economics* 27, 2003, pp.275–285; David

Throsby, 'The value of cultural heritage: What can economics tell us?' in Clark, K. (ed.), *Capturing the Public Value of Heritage: The Proceedings of the London Conference 25–26 January 2006*, London: English Heritage pp.40–44; and John Holden, *Capturing Cultural Value*, London: Demos, 2004.

24 See John Holden, *Cultural Value and the Crisis of Legitimacy*, Demos, 2006, Chapter 3, for a full discussion of these categories.

25 These reports are available to be downloaded from the RSC website. http://www.rsc.org.uk/education/how-our-work-makes-a-difference/research-case-studies/external-evaluations.aspx

26 The figures, in fact, remained statistically very high. Over the subsequent five years, the average completion rate was 87 per cent.

27 Colin Chambers, *Inside the Royal Shakespeare Company: Creativity and the Institution*, London and New York: Routledge, 2004, pp.188–189.

28 Helen Nicholson, *Theatre, Education and Performance*, London: Palgrave Macmillan, 2011, p.208.

29 Helen Nicholson, *Theatre, Education and Performance*, London: Palgrave Macmillan, 2011, p.208.

Chapter 2

1   See 'Shakespeare: Iconic or Relevant?' in Martin Blocksidge (ed.), *Shakespeare in Education*, London: Continuum, 2003, and Tracy Irish, *A History of the Teaching of Shakespeare in England*, 2008, accessed April 2013, and available on the RSC website at http://www.rsc.org.uk/downloads/rsc_history_teaching_shakespeare_171210.pdf. See also Janet Bottoms 'Doing Shakespeare: How Shakespeare became a school "subject" ', *Shakespeare Survey*, vol. 66, 2013.

2   See Matthew Arnold, *Culture and Anarchy*, first published in 1869, and his introduction to T.H. Ward's *The English Poets*, published in 1880.

3   A.C. Bradley's *Shakespearean Tragedy* was first published in 1904 and Walter Raleigh's *William Shakespeare* in 1907.

4   The English Association, *The Teaching of English in Schools* (Leaflet No. 7, 1908), referenced by Blocksidge and also Irish (see note 1).

5   See J.W. Patrick Kreber, *Sense and Sensitivity*, University of London Press, 1965, and Frank Whitehead, *The Disappearing Dias*, London: Chatto & Windus, 1966.

6   *Saved* was first performed at the Royal Court Theatre in 1965.

7   Jonathan Bate in an interview with the author, 29 April 2013.

8   In Chapter 7 of *The Genius of Shakespeare*, London: Picador, 1997.

9   See essays in Jonathan Dollimore and Alan Sinfield (eds), *Political Shakespeare: New Essays in Cultural Materialism*, Manchester University Press, 1985.

10 For comments on Kenneth Baker as editor of the 1988 edition of *The Faber Book of English History in Verse*, see Dollimore and Sinfield, p.198. For details of Michael Portillo's speech to the Conservative Way Forward group in 1994, see Jonathan Bate, *The Genius of Shakespeare*, London: Picador, 1997,

pp.187–189. For details of the so-called 'Battle of the Bard' see Tracy Irish, *A History of the Teaching of Shakespeare in England*, 2008, p.5.

11 This extract was first published in the *Independent on Sunday* and is quoted on the cover of the paperback edition, as is the later quote from Sir Peter Hall.

12 See Alan Sinfield, 'Royal Shakespeare: Theatre and the Making of Ideology' in Jonathan Dollimore and Alan Sinfield (eds), *Political Shakespeare: New Essays in Cultural Materialism*, Manchester University Press, 1985. For a telling critique of his understanding of theatrical character, see Miriam Gilbert 'A Test of Character' in G.B. Shand (ed.), *Teaching Shakespeare: Passing it On*, Chichester: Wiley-Blackwell, 2009, p.93. Peter Brook's *The Empty Space* was originally published in 1968 by McGibbon and Key. This quote is taken from the 1990 reprint by Penguin Books, pp.12–13.

13 Jonathan Bate, *The Genius of Shakespeare*, London: Picador, 1997, pp.213–214.

14 Jonathan Bate, *English Literature: A Very Short Introduction*, Oxford University Press, 2010, p.65.

15 The quotations in this paragraph are taken from his interview with the author, 29 April 2013.

16 Jonathan Bate, *The Genius of Shakespeare*, London: Picador, 1997, pp.248–250.

17 Jonathan Bate, *The Genius of Shakespeare*, London: Picador, 1997, p.316.

18 Jonathan Bate, *The Genius of Shakespeare*, London: Picador, 1997, p.327.

19 Jonathan Bate, *The Genius of Shakespeare*, London: Picador, 1997, p.330.

20 Jonathan Bate, *The Genius of Shakespeare*, London: Picador, 1997, p.332.

21 Jonathan Bate, *The Genius of Shakespeare*, London: Picador, 1997, p.330.

22 Jonathan Bate, *The Genius of Shakespeare*, London: Picador, 1997, p.336.

23 Jonathan Bate in an interview with the author, 29 April 2013. See also Bate's *The Genius of Shakespeare*, pp. 108–112, where he elaborates on this and other points relating to *King Lear*.

24 Michael Boyd, in an interview with the author, 25 April 2013.

25 For this and other quotes from Michael Boyd in this paragraph, see his Foreword in Jonathan Bate and Eric Rasmussen (eds), *The RSC William Shakespeare Complete Works*, Basingstoke: Macmillan, 2007, p.64.

26 Interviews with Charlie Rose in August 2011, and January 2012, accessed in April 2013 on www.theatrevoice.com/2173/shakespeare

27 Michael Boyd in an interview with the author, 25 April 2013.

28 Jonathan Bate in an interview with the author, 29 April 2013.

29 In our interview Bate emphasized to me his belief that young people can rise to the challenge of what is difficult in Shakespeare and that we should not too readily patronize them by always seeking to make him appear easy.

30 Jonathan Bate in an interview with the author, 29 April 2013.

31 An undergraduate module that resulted from this collaboration was entitled 'Shakespeare without Chairs' and is currently taught by Carol Chillington Rutter. See references to this in her chapter 'Playing Hercules or Labouring in

my Vocation' in G.B. Shand (ed.), *Teaching Shakespeare: Passing it On*, Chichester: Wiley-Blackwell, 2009.

32 Unsurprisingly, he believes this pedagogy should be complemented by literary approaches, not substituted for them, a point I return to in Chapter 7.

Chapter 3

1 Taken from http://en.wikipedia.org/wiki/Cicely_Berry [accessed July 2013].

2 See Foreword by Michael Boyd in Cicely Berry, *From Word to Play: a Handbook for Directors*, London: Oberon Books, 2008, p.vii.

3 In Cicely Berry, *Working Shakespeare: The Work Book*, New York: Applause Theatre and Cinema Books, 2004, p.9.

4 Cicely Berry, *Working Shakespeare: The Work Book*, New York: Applause Theatre and Cinema Books, 2004, p.8.

5 Cicely Berry in interview with the author, 24 April 2013.

6 Cicely Berry in interview with the author, 24 April 2013.

7 See books and DVD referenced elsewhere in this chapter.

8 Cicely Berry in interview with the author, 24 April 2013.

9 In Cicely Berry, *Working Shakespeare: The Work Book*, New York: Applause Theatre and Cinema Books, 2004, p.10.

10 Cicely Berry, *Working Shakespeare: The Work Book*, New York: Applause Theatre and Cinema Books, 2004, p.10.

11 Jeremy Irons in the introduction to the DVD *Working Shakespeare, Workshop 1: Muscularity of Language*, New York: The Working Arts Library.

12 The quote is from *English for Ages 5–16*, and is taken from an un-numbered page opposite the introduction in Rex Gibson (ed.), *Secondary School Shakespeare: Classroom Practice*, Cambridge: Cambridge Institute of Education, 1990.

13 Rex Gibson (ed.), *Secondary School Shakespeare: Classroom Practice*, Cambridge: Cambridge Institute of Education, 1990, p.6.

14 The sales figures are taken from the obituary for Rex Gibson, *The Independent*, 8 June 2005. *Teaching Shakespeare* was written by Rex Gibson and published by Cambridge University Press in 1998. It was reprinted twelve times within the next ten years.

15 Rex Gibson, *Teaching Shakespeare*, Cambridge: Cambridge University Press, 1998, p.xii

16 Rex Gibson, *Teaching Shakespeare*, Cambridge: Cambridge University Press, 1998, p.8.

17 Sarah Olive, a persistent critic of the RSC's approaches, offered this criticism in a workshop for Masters students led by Mary Johnson at the Shakespeare Institute in Stratford-upon-Avon in 2012. Her overall criticisms are examined in more detail, and responded to, in Chapter 7.

18 See, for example, Michael Boyd's paragraph on the influence of Cicely Berry in
    the introduction to *The RSC Shakespeare Toolkit for Teachers*, London:
    Bloomsbury Methuen Drama, 2010, p.5.

19 Rex Gibson, from the foreword presented in each volume of the *Cambridge
    School Shakespeare* series.

20 See, for example, the activities described as *Walking the Punctuation* (p.167);
    Good Angel / Bad Angel (170); and *Echoes* (p.178) in *Teaching Shakespeare*.

21 See Rex Gibson, *Teaching Shakespeare*, Cambridge: Cambridge University
    Press, 1998, pp.158–161. See also Chapter 5 of Cecily Berry's *From Word to
    Play: A Handbook for Directors* (Oberon Books, 2008), in particular p.106.

22 Mary Johnson in an email to the author, 4 August 2013.

23 Mary Johnson in an interview with the author, 27 June 2013.

24 See David Kolb's book *Experiential Learning: Experience as the Source of
    Learning and Development*, Englewood Cliffs, NJ; London: Prentice Hall,
    1984.

25 The workshop is quoted and referred to here with the permission of Mary
    Johnson.

26 Jonothan Neelands in an interview with the author, 6 June 2013. The reference
    is to Pierre Bourdieu, the influential social theorist. See Pierre Bourdieu,
    Distinction: A Social Critique of the Judgment of Taste, trans. R. Nice,
    London: Routledge and Kegan Paul, 1984.

27 Jonothan Neelands in an interview with the author, 6 June 2013.

28 For the common bank of activities and terms, see *The Shakespeare Toolkit for
    Teachers*, pp.289–301. See also Neelands, *Structuring Drama Work*,
    Cambridge: Cambridge University Press, 1991. Jacqui O'Hanlon has told me
    that many of these activities are no longer core to the RSC's pedagogy. She sees
    them as part of their early articulation of practice but not part of their current
    work: 'In order to be as authentic as possible, we increasingly say, if it doesn't
    happen in a rehearsal room, then we shouldn't do it.' (Email to the author,
    September 2013.) Many have been removed from the more recently edited
    version of the *Toolkit for Primary Schools*, published in 2014.

29 The workshop took place in London in 2008 and is referred to here with the
    permission of Jonothan Neelands.

Chapter 4

1 Rachel Gartside interviewed by the author, 27 September 2013. All other
   quotes from Rachel Gartside in this chapter are taken from this interview.

2 Rebecca Gould had been director of education at Plymouth Theatre Royal. At
   the time she was working with teachers in the second year of their PG
   Certificate, helping them plan for and stage performances.

3 The statistics are taken from a report written by the RSC for internal
   dissemination only. The company's Head of Audience Insight advises that thirty
   responses are sufficient to provide a credible sample size. In March 2014, the

Department for Education awarded the RSC a second grant to distribute a specially edited version of the *Toolkit* to every state-maintained primary school in England (16,786 schools in all).

4 Jacqui O'Hanlon interviewed by the author, 26 September 2013. All other quotes from Jacqui O'Hanlon in this chapter are taken from this interview.

5 See Chapter 1 for details of how the LPN is organized around hubs and clusters. Later chapters will detail how this developed to include regional theatres in the hub.

6 See, for example, *Beginning Drama 4–11*, *Beginning Shakespeare 4–11* (both co-authored with Joe Winston, the former published in Mandarin Chinese in 2008) and *Creating Writers* (with Jo Howell).

7 These production videos were accessed on the RSC website in March 2014, on http://www.rsc.org.uk/whats-on/richard-ii/video-production-diary.aspx. The quote from Gregory Doran is taken from the first of these.

8 In this production, Hamlet was played by Jonathan Slinger. Miles saw his as a particularly male portrayal of grief, with Hamlet emotionally isolating himself and wishing to deal with his grief alone.

9 This is, of course ground that Grotowski explored in detail and made central to his processes of rehearsal. See Jerzy Grotowski, *Towards a Poor Theatre*, London: Routledge, 2002.

10 See http://www.bbc.co.uk/hamlet/past_productions/rsc_stage_1997.shtml

11 Jacqui O'Hanlon comments: 'This exercise is one that I have seen Cicely Berry do with every *Hamlet* acting company since I've been with the RSC. She feels it puts the actors in touch with "the other"; the sense of spirit that the scene is full of and which actors need to discover for themselves. It is electric to do this work in a studio space, as I've seen her do, with the lights off. All that we have is the language. The discoveries that the actors make during this sequence are very similar to the ones noted here from the teachers. And the impact of Cicely's work on this scene always finds its way into the final production.' (Email to the author, November, 2013.)

12 For the origin of this particular exercise, see Andy Kempe, 'Drama and the Development of Literacy', *NADIE Journal*, no. 24, 2000.

13 Miles used the word 'unfolding' here and alluded interestingly to the use of this very word at the start of the play when Francisco declares 'Stand and unfold yourself', meaning reveal your identity.

14 Jacqui O'Hanlon comments on this particular exercise that 'it is useful to think about a soliloquy as a dialogue – perhaps with the audience. We're always looking for ways to help the speech be dynamic and active as opposed to reflective and passive. So we might use this kind of approach with an actor as they start to explore a particular speech or soliloquy to help them find the argument within it.' (Email to the author, November 2013.)

15 See Jerome Bruner, *Towards a Theory of Instruction*, Cambridge MA: Harvard University Press, 1974. In actual fact, some young actors arrive for rehearsals with the same anxieties and even prejudices that one might find in students. As Jacqui O'Hanlon comments: 'Actors do not come on day one knowing the whole play; they need to find it together.'

16 See Eric Booth http://ericbooth.net/three-and-a-half-bestsellers/ [accessed April, 2014].

17 See Jerome Bruner, 'The Role of Dialogue in Language Acquisition', in Anne Sinclair, Robert J. Jarvella and Willem J. M. Levelt (eds), *The Child's Concept of Language,* New York: Springer Verlag, 1978.

Chapter 5

1 *The RSC Shakespeare Toolkit for Teachers*, London: Bloomsbury Methuen Drama, 2010, p.8.

2 *The RSC Shakespeare Toolkit for Teachers*, London: Bloomsbury Methuen Drama, 2010, p.9.

3 John Dewey, *Democracy and Education*, California, US: Simon & Brown, 2011 (first published by MacMillan, 1916), p.7.

4 Kate McLuskie, 'Dancing and Thinking: Teaching "Shakespeare" in the Twenty-First Century' in G.B. Shand (ed.), *Teaching Shakespeare: Passing it On*, Chichester: Wiley-Blackwell, 2009, p.131.

5 See also Joe Winston, *Drama and English at the Heart of the Curriculum*, London: David Fulton, 2004, pp.9–10.

6 Johan Huizinga, *Homo Ludens*, London: Paladin, 1971 (first published 1949). Richard Schechner, *Performance Theory*, New York: Ralph Pine, 1977.

7 Guy Cook, *Language Play, Language Learning*, Oxford: Oxford University Press, 2000.

8 Nessa Wolfson, 'The Bulge: A theory of speech behaviour and social distance', *Penn Working Papers in Educational Linguistics*, vol. 2, no. 1, 1990.

9 Guy Cook, *Language Play, Language Learning*, Oxford: Oxford University Press, 2000, p.62.

10 Rex Gibson, *Teaching Shakespeare*, Cambridge: Cambridge University Press, 1998, pp.198–199.

11 John Dewey, *Education as Experience*, New York: Touchstone, 1938/1997, pp.26–27.

12 John Dewey, *Education as Experience*, New York: Touchstone, 1938/1997, p.27.

13 John Dewey, *Education as Experience*, New York: Touchstone, 1938/1997, p.28.

14 Jonothan Neelands and Jacqui O'Hanlon, 'There is Some Soul of Good: An action-centred approach to teaching Shakespeare in schools', *Shakespeare Survey*, vol. 64, 2011, p.240.

15 Jonothan Neelands and Jacqui O'Hanlon, 'There is Some Soul of Good: An action-centred approach to teaching Shakespeare in schools', *Shakespeare Survey*, vol. 64, 2011, p.242. The quote is originally from John Dewey, *Democracy and Education* (New York: Macmillan, 1916; repr Teddington, 2007), p.167.

16 This is my own summary. For a more detailed and nuanced interpretation, see Neelands and O'Hanlon, 'There is Some Soul of Good: An action-centred

approach to teaching Shakespeare in schools', *Shakespeare Survey*, vol. 64, 2011, pp.242–243.

17 Keeton M. and Tate P., cited in David Kolb, *Experiential Learning: Experience as the Source of Learning and Development*, Englewood Cliffs, NJ: Prentice Hall, 1984, p.5

18 Neelands and O'Hanlon expand on this; see 'There is Some Soul of Good: An action-centred approach to teaching Shakespeare in schools', *Shakespeare Survey*, vol. 64, 2011, pp.245-247. See also Helen Nicholson, *Theatre, Education and Performance*, Basingstoke: Palgrave Macmillan, 2011, pp.41–43

19 John Dewey, *Art as Experience*, New York: Penguin 1934/2005, p.270.

20 John Dewey, *Art as Experience*, New York: Penguin 1934/2005, p.58.

21 John Dewey, *Art as Experience*, New York: Penguin 1934/2005, p.40.

22 John Dewey, *Art as Experience*, New York: Penguin 1934/2005, p.58.

23 *The RSC Shakespeare Toolkit for Teachers*, p.8.

24 See Richard Sennett, *The Craftsman*, London: Allen Lane, 2008. All quotes here are from p.289.

25 Rex Gibson, 'Narrative Approaches to Shakespeare: Active Storytelling in Schools' in the *Shakespeare Survey*, vol. 53, 2000, p.154

26 Kate McLuskie, 'Dancing and Thinking: Teaching "Shakespeare" in the Twenty-First Century' in G.B. Shand (ed.), *Teaching Shakespeare: Passing it On,* Chichester: Wiley-Blackwell, 2009, p.139.

27 Mark Johnson, *The Meaning of the Body: Aesthetics of Human Understanding*, Chicago: University of Chicago Press, 2008, p.11. Interest in the relationship between embodiment and cognition is very current in Theatre and Performance Studies, including Shakespeare studies. See, for example, Nicola Shaughnessy (ed.), *Affective Performance and Cognitive Science: Body, Brain and Being*, London: Methuen Drama, 2013; and Laurie Johnson, John Sutton and Evelyn Tribble (eds.) *Embodied Cognition and Shakespeare's Theatre: The Early Modern Body-Mind*, London: Routledge Studies in Shakespeare, 2014.

28 Mark Johnson, *The Meaning of the Body: Aesthetics of Human Understanding*, Chicago: University of Chicago Press, 2008, p.13.

29 Mark Johnson, *The Meaning of the Body: Aesthetics of Human Understanding*, Chicago: University of Chicago Press, 2008, p.15.

30 Richard Sennett describes how professional musicians communicate with one another through their art rather than through words. He writes: 'When musicians want to explain something, they more frequently show rather than tell, that is, they play a particular passage to others, leaving the others to interpret what they are doing.' See *Together: The Rituals, Pleasures and Politics of Co-operation*, London: Allen Lane, 2012, p.18.

31 Mark Johnson, *The Meaning of the Body: Aesthetics of Human Understanding*, Chicago: University of Chicago Press, 2008, p.45.

32 The quote is from John Armstrong. See Armstrong, *The Intimate Philosophy of Art*, Harmondsworth: Penguin, 2005, p.83. See also Joe Winston, *Beauty and Education*, New York: Routledge, 2010, pp.72–74.

33 This was originally published in *The Stage*, 2 April 2009. I have taken it from Neelands and O'Hanlon, 'There is Some Soul of Good: An action-centred approach to teaching Shakespeare in schools', *Shakespeare Survey*, vol. 64, 2011, p.247.

34 Gregory Doran speaking on the first of the video production diaries, accessed March, 2014. See http://www.rsc.org.uk/whats-on/richard-ii/video-production-diary.aspx

35 Jonothan Neelands and Jacqui O'Hanlon, 'There is Some Soul of Good: An action-centred approach to teaching Shakespeare in schools', *Shakespeare Survey*, vol. 64, 2011, p.245.

36 Helen Nicholson, *Applied Drama: The Gift of Theatre*, Basingstoke: Palgrave Macmillan, 2005, p.59.

37 Richard Sennett, *Together: The Rituals, Pleasures and Politics of Co-operation*, London: Allen Lane, 2012, p.16.

38 Richard Sennett, *Together: The Rituals, Pleasures and Politics of Co-operation*, London: Allen Lane, 2012, p.18.

39 This quote was originally cited in the RSC Histories Cycle Programme Notes, 2007. I have taken it from Jonothan Neelands and Jacqui O'Hanlon, 'There is Some Soul of Good: An action-centred approach to teaching Shakespeare in schools', *Shakespeare Survey*, vol. 64, 2011, p.247.

40 See, in particular, Joe Winston, 'A Place for Beauty in Arts Education' in Michael Fleming *et al* (eds), *The International Handbook of Arts Education*, London and New York: Routledge, 2014. For a lengthier consideration of the issues discussed in this section, see also Joe Winston, *Beauty and Education*, New York: Routledge, 2010.

41 Kant was not the first to propose these distinctions but he was the most influential. For a fuller discussion of the implications of Kant's theories of beauty for education, see Winston, *Beauty and Education*, pp.19–31.

42 Iris Murdoch, *The Sovereignty of Good*, London: Routledge, 1970/1989. See also Winston, *Beauty and Education*, pp.50–54.

43 This example is drawn from Elaine Scarry, *On Beauty and Being Just*, London: Duckworth, 2001, p.33.

44 Cicely Berry, *From Word to Play: A Handbook for Directors*, London: Oberon Books, 2008, p.6.

Chapter 6

1 See, for example, Helen Freshwater ' "You say something": Audience Participation and *The Author*', *Contemporary Theatre Review*, vol. 21, no. 4, 2011. See also Helen Iball, 'A mouth to feed me: Reflections inspired by the poster for Tim Crouch's *The Author*' in the same issue.

2 See *Contemporary Theatre Review*, vol. 21, no. 4, 2011. The quote by Stephen Bottoms is taken from the introduction to Tim Crouch, *Plays One*, London: Oberon Books, 2011.

3   Taken from a review by Joyce McMillan in *The Scotsman* accessed from the website http://www.timcrouchtheatre.co.uk [accessed September 2012].

4   Tim Crouch in an interview with the author, at the Unicorn Theatre in London, 12 October 2012. All quotes by Tim in the first half of this chapter are taken from this interview unless otherwise stated.

5   Tim Crouch speaking 13 October 2011, www.youtube.com/ watch?v=6MFBia3chTU Uploaded by the RSC [accessed September 2013].

6   Tim Crouch speaking 13 October 2011, www.youtube.com/ watch?v=6MFBia3chTU Uploaded by the RSC [accessed September 2013].

7   Jonathan Bate, 'The Taming of the Shrew: Introduction' in Jonathan Bate and Eric Rasmussen (eds), *William Shakespeare Complete Works*, London: Macmillan, 2007, p.526.

8   Tim Crouch speaking 13 October 2011, www.youtube.com/ watch?v=6MFBia3chTU Uploaded by the RSC [accessed September 2013].

9   See, for example, Jonathan Bate, The Taming of the Shrew: Introduction' in Jonathan Bate and Eric Rasmussen (eds), *William Shakespeare Complete Works*, London: Macmillan, 2007, p.527. See also Sean McEvoy, *Shakespeare: The Basics*, London: Routledge, 2006, p.145.

10 Jacques Rancière, *The Emancipated Spectator*, London: Verso, 2009. Trans. Gregory Eliot. See in particular p.14.

11 The original speech is 44 lines in length, of which Tim's edit kept 28.

12 Tim Crouch speaking 13 October 2011, www.youtube.com/watch? v=6MFBia3chTU Uploaded by the RSC [accessed September 2013].

13 Dominic Cavendish, *Daily Telegraph*, 4 October 2011.

14 Rehearsal attended 22 June 2011.

15 Tim Crouch interviewed by Miles Tandy of the RSC in Stratford-upon-Avon, 14 June 2013. All quotes from Tim in the rest of this chapter are taken from this interview unless otherwise stated.

16 See for example 'Cap O'Rushes' in Joseph Jacobs, *English Fairy Tales*, London: Everyman, 1993 (first published 1892); and in particular 'Dear As Salt' in Italo Calvino's *Italian Folktales*, Harmondsworth: Penguin, 1982, trans. George Martin.

17 This is edited from Tim's interview with Miles Tandy.

18 The figures were compiled for inhouse company information, not for publicity purposes, as were the selection of quotes from audience feedback that I have included here.

19 http://www.yorktheatreroyal.co.uk/handheld/review/review_28_11_12_king_ lear.php [accessed September 2013].

20 This is something the RSC is aware of and is currently making efforts to address – there is a tension between the desire of some schools to ensure that as many of their students as possible see the production and the Company's strong wish that it must be an enjoyable experience for all who watch it, not a physically uncomfortable one.

21 See Joe Winston 'Between the aesthetic and the ethical: analysing the tension at the heart of Theatre in Education', *Journal of Moral Education*, vol. 34, no. 3,

2005; and also Joe Winston, 'Tapestry and the aesthetics of theatre in education as dialogic encounter and civic exchange', in *Research in Drama Education*, vol. 18, no. 1, 2013.

Chapter 7

1 Sarah Olive, 'The Royal Shakespeare Company as "cultural chemist" ' in Peter Holland (ed.), *Shakespeare Survey*, vol. 64, 2011, p.252.

2 Sarah Olive, 'The Royal Shakespeare Company as "cultural chemist" ' in Peter Holland (ed.), *Shakespeare Survey*, vol. 64, 2011, p.254.

3 Sarah Olive, 'The Royal Shakespeare Company as "cultural chemist" ' in Peter Holland (ed.), *Shakespeare Survey*, vol. 64, 2011, p.255.

4 Sarah Olive, 'The Royal Shakespeare Company as "cultural chemist" ' in Peter Holland (ed.), *Shakespeare Survey*, vol. 64, 2011, p.257.

5 Sarah Olive, 'The Royal Shakespeare Company as "cultural chemist" ' in Peter Holland (ed.), *Shakespeare Survey*, vol. 64, 2011, p.254.

6 Sarah Olive, 'The Royal Shakespeare Company as "cultural chemist"' in Peter Holland (ed.), *Shakespeare Survey*, vol. 64, 2011, p.252.

7 Jacqui O'Hanlon makes the following comment: 'When we ask the 1,100 schools and 2,500 teachers who work with us each year "what do you need from us?", they say, "evidence that your methods raise attainment; evidence that your approaches will support the learning objectives that I need to deliver". We try hard to preserve the artistic integrity and authenticity of our work, but we also speak to schools and teachers in a language they tell us they need us to speak in, otherwise they can't justify working with us.' Email to the author, October, 2013.

8 See, for example, Tracy Irish, *Classroom Research: Findings from the Action Research Projects Carried Out by Teachers during 2006–07 to Assess the Effectiveness of Theatre-based Approaches to Teaching Shakespeare in the English/Literacy Classroom*, RSC, 2008. Page 5 is devoted entirely to this issue.

9 Many examples of this can be found in the articles, research reports and teachers' research assignments referred to throughout the rest of this chapter and available on the RSC website.

10 Bloom is, of course, famous for his comment that *King Lear* is better read than performed, as a performance can never do it justice. See Harold Bloom, *Shakespeare: The Invention of the Human*, London: Fourth Estate, 1999, where he also quips: '*Hamlet* has survived everything, even Peter Brook' (p.391). Personally, I am a great admirer of his writings, even if I don't always agree with him.

11 Jonathan Bate in an interview with the author, 29 April 2013.

12 Jacqui O'Hanlon, interview with the author, 23 May 2013.

13 Tracy Irish, 'Would you risk it for Shakespeare? A case study of using active approaches in the English classroom', *English in Education*, vol. 5, no. 1, Spring 2011. Available from the RSC on: http://www.rsc.org.uk/education/how-our-work-makes-a-difference/research-case-studies/articles-reports.aspx

I have used the pagination provided for the article on this site in the references below.

14 For readers based outside England, the GCSE is the national examination current at the time of the research, taken by sixteen-year-olds in Year 11. Year 10 is when they would have begun their coursework for this.

15 Tracy Irish, 'Would you risk it for Shakespeare? A case study of using active approaches in the English classroom', *English in Education*, vol. 5, no. 1, Spring 2011, p.5.

16 Tracy Irish, 'Would you risk it for Shakespeare? A case study of using active approaches in the English classroom', *English in Education*, vol. 5, no. 1, Spring 2011, p.6.

17 Tracy Irish, 'Would you risk it for Shakespeare? A case study of using active approaches in the English classroom', *English in Education*, vol. 5, no. 1, Spring 2011, p.8.

18 Tracy Irish, 'Would you risk it for Shakespeare? A case study of using active approaches in the English classroom', *English in Education*, vol. 5, no. 1, Spring 2011, p.9.

19 Tracy Irish, 'Would you risk it for Shakespeare? A case study of using active approaches in the English classroom', *English in Education*, vol. 5, no. 1, Spring 2011, p.10.

20 Deborah Britzman, *Practice Makes Practice: A Critical Study of Learning to Teach*, New York: State University of New York Press, 1991, p.8.

21 Referred to in Britzman, *Practice Makes Practice: A Critical Study of Learning to Teach*, New York: State University of New York Press, 1991, p.52.

22 Pat Thomson *et al*, *A Study of the Learning and Performance Network, An education Programme of the Royal Shakespeare Company*, published by Creativity, Culture and Education, October 2010, p.26. Available from the RSC on: http://www.rsc.org.uk/education/how-our-work-makes-a-difference/research-case-studies/external-evaluations.aspx

23 See Chapter 1 of this volume for a clear breakdown of the structure and organization of the LPN.

24 Pat Thomson *et al*, *A Study of the Learning and Performance Network, An education Programme of the Royal Shakespeare Company*, published by Creativity, Culture and Education, October 2010, p.22.

25 Jonothan Neelands *et al*, *An Evaluation of* Stand up for Shakespeare, *The Royal Shakespeare Company's Learning and Performance Network, 2006–09*, CEDAR, University of Warwick, 2009, pp.38–54. Available from the RSC on: http://www.rsc.org.uk/education/how-our-work-makes-a-difference/research-case-studies/external-evaluations.aspx

26 Pat Thomson *et al*, *A Study of the Learning and Performance Network, An education Programme of the Royal Shakespeare Company*, published by Creativity, Culture and Education, October 2010, p.19.

27 Pat Thomson *et al*, *A Study of the Learning and Performance Network, An education Programme of the Royal Shakespeare Company*, published by Creativity, Culture and Education, October 2010, p.26.

28 Jonothan Neelands *et al*, *An Evaluation of* Stand up for Shakespeare, *The Royal Shakespeare Company's Learning and Performance Network, 2006–09*, CEDAR, University of Warwick, 2009, pp.52–53.

29 Jonothan Neelands *et al*, *An Evaluation of* Stand up for Shakespeare, *The Royal Shakespeare Company's Learning and Performance Network, 2006–09*, CEDAR, University of Warwick, 2009, p.53.

30 Tracy Irish, *Classroom Research: Findings from the Action Research Projects Carried Out by Teachers during 2006–07 to Assess the Effectiveness of Theatre-based Approaches to Teaching Shakespeare in the English/Literacy Classroom*, RSC, 2008, p.4

31 Jonothan Neelands *et al*, *An Evaluation of* Stand up for Shakespeare, *The Royal Shakespeare Company's Learning and Performance Network, 2006–09*, CEDAR, University of Warwick, 2009, p.52.

32 Jonothan Neelands *et al*, *An Evaluation of* Stand up for Shakespeare, *The Royal Shakespeare Company's Learning and Performance Network, 2006–09*, CEDAR, University of Warwick, 2009, p.54.

33 Tracy Irish, *Classroom Research: Findings from the Action Research Projects Carried Out by Teachers during 2006–07 to Assess the Effectiveness of Theatre-based Approaches*, p.5.

34 Jonothan Neelands *et al*, *An Evaluation of* Stand up for Shakespeare, *The Royal Shakespeare Company's Learning and Performance Network, 2006–09*, CEDAR, University of Warwick, 2009, p.54.

35 Jonothan Neelands *et al*, *An Evaluation of* Stand up for Shakespeare, *The Royal Shakespeare Company's Learning and Performance Network, 2006–09*, CEDAR, University of Warwick, 2009, p.62.

36 Jonothan Neelands *et al*, *An Evaluation of* Stand up for Shakespeare, *The Royal Shakespeare Company's Learning and Performance Network, 2006–09*, CEDAR, University of Warwick, 2009, p.63.

37 Tracy Irish, *Classroom Research: Findings from the Action Research Projects Carried Out by Teachers during 2006–07 to Assess the Effectiveness of Theatre-based Approaches*, p.6.

38 Tracy Irish, *Classroom Research: Findings from the Action Research Projects Carried Out by Teachers during 2006–07 to Assess the Effectiveness of Theatre-based Approaches*, p.6.

39 Tracy Irish, *Classroom Research: Findings from the Action Research Projects Carried Out by Teachers during 2006–07 to Assess the Effectiveness of Theatre-based Approaches*, p.6.

40 Tracy Irish, *Classroom Research: Findings from the Action Research Projects Carried Out by Teachers during 2006–07 to Assess the Effectiveness of Theatre-based Approaches*, p.1.

41 Jonothan Neelands *et al*, *An Evaluation of* Stand up for Shakespeare, *The Royal Shakespeare Company's Learning and Performance Network, 2006–09*, CEDAR, University of Warwick, 2009, p.68.

42 Tracy Irish, *Classroom Research: Findings from the Action Research Projects Carried Out by Teachers during 2006–07 to Assess the Effectiveness of Theatre-based Approaches*, p.8.

43 Jonothan Neelands *et al*, *An Evaluation of* Stand up for Shakespeare, *The Royal Shakespeare Company's Learning and Performance Network, 2006–09*, CEDAR, University of Warwick, 2009, p.69.

44 Pat Thomson *et al*, *A Study of the Learning and Performance Network, An education Programme of the Royal Shakespeare Company*, published by Creativity, Culture and Education, October 2010, p.20.

45 Pat Thomson *et al*, *A Study of the Learning and Performance Network, An education Programme of the Royal Shakespeare Company*, published by Creativity, Culture and Education, October, p.22.

46 Pat Thomson *et al*, *A Study of the Learning and Performance Network, An education Programme of the Royal Shakespeare Company*, published by Creativity, Culture and Education, October 2010, p.23.

47 The substance of their suggestion is that the research project be redesigned with different reflective stages that encourage teachers to critique and experiment with practice over the year in a more structured fashion. Assessment of the programme was redesigned in order to respond to this for the 2012 cohort and beyond.

48 I conducted my own meta-analysis of the assignments of twenty-seven teachers from the 2009–2011 cohorts and this very much reflects the findings of these earlier studies. Fourteen of the assignments concentrated on issues related to attainment and/or raising standards of writing, for example, with just two focusing precisely on whether using rehearsal room pedagogy had deepened student understanding of the plays. Others focused on evaluating the pedagogy's impact on the social health of particular classes, on the engagement of boys, and its effects on the learning of particular student groups, such as those with special educational needs or English as an Additional Language. A minority testify to ongoing difficulties and disappointments or to a lack of improvement in the grades that they were hoping for, but most write enthusiastically of changes both in attitude and attainment and the warm, emotive words pointed to by Thomson *et al* continue to be in evidence. One teacher, for example, writes of how Shakespeare inspired the writing of her own class in the following words: 'As a class we built up a speech for Juliet and the effect was dynamic. I was amazed at the intensity of feeling and richness of language that emerged. In some instances many children had assimilated and incorporated the language of Shakespeare, merging it with their own. The children felt that they had enabled Juliet to speak out.' Another teacher designed a consciously rigorous research project intended to gauge as accurately as possible the impact of Shakespeare on her students' writing and I will look closely at her findings in the next chapter.

49 Jonothan Neelands *et al*, *An Evaluation of* Stand up for Shakespeare, *The Royal Shakespeare Company's Learning and Performance Network, 2006–09*, CEDAR, University of Warwick, 2009, p.81.

50 Jonothan Neelands *et al*, *An Evaluation of* Stand up for Shakespeare, *The Royal Shakespeare Company's Learning and Performance Network, 2006–09*, CEDAR, University of Warwick, 2009, p.81.

51 Jonothan Neelands *et al*, *An Evaluation of* Stand up for Shakespeare, *The Royal Shakespeare Company's Learning and Performance Network, 2006–09*, CEDAR, University of Warwick, 2009, p.80.

52 Pat Thomson *et al*, *A Study of the Learning and Performance Network, An education Programme of the Royal Shakespeare Company*, published by Creativity, Culture and Education, October 2010, p.23.

53 Michelle was one of several teachers I could have spoken to. I chose her out of
    geographical convenience, as she lives in driving distance from the university
    where I work.

54 Interview with the author, 25 October 2013. All subsequent quotes from
    Michelle in this chapter are taken from this interview. The interview took place
    in her home.

55 Jacqui O'Hanlon, interview with the author, 23 May 2013.

56 Elaine Scarry, *On Beauty and Being Just*, London: Duckworth, 2001.

57 Joe Winston, *Beauty and Education*, New York: Routledge, 2010, p.134.

Chapter 8

1   This final section of the chapter is drawn largely from Joe Winston, ' "Play
    is the thing": Shakespeare, language play and drama pedagogy in the
    early years', *Journal of Aesthetic Education*, vol. 47, no. 2, Summer 2013,
    pp.1–15.

2   This quote is taken from Sheila Galloway and Steve Strand, *Creating a
    Community of Practice: Final Report to the Royal Shakespeare Company's
    Learning and Performance Network*, CEDAR, University of Warwick, March
    2010. An executive summary of the 2007 and 2009 Student Attitude Surveys
    can be found pp.21–31 with a full technical report explaining the quantitative
    methodology and analysis in Appendix 1, pp.43–90. To access the full report go
    to: http://www.rsc.org.uk/education/how-our-work-makes-a-difference/
    research-case-studies/external-evaluations.aspx

3   Confidence intervals are a statistical concept and are used to calculate the
    reliability of an estimate. For a full explanation see: http://en.wikipedia.org/
    wiki/Confidence_interval#Conceptual_basis

4   A t-test can be used to determine if two sets of data are significantly different
    from each other. For a fuller explanation see: http://en.wikipedia.org/wiki/
    Student's_t-test

5   See Jonothan Neelands, 'Acting together: ensemble as a democratic process in
    art and life', *Research in Drama Education: The Journal of Applied Theatre and
    Performance*, vol. 14, no. 2, 2009, pp.173–190.

6   Jackie, interview with the author, 23 October 2013. All quotations are from this
    interview. References to her assignment are made with her permission.

7   Taken from Appendix J in Jackie's assignment, which includes the transcript of
    an interview between the four boys and a member of the local Behaviour
    Support Services. Although she was known to the boys, the support officer was
    completely removed from the Shakespeare project and so, it was felt, could
    solicit honest responses.

8   Taken from Appendix M of Jackie's assignment.

9   See, for example, Joe Winston, *Drama and English at the Heart of the
    Curriculum*, London: David Fulton, 2004. See also Julie Dunn *et al*, 'Drama

and Writing: Overcoming the hurdle of the Blank Page' in Michael Anderson and Julie Dunn (eds), *How Drama Activates Learning: Contemporary Research and Practice*, London: Bloomsbury, 2013, pp.245–259.

10 *ECAT* uses four categories of what it calls 'typical stages of speech, language and communication development': listening and attention; understanding of language; speech, sounds and talk; social skills. These are levelled at six-to-twelve-month intervals with detailed descriptors at each level to enable assessment.

11 Guy Cook, *Language Play, Language Learning,* Oxford: Oxford University Press, 2000.

12 See Chapter 3 in Joe Winston and Miles Tandy, *Beginning Shakespeare, 4–11,* London: David Fulton, 2012, for a detailed description of this teaching scheme.

13 Ann Levy, 'The Language of Play: The Role of Play in Language Development. A Review of the Literature' in Sue Burroughs and Roy Evans (eds), *Play, Language, and Socialisation: Perspectives on Adult Roles,* New York: Gordon and Breach, 1986; Jerome Bruner, Alison Jolly, and Kathy Sylva (eds), *Play: Its Role in Development and Evolution,* New York: Basic Books, 1976; Lev Vygotsky, *Thought and Language,* trans. E. Hanfman and G. Valar, Cambridge, MA: MIT Press, 1962.

14 Roger Caillois, *Man, Play, and Games,* trans. Meyer Barash, Urbana, IL: University of Illinois Press, 2001; Johan Huizinga, *Homo Ludens,* London: Paladin, 1971.

15 Guy Cook, *Language Play, Language Learning*, Oxford: Oxford University Press, 2000, p.21.

16 Nessa Wolfson, 'The Bulge: A theory of speech behavior and social distance,' *Penn Working Papers in Educational Linguistics*, vol. 2, no. 1, 1990, pp.55–83.

17 For a critical perspective on such views, see Penny Holland, *We Don't Play with Guns Here: War, Weapons, and Superhero Play in the Early Years,* Maidenhead, UK: Open University Press, 2003.

18 Iona and Peter Opie, *The Lore and Language of Schoolchildren,* Oxford: Oxford University Press, 1959.

19 This point has been made by Michael Boyd but he is in good company here; the German philosopher Friedrich Schiller noted this over 200 years ago. See Friedrich Schiller, *On the Aesthetic Education of Man in a Series of Letters*, ed. and trans. E. M. Wilkinson and L. A. Willoughby, Oxford: Clarendon Press, 1967. See also Joe Winston, *Beauty and Education,* New York: Routledge, 2010.

20 For a particularly enlightening reading of this speech, see Chapter 6 of Jonathan Bate, *Soul of the Age: The Life, Mind, and World of William Shakespeare,* London: Penguin Books, 2009.

21 Iona and Peter Opie *The Lore and Language of Schoolchildren,* Oxford: Oxford University Press, 1959, p.45.

22 Guy Cook, *Language Play, Language Learning,* Oxford: Oxford University Press, 2000, p.128.

23 This is a specific adaptation of the strategy known as the 'Whoosh' and included in the RSC *Toolkit*.

24 One of his more amusing examples is of a child who thought that the hymn 'Gladly the Cross I'd Bear', which he sang regularly at school, was about a cross-eyed bear named Gladly!

25 All of the children's names used here are pseudonyms.

26 Guy Cook, *Language Play, Language Learning*, Oxford: Oxford University Press, 2000, p.124.

27 Cicely Berry, *From Word to Play: A Handbook for Directors*, London: Oberon Books, 2008, Chapter 5.

28 Cicely Berry, *From Word to Play: A Handbook for Directors*, London: Oberon Books, 2008, p.105.

29 Cicely Berry, *From Word to Play: A Handbook for Directors*, London: Oberon Books, 2008, p.142.

30 See Iris Murdoch, *The Sovereignty of Good*, London: Routledge, 1989, pp.84–85; and Joe Winston, *Beauty and Education*, pp. 50–54.

31 See Chapter 3 of Theodor Todorov, *Genres in Discourse*, trans. C. Porter, Cambridge: Cambridge University Press, 1990.

32 Guy Cook, *Language Play, Language Learning*, Oxford: Oxford University Press, 2000, p.201.

Chapter 9

1 Keynote address at the British Library on 4 February 2014, in a provocation organized as part of the Warwick Commission on the Future of Cultural Value. A video of this can be accessed on: http://www2.warwick.ac.uk/research/warwickcommission/futureculture/events/provocation1/videos/

2 This and other quotes by Catherine Mallyon are taken from an interview with the author, 2 April 2014.

3 Quotes taken from page 5 of the *RSC Toolkit for Primary Teachers*, London: Methuen Drama, 2014.

4 The quote is taken from Gregory Doran's contribution to the programme notes for his 2014 production of *Henry IV Part 1*. In it he also details how the assistant director, Owen Horsley, pulled some of the company together to stage a version of *The Famous Victories* during rehearsal. The future *First Encounter* production would seem to illustrate a continuing close relationship between artistic experiment and education within the company.

5 These quotes and statistics were obtained from audience research conducted by the RSC and published for the company's own internal use in January 2014.

6 On 22 March 2014, at the Clore Learning Centre in Stratford.

7 The RSC does have a formal education advisory group which meets quarterly, attended not only by the Head of Education but also by either the artistic or

executive director. Two of its governors are also head teachers, one from the private and the other from the state sector, the latter being also a member of the board.

8 The regional partner theatres are: Grand Theatre, Blackpool; The Alhambra Theatre, Bradford; The Marlow Theatre, Canterbury; Curve, Leicester; Intermission Youth Theatre; Hall for Cornwall, Cornwall; Hull Truck Theatre, Hull; Newcastle Theatre Royal, Newcastle; The New Vic Theatre, Newcastle-under-Lyme; Nuffield Theatre, Southampton; York Theatre Royal, York.

9 See Sheila Galloway and Steve Strand, *Creating a Community of Practice: Final Report to the Royal Shakespeare Company's Learning and Performance Network. Research and Development Programme for the Evaluation of the RSC's Learning and Performance Network 2007–2009*. This can be accessed on: http://www.rsc.org.uk/education/how-our-work-makes-a-difference/research-case-studies/external-evaluations.aspx

10 Jean Lave and Etienne Wenger, *Situated Learning: Legitimate Peripheral Participation,* Cambridge: Cambridge University Press, 1991. See also Etienne Wenger, *Communities of Practice: Learning, Meaning and Identity*, Cambridge: Cambridge University Press, 1998.

11 This summary and the ensuing quotes are taken from Chapter 2 of Wenger's *Communities of Practice* (1998).

12 Etienne Wenger, *Communities of Practice: Learning, Meaning and Identity*, Cambridge: Cambridge University Press, 1998, p.85.

BIBLIOGRAPHY

Armstrong, John, *The Intimate Philosophy of Art*, Harmondsworth: Penguin, 2005.

Arnold, Matthew, *Culture and Anarchy*, Cambridge: Cambridge University Press, 1996. (First published 1869.)

Banks, Fiona, *Creative Shakespeare: The Globe Education Guide to Practical Shakespeare*, London: Bloomsbury, 2014.

Bate, Jonathan, *The Genius of Shakespeare*, London: Picador, 1997.

Bate, Jonathan, *Soul of the Age: The Life, Mind, and World of William Shakespeare*, London: Penguin Books, 2009.

Bate, Jonathan, *English Literature: A Very Short Introduction*, Oxford: Oxford University Press, 2010.

Bate, Jonathan and Rasmussen, Eric (eds), *The RSC William Shakespeare Complete Works*, Basingstoke: Macmillan, 2007.

Berry, Cicely, *From Word to Play: A Handbook for Directors*, London: Oberon Books, 2008.

Berry, Cicely, *Working Shakespeare: The Work Book*, New York: Applause Theatre and Cinema Books, 2004.

Blocksidge, Martin (ed.), *Shakespeare in Education*, London: Continuum, 2003.

Bloom, Harold, *Shakespeare: The Invention of the Human*, London: Fourth Estate, 1999.

Bottoms, Janet, 'Doing Shakespeare: How Shakespeare became a school "subject" ', *Shakespeare Survey*, vol. 66, 2013.

Bourdieu, Pierre, *Distinction: A Social Critique of the Judgment of Taste*, trans. Nice, R., London: Routledge and Kegan Paul, 1984.

Bradley, A.C., *Shakespearean Tragedy*, Basingstoke: MacMillan, 1992. (First published 1904.)

Britzman, Deborah, *Practice Makes Practice: A Critical Study of Learning to Teach*, New York: State University of New York Press, 1991.

Brook, Peter, *The Empty Space*, Harmondsworth: Penguin, 1990. (First published 1968.)

Bruner, Jerome, *Towards a Theory of Instruction*, Cambridge MA: Harvard University Press, 1966.

Bruner, Jerome, Jolly, Alison and Sylva, Kathy (eds), *Play: Its Role in Development and Evolution*, New York: Basic Books, 1976.

Bruner, Jerome, 'The Role of Dialogue in Language Acquisition' in Sinclair, Anne, Jarvella, Robert J. and Levelt, Willem J. M. (eds), *The Child's Concept of Language*. New York: Springer Verlag, 1978.

Caillois, Roger, *Man, Play, and Games*, trans. Barash, Meyer, Urbana, IL: University of Illinois Press, 2001.

Calvino, Italo, *Italian Folktales*, trans. Martin, George, Harmondsworth: Penguin, 1982.

Chambers, Colin, *Inside the Royal Shakespeare Company: Creativity and the Institution*, London and New York: Routledge, 2004.

Chillington Rutter, Carol, 'Playing Hercules or Labouring in my Vocation' in Shand, G.B. (ed.), *Teaching Shakespeare: Passing it On*, Chichester: Wiley-Blackwell, 2009.

Cook, Guy, *Language Play, Language Learning*, Oxford: Oxford University Press, 2000.

Crouch, Tim, *Plays One*, London: Oberon Books, 2011.

Dewey, John, *Democracy and Education*, California, US: Simon & Brown, 2011. (First published by Macmillan, 1916.)

Dewey, John, *Art as Experience*, New York: Penguin, 2005. (First published 1934.)

Dewey, John, *Education as Experience*, New York: Touchstone, 1997. (First published 1938.)

Dollimore, Jonathan and Sinfield, Alan (eds), *Political Shakespeare: New essays in Cultural Materialism*, Manchester: Manchester University Press, 1985.

Dunn, Julie, Harden, Annette and Marino, Sarah, 'Drama and Writing: Overcoming the Hurdle of the Blank Page' in Anderson, Michael and Dunn, Julie (eds), *How Drama Activates Learning: Contemporary Research and Practice*, London: Bloomsbury, 2013.

Folger Education, *Shakespeare Set Free Toolkit: Resources for Teaching and Learning*, Washington DC: Folger Shakespeare Library, 2009.

Freshwater, Helen, ' "You say something": Audience participation and *The Author*', *Contemporary Theatre Review*, vol. 21, no.4, 2011.

Gibson, Rex (ed.), *Secondary School Shakespeare: Classroom Practice*, Cambridge: Cambridge Institute of Education, 1990.

Gibson, Rex, *Teaching Shakespeare*, Cambridge: Cambridge University Press, 1998.

Gibson, Rex, 'Narrative approaches to Shakespeare: Active storytelling in schools' in *The Shakespeare Survey*, vol. 53, 2000.

Gilbert, Miriam, 'A Test of Character' in Shand, G.B. (ed.), *Teaching Shakespeare: Passing it On*, Chichester: Wiley-Blackwell, 2009.

Grotowski, Jerzy, *Towards a Poor Theatre*, London: Routledge, 2002. (First published 1968.)

Holden, John, *Capturing Cultural Value*, London: Demos, 2004.

Holden, John, *Cultural Value and the Crisis of Legitimacy*, Demos, 2006.

Holland, Penny, *We Don't Play with Guns Here: War, Weapons, and Superhero Play in the Early Years*, Maidenhead: Open University Press, 2003.

Huizinga, Johan, *Homo Ludens*, London: Paladin, 1971. (First published 1949.)

Iball, Helen, 'A mouth to feed me: Reflections inspired by the poster for Tim Crouch's *The Author*', *Contemporary Theatre Review*, vol. 21, no.4, 2011.

Irish, Tracy, 'Would you risk it for Shakespeare? A case study of using active approaches in the English classroom', *English in Education*, vol. 5, no. 1, Spring 2011.

Jacobs, Joseph, *English Fairy Tales*, London: Everyman, 1993. (First published 1892.)

Johnson, Laurie, Sutton, John and Tribble, Evelyn (eds), *Embodied Cognition and Shakespeare's Theatre: The Early Modern Body-Mind*, London: Routledge Studies in Shakespeare, 2014.

Johnson, Mark, *The Meaning of the Body: Aesthetics of Human Understanding*, Chicago: University of Chicago Press, 2008.

Kempe, Andy, 'Drama and the Development of Literacy', *NADIE Journal*, no. 24, 2000.

Kolb, David, *Experiential Learning: Experience As the Source of Learning and Development*, Englewood Cliffs, NJ; London: Prentice Hall, 1984.

Kreber, J.W. Patrick, *Sense and Sensitivity*, London: University of London Press, 1965.

Lave, Jean and Wenger, Etienne, *Situated Learning: Legitimate Peripheral Participation*, Cambridge: Cambridge University Press, 1991.

Levy, Ann, 'The Language of Play: The Role of Play in Language Development. A Review of the Literature' in *Play, Language, and Socialisation: Perspectives on Adult Roles*, Burroughs, Sue and Evans, Roy (eds), New York: Gordon and Breach, 1986.

McEvoy, Sean, *Shakespeare: The Basics*, London: Routledge, 2006.

McLuskie, Kate, 'Dancing and Thinking: Teaching "Shakespeare" in the Twenty-First Century', in Shand, G.B. (ed.), *Teaching Shakespeare: Passing it On*, Chichester: Wiley-Blackwell, 2009.

Milsom, Patricia, *The History and Development of the Royal Shakespeare Education Department: Glorious Hybrids*, unpublished MPhil Dissertation, University of Birmingham, 2003.

Monk, Nicholas, Chillington Rutter, Carol, Neelands, Jonothan and Heron, Jonathan, *Open Space Learning: A Study in Trans-disciplinary Pedagogy*, London: Bloomsbury, 2011.

Murdoch, Iris, *The Sovereignty of Good*, London: Routledge, 1989. (First published 1970.)

Neelands, Jonothan, *Structuring Drama Work*, Cambridge: Cambridge University Press, 1991.

Neelands, Jonothan, 'Acting together: ensemble as a democratic process in art and life', *Research in Drama Education: The Journal of Applied Theatre and Performance*, vol.14, no. 2, 2009.

Neelands, Jonothan and O'Hanlon, Jacqui, 'There is Some Soul of Good: An action-centred approach to teaching Shakespeare in schools', *Shakespeare Survey*, vol. 64, 2011.

Nicholson, Helen, *Applied Drama: The Gift of Theatre*, Basingstoke: Palgrave Macmillan, 2005.

Nicholson, Helen, *Theatre, Education and Performance*, London: Palgrave Macmillan, 2011.

O'Brien, Dave, *Measuring the Value of Culture: A Report to the Department of Culture, Media and Sport*, December 2010.

Olive, Sarah, 'The Royal Shakespeare Company as "cultural chemist" ', *Shakespeare Survey*, vol. 64, 2011.

Opie, Iona and Peter, *The Lore and Language of Schoolchildren*, Oxford: Oxford University Press, 1959.

Rancière, Jacques, *The Emancipated Spectator*, trans. Eliot, Gregory, London: Verso, 2009.

Royal Shakespeare Company, *The RSC Shakespeare Toolkit for Teachers*, London: Bloomsbury Methuen Drama, 2010.

Royal Shakespeare Company, *The RSC Shakespeare Toolkit for Primary Teachers*, London: Methuen Drama, 2014.

Scarry, Elaine, *On Beauty and Being Just*, London: Duckworth, 2001.

Schechner, Richard, *Performance Theory*, New York: Ralph Pine, 1977.

Schiller, Friedrich, *On the Aesthetic Education of Man in a Series of Letters*, ed. and trans. Wilkinson, E. M. and Willoughby, L. A., Oxford: Clarendon Press, 1967.

Sennett, Richard, *The Craftsman*, London: Allen Lane, 2008.

Sennett, Richard, *Together: The Rituals, Pleasures and Politics of Co-operation*, London: Allen Lane, 2012.

Shaughnessy, Nicola (ed.) *Affective Performance and Cognitive Science: Body, Brain and Being*, London: Bloomsbury Methuen Drama, 2013.

Sinfield, Alan, 'Royal Shakespeare: Theatre and the Making of Ideology' in Dollimore, Jonathan and Sinfield, Alan (eds), *Political Shakespeare: New Essays in Cultural Materialism*, Manchester: Manchester University Press, 1985.

Tandy, Miles and Howell, Jo, *Creating Writers in the Primary School*, Abingdon, Oxon: Routledge, 2008.

Throsby, David, 'Determining the value of cultural goods: How much (or little) does contingent valuation tell us?', *Journal of Cultural Economics* 27, 2003, pp.275–285.

Throsby, David, 'The Value of Cultural Heritage: What Can Economics Tell Us?' in Clark, K. (ed.), *Capturing the Public Value of Heritage: The Proceedings of the London Conference 25–26 January 2006*, London: English Heritage pp.40–44.

Todorov, Theodor, *Genres in Discourse*, trans. Porter, C., Cambridge: Cambridge University Press, 1990.

Vygotsky, Lev, *Thought and Language*, trans. Hanfman, E. and Valar, G., Cambridge, MA: MIT Press, 1962.

Ward, Thomas Humphry, *The English Poets: Selections with Critical Introductions by Various Writers and a General Introduction by Matthew Arnold*, London and New York: Macmillan, vol. 1, 1880.

Wenger, Etienne, *Communities of Practice: Learning, Meaning and Identity*, Cambridge: Cambridge University Press, 1998

Whitehead, Frank, *The Disappearing Dias*, London: Chatto & Windus, 1966.

Winston, Joe and Tandy, Miles, *Beginning Drama: 4–11*, London: David Fulton Press, 1997.

Winston, Joe, *Drama and English at the Heart of the Curriculum*, London: David Fulton, 2004.

Winston, Joe, 'Between the aesthetic and the ethical: analysing the tension at the heart of Theatre in Education', *Journal of Moral Education*, vol. 34, no. 3, 2005.

Winston, Joe, *Beauty and Education*, New York: Routledge, 2010.

Winston, Joe and Tandy, Miles, *Beginning Shakespeare: 4–11*, Abingdon, Oxon: Routledge, 2012.

Winston, Joe, 'Tapestry and the aesthetics of theatre in education as dialogic encounter and civic exchange', in *Research in Drama Education: The Journal of Applied Theatre and Performance*, vol. 18, no. 1, 2013.

Winston, Joe, ' "Play is the thing": Shakespeare, language play and drama pedagogy in the early years', *Journal of Aesthetic Education*, vol. 47, no. 2, Summer 2013.

Winston, Joe, 'A Place for Beauty in Arts Education' in Fleming, Michael, O'Toole, John and Bresler, Liora (eds), *The International Handbook of Arts Education*, London and New York: Routledge, 2014.

Wolfson, Nessa, 'The Bulge: A theory of speech behaviour and social distance', *Penn Working Papers in Educational Linguistics*, vol. 2, no. 1, 1990.

Research reports accessed from the RSC website

Galloway, Sheila and Strand, Steve, *Creating a Community of Practice: Final Report to the Royal Shakespeare Company's Learning and Performance Network*, CEDAR, University of Warwick, March 2010.

Irish, Tracy, *Classroom Research: Findings from the action research projects carried out by teacher during 2006–07 to assess the effectiveness of theatre-based approaches to teaching Shakespeare in the English/Literacy Classroom*, RSC, 2008.

Irish, Tracy, *A History of the Teaching of Shakespeare in England*, RSC, 2008.

Neelands, Jonothan, Galloway, Sheila and Lindsay, Geoff, *An Evaluation of* Stand up for Shakespeare, *The Royal Shakespeare Company's Learning and Performance Network, 2006–09*, CEDAR, University of Warwick, May, 2009.

Thomson, Pat, Hall, Chris, Thomas, Deborah, Jones, Ken, Franks, Anton, *A Study of the Learning and Performance Network, an Education programme of the Royal Shakespeare Company*, published by Creativity, Culture and Education, October 2010.

DVDs

Working Shakespeare, Workshop 1: Muscularity of Language, New York: The Working Arts Library, 2002.

INDEX

All works are by William Shakespeare unless otherwise indicated.